EMOTION-REGULATING PLAY THERAPY WITH ADHD CHILDREN

EMOTION-REGULATING PLAY THERAPY WITH ADHD CHILDREN

Staying With Playing

ENRICO GNAULATI

JASON ARONSON

Lanham • Boulder • New York • Toronto • Plymouth, UK

Published in the United States of America
by Jason Aronson
An imprint of Rowman & Littlefield Publishers, Inc.

A wholly owned subsidary of
The Rowman & Littlefield Publishing Group, Inc.
4501 Forbes Boulevard, Suite 200, Lanham, Maryland 20706
www.rowmanlittlefield.com

Estover Road
Plymouth PL6 7PY
United Kingdom

British Library Cataloging in Publication Information Available

Library of Congress Cataloging-in-Publication Data

Gnaulati, Enrico.
  Emotion regulating play therapy with ADHD children : staying with playing /
Enrico Gnaulati.
     p. ; cm.
  Includes bibliographical references and index.
  ISBN-13: 978-0-7657-0522-8 (alk. paper)
  ISBN-10: 0-7657-0522-2 (alk. paper)
  ISBN-13: 978-0-7657-0523-5 (alk. paper)
  ISBN-10: 0-7657-0523-0 (alk. paper)
 1. Attention-deficit disorder—Treatment. 2. Play therapy. 3. Emotions. I.
Title.
  [DNLM: 1. Attention Deficit Disorder with Hyperactivity—therapy. 2. Child.
3. Emotions. 4. Play Therapy—methods. WS 350.8.A8 G571e 2008]

  RJ506.H9G57 2008
  618.92'891653--dc22   2007037580

Printed in the United States of America

⊚™ The paper used in this publication meets the minimum requirements of
American National Standard for Information Sciences—Permanence of Paper for
Printed Library Materials, ANSI/NISO Z39.48-1992.

CONTENTS

PREFACE

I wrote this book for an assortment of reasons. In midlife, an ethical and pragmatic spirit has descended upon my intellectual pursuits such that the more my reading and thinking opened up intriguing explanatory vistas into ADHD phenomena, and the more I encountered children, so afflicted, in need of help, the louder the voice in my head became to forge ahead with the book. Furthermore, it would be disingenuous of me to sidestep stating how this book also reflects my disenchantment with medicalized and neurocognitivist accounts of ADHD, at least in its milder form. I have seen as many ADHD children disserviced as serviced by a quickness to medicate and by psychotherapy being relegated to a peripheral role. In my opinion, medicalized and neurocognitivist accounts of ADHD have assumed a level of paradigm dominance of the sort that has stifled novel thinking about the disorder. And yet, we are seeing a flowering of theory and research on children's emotional development and of the impact of emotional experiences on early brain development, which could have relevance for the etiology and treatment of ADHD, making it imperative that paradigm openness be courted.

There are other compelling reasons for me to write the book: I wanted to articulate and consolidate for myself the direction my thinking about and way of working with ADHD children was heading; and I wanted to write a book that would actually be read and considered useful in lessening the real suffering of real children and families. This may seem like a peculiar, if not quaint, thing to say. However, having previously written a dissertation and a variety of research articles that were read by a handful of academics and continue to do little but gather dust, I could not live with the disillusionment! I also wanted to write the sort of book that would be of practical benefit to a range of professionals and laypersons—to child therapists, academics, researchers, and educated parents alike. To reiterate, there is something about midlife (not to mention my Scottish origins!) that imbues one with pragmatism, the urge to produce something of real utility, not just to satisfy one's intellectual curiosity, nor engage in mere academic exercise.

A host of people merit my appreciation and gratitude. I am profoundly fortunate to have had professors throughout my undergraduate and graduate college years who were quintessential mentors. Art Hansen, Steen Halling, and John Broughton were as close to guardian angels as it gets, extending themselves in ways that helped an insecure, intellectually starved, working-class young man gradually develop a belief in himself as having a keen mind. This book is a gift back to them. Steven Williams, forever a friend, continues to show me the sheer pleasure that can be derived from discussing ideas. I am indebted to the faculty and my mid-1980s graduate cohort in the Existential-Phenomenological Psychology program at Seattle University where I acquired a rock-solid foundation in the humanistic dimensions of clinical work in a milieu where humanism was both espoused and embodied. Rosalea Schonbar, Stephen Mitchell, and Barry Farber broadened my exposure to psychoanalytic thought while I was a doctoral student in the clinical psychology program at Teachers College, Columbia University. Alan Karbelnig and Tom Peters have tacitly taught me that it is possible to be a professional of high regard, be intellectually vital, and still be unpretentious, retain a sense of humor, and be delightfully irreverent. Sam Alibrando, Marilyn Simpson, Steve Moss, Linda Bortell, Linda Krippner, and Mona Kumar have been generous listeners and insightful co-consultants. My friends and child psychiatry colleagues, Rick Lasarow and Larry Braslow, keep me both heartened and realistic about the advantages and disadvantages of medicating children. James Grotstein kindly read versions of the book and offered valuable feedback.

A host of authors have had transformative effects on my clinical thinking over the years: Erich Fromm, R. D. Laing, D. W. Winnicott, Medard Boss, Helen Merrell Lynd, Peter Lomas, Carolyn Saarni, Susanne Denham, Stephen Mitchell, Lewis Aaron, Anthony Stevens, Robert Stolorow, Donnel Stern, Martha Stark, Karlen Lyons-Ruth, Arietta Slade, Paul Wachtel, Allan Schore—to name but a few. The traces of their thinking can be found in these pages.

My parents, Carmen and Rodolfo Gnaulati, by example, have shown me that something good can come of commitment, hard work, and endurance. My father-in-law, Don Chunn, a therapist himself, sowed the seeds of this being an attractive professional choice for me.

The untold numbers of children and families who have crossed my office threshold are deserving of credit. You have covertly communicated to me what you need to get better, and in my more humble, mindful moments I have taken note.

Most of all this book is dedicated to Janet, my loved and loving wife, life companion, and true co-parent who recurringly and willingly freed me up to check out of life and "enter the writing trance" that made this book possible; and, to my dear son, Marcello, who gives me daily lessons on the normalcy of boyish exuberance and rambunctiousness.

INTRODUCTION

I t is ironic that the stock and trade of child therapists, play therapy, in many circles is considered irrelevant to remedy the most common psychological affliction in children, Attention-Deficit Hyperactivity Disorder (ADHD). ADHD has become so thoroughly medicalized in our collective consciousness that to advance play therapy as a treatment option places one at risk for being seen as quaint, befogged, or even negligent. It is tempting to lay the blame for this state of affairs squarely on the doorsteps of the pharmaceutical industry. The argument goes something like this: the meaty profits gained from selling ADHD as a "brain disorder," treatable first and foremost with medications, ensures that nonmedical approaches do not get a fair hearing. There is merit to this viewpoint, which is not to say that medications for ADHD do not have their place, as we discuss further in this book. Yet, the narrow manner in which the disorder is typically conceptualized by academics has also contributed to the marginalization of play therapy as a useful modality with ADHD children. Moreover, play therapy as a discipline is worthy of reproach. All too often what is emphasized in child work is the therapist's disengaged reflectiveness and the child's expectable gravitation toward low-key, object-mediated, talk-heavy, symbolic play—conditions that are hardly amenable to helping the action-oriented child.

Neurocognitive definitions of ADHD have gained ascendancy among academics. It is commonplace to frame standard ADHD symptoms (i.e., motor restlessness, impulsivity, excessive talking, distractibility, forgetfulness, and problems listening, waiting one's turn, and completing mentally effortful tasks) as deficits in self-control and cognitive inefficiencies deriving from abnormal neurology. Favored explanations are those tilted in the direction of according causal significance to faulty brain structures and biochemical processes (Himelstein, Schultz, Newcorn, and Halperin, 2000).

Several assumptions are embedded in this neurocognitive framework that have sorry implications for the utility of play therapy with ADHD children. First is the notion that there is little to be gained from viewing ADHD symptoms as intra- or interpersonally meaningful in any fundamental way. Conceiving of ADHD symptoms mainly as neurological outcroppings renders them something to be managed and controlled, more so than understood. It becomes pointless to base a treatment for ADHD on discerning and reworking the purposes and functions symptoms serve the child in everyday human contexts. Next, given that the causal agent of ADHD symptoms is thought to be the ADHD brain, the architecture of which is largely predetermined by relatively fixed biogenetic events, it stands to reason that contemplating and crafting corrective therapeutic interventions based on etiological factors that are not ostensibly organic is a dubious enterprise; this, despite the abundance of neurological research underscoring the plasticity of the brain and how constitutional factors and social experiences interact in its formation and transformation (Goldschmidt, 2006).

Yet it goes without saying that any viable role for play therapy with ADHD requires an understanding of the disorder that is sufficiently teleological, where symptoms represent purposeful attempts at communication, interaction, self-expression, fulfillment of developmental needs, or the like, that lend themselves to salutary transformation through therapeutic play. Herein lies one agenda of this book. The reader will encounter a rich framework for understanding and treating the myriad developmental and psychosocial needs and motives undergirding ADHD.

Another aim of this book is to enlarge our understanding of the etiology of ADHD by drawing upon available knowledge on how children in general acquire the social and emotional competencies that at problematic levels constitute ADHD symptoms. Excluding severe cases, I do not view ADHD children and non-ADHD children as categorically different but take the position that there are social and emotional challenges that children face in early childhood, and when there are significant and long-standing setbacks in salient areas a diagnosis of ADHD arises as a possibility. This is tantamount to me viewing symptoms as incomplete developmental achievements and believing it to be instructive to extrapolate from knowledge of typical childhood development to shed light on atypical outcomes. This is also tantamount to me having a developmental and functionalist rendering of the ADHD diagnosis. I do not view ADHD as a "disease entity," something attributable to the child independent of developmental and contextual factors. Rather I see the diagnosis as comprising a useful set of criteria to distinguish children who are in need of intervention because their nonnormative rate of socioemotional development has made it difficult for them to function in the everyday environments in which they find themselves.

Of course, there are those severe cases of ADHD more confidently understood through the lens of organic damage and neurologic impairment, where symptoms remain acute independent of agreeable environmental changes and where problems with impulse control, frustration tolerance, aggressivity, and cognitive disorganization are so intractable and chronic that typical developmental explanations seem not to apply. However, in my estimation these more extreme cases are in the minority and we can largely extrapolate from normative developmental phenomena to understand most cases of ADHD and upon which to base treatment interventions. It goes without saying that the explanatory model and play therapy approach supplied in this book is geared toward mild and moderate cases of ADHD, those where symptoms wax and wane based on favorable or unfavorable environmental conditions and which indeed seem developmentally intelligible.

Stated more explicitly, the central premise of this book is that ADHD, in most cases, is best accounted for and treated in terms of various deficits in children's self-regulation of emotion in social contexts. This approach to ADHD appears to be unprecedented in the literature and the hope is that it stands as a refreshing alternative to the neurocognitive one that has come to dominate the field (Barkley, 2006; Douglas, 2005; Hinshaw, Carte, Fan, Jassy, and Owens, 2007). Robust self-regulation of emotion in children is reflected in the likes of: stoking up or toning down the intensity of affective communications to achieve desired interpersonal goals; staying relatively focused and organized in one's thoughts and actions when emotionally aroused; tolerating the frustration accompanying task persistence and independent task mastery; displaying negative emotions in nonprotracted ways; versatility in negotiating other's emotions; and skill at using language and symbolic play to achieve high-order expressive mastery of emotion. Upon close scrutiny, the parallels between diminished emotion-regulation skills and ADHD phenomena are striking. For example, the child who is easily emotionally flooded is likely to be so preoccupied with scanning the surround for potential sources of emotional danger that he or she frequently is motorically restless and ill-attuned to the task at hand. This is but one example of the interface between emotional dysregulation and ADHD symptoms. Many more are covered in this book.

In the beginning section of the book I painstakingly lay out a host of pathways to the attainment of optimal self-regulation of emotion in early childhood, cutting a wide swathe that incorporates such factors as: optimal patterns of affect matching and mismatching in the caregiver-infant dyad; secure attachment; parenting practices that fortify children's differentiated emotional responsiveness, willingness to listen and comply with directives, and frustration tolerance as they strive for independent task mastery; relatively easy infant temperament; good sleep routines; preschool experiences that underscore social and emotional learning; and occasions for active play in the father-child relationship. This is not intended to be an academic exercise. Rather, we can reason backwards from factors that facilitate children's emotional mastery to deduce etiological insights into ADHD. Moreover, many of the practices that boost emotion regulation in early childhood have ramifications for how play therapy techniques with ADHD are best devised, as well as how caregivers during adjunctive parent sessions are best advised.

As mentioned above, traditional play therapy has shortcomings that have led to it being sidelined as a treatment modality with ADHD children. There are various reasons why sedentary, talk-heavy, object-mediated symbolic play and its interpretation alienates and is ineffective with ADHD children. The play of such children tends to be active, void of reflective disclosures, person mediated, and concrete. To expect an ADHD child to use toy figures to mediate communication, engage in sedentary play, and reflect on and absorb interpretations as to its meaning is to expect him or her to be cured as a prerequisite for treatment. Moreover, to recurringly adopt a "neutral," nondirective stance in the face of a child's provocativeness, impulsivity, or disorganized behavior is to court symptom aggravation rather than amelioration.

As will become apparent to the reader, if play therapy is to be advantageous to the ADHD child it must allow for a participatory stance on the part of the therapist. Progressive emotional mastery is not an emergent competency of the child that flowers when he or she is provided with free play experiences and nondirective understanding by the therapist. For that matter, the range, type, and intensity of emotions experienced by the child in therapy is not strictly internal to the child, solely governed by the child's inhibitedness or lack thereof, but is governed also by what is evoked in the play interaction with the therapist. What feelings are felt by the child, how intensely and for how long, depends, in part, on the therapist's skill at throwing him or herself into the play in sensitive and sensitizing ways. Indeed, the child's capacity for prolonging or foreshortening emotional expressions based on what the interaction permits; recovering from noxious levels of excitement or agitation; staying organized in the face of emotional arousal; displaying feelings in socially finessed ways; persisting with goal-directed play without imploding in frustration, and so on, is inextricably linked to the therapist's active subjective input.

Emphasis on children's play content and its symbolism has obscured the therapeutic value of the play process itself. Indulging the ADHD child's gravitation toward person-focused, kinesthetic, concrete play, without undue demands for self-reflection, can be instrumental in making treatment possible. For example, the therapist's willingness to engage in an animated sword fight with the child is tacit acceptance of him or her as a person embodying a high activity level. Vigorous play is often the precondition for the child becoming symptomatic, exhibiting socioemotional vulnerabilities in here-and-now mutual enactments with the therapist that can then be constructively handled. Predictable occasions for active play with the therapist may even be what enables some children to punctuate play with talk about troubling life events. "Down time," resting between active play sequences, finds the child in a state of quietude conducive to self-disclosure and reflection.

In the pages that follow I flesh out the enlivening and organizing benefits of the play process with ADHD children. Along the way, extracting from contemporary psychoanalytic theory, I substantiate a role for the therapist's authentic use of self in the play process to engender a capacity for mutual relatedness and improved social know-how in the child. The latter is especially relevant with ADHD children who often have sufficient knowledge of social etiquette but run into difficulty converting such knowledge into action. I redefine the role of interpretation in child work, argue in favor of the therapeutic potential of mutual enactments, address the circumstances under which the therapist might function as a mentor for the child, and discuss how conjoint work with parents best takes shape. Concepts and techniques are backed up with ample clinical examples and case studies.

For practitioners like myself, the dominance of neurocognitive and medicalized accounts of ADHD has had a stultifying effect on writing and thinking about its possible remediation through therapeutic play. If the reader finds this book to be a welcome antidote to this situation I will have accomplished my task.

1

EARLY-CHILDHOOD PATHWAYS TO SELF-REGULATION OF EMOTION

EMOTION REGULATION DEFINED

A convergence of knowledge from fields as diverse as psychoanalysis, infant research, attachment theory, early-childhood education, and academic psychology increasingly points to the centrality of emotion in the psychological health and ill-health of children. It is not just children's competency at distinguishing and verbally expressing specific emotions, or even blended ones, that has taken on investigatory significance, but the vicissitudes of intra- and interpersonally negotiating emotions in general. It is primarily the latter that has come to be known as *affect regulation*. The emphasis is on the temporal, intensive, and social-communicative dimensions of emotion: how quickly affective states emerge and are recovered from; how long they last; how faintly or intensely they are experienced; one's adeptness at altering and modulating the outward expression of emotion to better realize interpersonal goals; and one's effectiveness in negotiating the emotionality of others. Affect regulation theorists also concern themselves with how emotional arousal promotes or interferes with organized cognition and behavior.

Extrapolating from the work of Thompson (1990, 1991, 1994), and others (Denham, 1998; Saarni, 1999; Sroufe, 1997), we can begin to formulate some descriptive criteria for optimal self-regulation of affect by the dawn of the school-age years. In the chapter that follows we systematically address links between faulty development of affect regulation and ADHD.

1

Modulating the Intensity of Emotion to Better Realize One's Interpersonal Goals

A core feature of enhanced affect regulation pertains to amplifying and deamplifying the intensity of emotions to improve the likelihood that interpersonal objectives will be realized. Being able to "down-regulate," or dampen intense affects, selecting words and embodying nonverbal behaviors that soften communications, may make the difference between being interacted with or shunned. It is one thing for a child to suddenly enter a friend's play space, brimming with excitement, pressuring for eye contact, in a high-pitched voice pleading to be played with, all the while oblivious to the friend's nonverbal and verbal conveyance of discomfort: "Juanita, wanna jump rope, wanna jump rope, let's do it, let's do it!" It is another thing to slowly enter a friend's play space, showing modulated enthusiasm and tacitly discerning how much eye contact, physical proximity, and excitement will secure a needed playmate.

Likewise, facility at "up-regulating," or boosting one's dim affective responses, can lend legitimacy to communications in certain social situations. It is one thing to cast a downward gaze, assume a limp posture, and in a hollow voice implore a child to stop playing so roughly in the form of a question. It is something else to look that child in the eye and, with a firm voice and erect posture, state a desire in the form of a directive: "Right now I am through playing with you because you're being too rough with me." In short, a routine pattern of being underwhelmed in emotionally charged situations might not serve a child well.

Continuous Display of Organized Thought and Behavior Despite High Levels of Distress or Excitement

Acquiring the ability to maintain organized thinking and behavior in the face of elevated distress or excitement are impressive developmental achievements. Take a simple game of "tag" on an unsupervised playground, at the end of a full school day where a child is being hotly pursued by a classmate who is sometimes a friend, at other times a foe, yet who is both revered and envied for his speed. It is no easy feat for the child to self-contain his arousal—fear, envy, excitement, aggression, the risk of shame, all welling up—carefully maneuvering his body, scoping out where to run to avoid being tagged, all the while being tinged with the affectivity of his pursuer. Likewise, consider the child who is administered an exam at school after a poor night's sleep due to studying late, only to find out that she had used the wrong study guide. Managing the attendant distress to enable herself to remember unstudied, yet relevant, material, and attend to and concentrate on exam content, although challenging, becomes necessary.

Emotional Responsiveness Supplanting Emotional Reactivity

Relatively speaking, if development is on course throughout early childhood and beyond, we see a predisposition for emotional responsiveness edging out that for emotional reactivity, with children steadily acquiring the capacity to delay responding to precipitating events. Thompson (1991) refers to this as *latency*. However, presumably, it is important to differentiate between impulsive reactions and spontaneity, per se. With the latter, there may be minimal delay between an event and an emotional response, yet the child likely experiences a measure of control over his or her expressive actions, having quickly processed much overt and covert social-emotional information, all the while feeling vitalized. On the other hand, impulsive reactions tend to be marked by loss of affective control, with a more constricted processing of social-emotional information.

Transitioning Out of Emotional Episode

One of the hallmarks of emotional maturation in childhood involves relative self-attenuation of and recovery from strong emotional reactions, with the intensity and duration of emotions felt and expressed being appropriate to the situation. It is the emotionally fluent child, who upon discovering that his elaborate Lego construction was accidentally knocked over by his dog, pounds his fist on his bed, spiritedly yelling, "I wish my dog would watch where he is going. I'm so mad. That Lego space station took two whole hours to build. I'm MAD, MAD, mad," yet picks up the salvageable sections, loud demonstrations of anger being supplanted by muted irritable muttering, thereafter turning to his father solemnly, although with a half-smile, asking: "What's for dinner? Dog stew?" Naturally, aptness to experience emotions as temporally impermanent presupposes access to a variety of words and phrases that capture their transitory nature (i.e., "Right now I am so upset with you," "Mum, I'm not going to stay mad at you forever you know," "This ice-cream is DELICIOUS! Once I've eaten it, it's back to cleaning up my room. Boo hoo").

Seeing Tasks Through to Completion Without Undue Frustration and Premature Discontinuance

Effortful dedication to and completion of everyday childhood tasks, pursuits, and activities involves self-dampening of frustration. The child may try and err, but if success is in the cards, attendant frustration has to be kept in abeyance. Self-soothing behaviors may be used to down-regulate tension (i.e., hand squeezing, playing with strands of hair, humming, deep breathing). Silent positive self-talk may help with perseverance (i.e., "I can do it. Hang in there. I know I can make three-point shots in the basket. I've done it before").

Negotiating Other's Emotions

Flexible handling of others' emotions also signifies optimal affect regulation. For instance, there are social benefits for the child who can share in someone else's excitement without routinely being overwhelmed by it, emotionally numbing him or herself, or physically fleeing the situation. The same applies to the child who is capable of being emotionally available to others in their distress, likewise without chronic tendencies to become overwhelmed, numb oneself, or take flight. What distinguishes these outcomes is the degree of existent self-other differentiation at the level of affect. *Empathic concern* is predicated on being able to emotionally join with another, be sensitized to his or her feelings, while remaining cognizant that these feelings mostly belong to the other person. On the other hand, *personal distress reactions* ensue when there is a sudden collapse in self-other boundaries and the child becomes overwhelmingly infused with and disorganized by another child's emotionality (Eisenberg et al., 1989). Personal distress reactions tend to short-circuit empathic gestures in that the child becomes so overcome by his or her own reactions to another child's emotionality that he or she requires relief, trumping the child originally in need.

Adept Use of Language and Symbolic Play to Facilitate Higher-Order Emotional Expressiveness

Higher order processing of affective experience necessitates efficacious use of language and other representational tools, such as symbolic play. It is the emotionally fluent child who has access to a broad vocabulary to label and elaborate upon a range of feelings. Such a child has also learned that the type of emotion words used has a bearing on whether his or her communications will be entertained by others and is handy at choosing words to effect desired social outcomes. For example, a child may be happily playing alone and become irate because someone else has entered her play space. She may desire that the other child leave. If she yells out, "Go away, you nasty girl, and leave me alone," the other child might start weeping and linger around, or approach the girl in anger, neither of which effect the desired social outcome, which is to be left alone to play. Saying, "Right now I am enjoying playing alone. Can you please leave me be," in a bold but kind voice would increase the likelihood of the girl's wish being met.

Being exposed to, retaining memory for, and self-generating words and phrases that capture the *transitory nature of feelings* and that are *nontotalistic in their appraisals of self and others* testify to a certain socioemotional adeptness ("Right now I am so mad at you. I don't know how I will feel later" versus "I am so mad at you, I'm through being your friend," "I get so sad when I am mean to my friends and they avoid me" versus "I am such a hateful person that nobody likes me").

Developmental advances in affect regulation can be seen in the symbolic play of children who are well versed in using toys and play materials as representational forms to convey textured meaning about themselves, important others, and their experiential worlds. Throwing themselves into symbolic play, they are able to displace potentially threatening feeling states onto play figures and fictional characters, thereby affording them with mastery over and deeper processing of such feeling states.

Now that the reader has been acquainted with the constituents of optimal emotion regulation, we can turn our attention to the developmental, attachment-related, neurobiological, and pedagogical processes that promote and compromise its formation throughout early childhood.

DEVELOPMENTAL CONSIDERATIONS

Substantial evidence exists showing how caregiver-infant dyadic regulatory processes impact the child's formative capacities for internally managing states of emotional arousal and de-arousal. It is generally assumed that what starts out as "external" regulation becomes psychologically incorporated as "internal," with qualitative features of early dyadic regulation serving as an inner template for the child's own emerging regulatory proclivities. Yet, the intersubjective nature of emotional experiences and communications in the caregiver-infant relationship precludes a strict delineation of external and internal, inner and outer.

Self-regulation of emotion may be the desired developmental end-point for children, but not without heavy reliance on caregivers in the beginning, giving way to partial reliance. Sroufe (1997) suggests that the normative trajectory is one from "caregiver-orchestrated," to "caregiver-guided," to self-regulation. An example will elucidate. The three-month-old infant may avert her gaze and stiffen her posture to signal that her mother's excitement has become momentarily unbearable. The mother may look away and tone down her excitement, allowing her infant time to reestablish emotional equilibrium and gesture a readiness to be reengaged (caregiver-orchestrated regulation).

However, the three-year-old toddler has a greater range of regulatory strategies and need not be so fundamentally reliant on her mother to recover from overarousal. When suddenly confronted by and infused with mother's excitement, the toddler may walk away to regain composure but still remain distressed. The mother may extend herself in ways to alleviate her toddler's discomfort: "Did my big happy feelings make you feel nervous? Maybe you were not ready to have me be next to you?" At which point the toddler may verbalize, "Me no like it when you run up to me and spook me," and the child may gradually transition out of a negative emotional state prompted, in part, by her mother suggesting a fun game of ring-toss together (caregiver-guided regulation).

The self-regulatory finesse of the eight-year-old child may be exemplified in her showing a modicum of empathy for her mother's excitement, indulging her for a few minutes, while communicating eagerness to return to the book she was reading before the encounter with her mother: "Mom, I know that you are a happy camper, and want to talk right now, but I am really, really, really enjoying reading this book!" Residual tension carrying over from the interaction may be coped with by putting on a soothing CD, getting under the blankets of the bed she was formerly lying on top of, or softly humming while reading (self-regulation).

Sroufe (1997) cogently articulates the tasks inherent in smooth self-regulation of emotion: "Children must delay, defer, and accept substitutions without becoming aggressive or disorganized by frustration, and they are expected to cope well with high arousal, whether due to environmental challenge or fatigue. At the same time they are spontaneous and exuberant when circumstances permit" (214).

Yet even the most emotionally mature child will become unduly taxed under stressful life conditions, regressing in ways that require varying degrees of caregiver input to deintensify and emerge from negative emotional states and segue into positive ones.

A more complete understanding of the pathways to optimal self-regulation of affect requires a step-by-step look at its dyadic precursors in the parent-infant relationship and regulatory socialization of toddlers and school-age children by caregivers and teachers.

Infancy

Stern (1971, 1977) is credited with recasting the image of newborns put forth by Mahler (Mahler, Pine, and Bergman, 1975), whereby we now think of infants as active, responsive, and communicative, displaying an expanding array of affectively suffused signals as to his or her need states, rather than relatively passive, nonresponsive, and noncommunicative (i.e., Mahler's autistic phase). There is general acceptance of bidirectionality in the caregiver-infant relationship, one dimension of which is recurrent mutual cuing. Caregiver and infant take their cues from each other regarding the foreshortening or prolongation, amplification or deamplification of affective states coexperienced. In the words of Beebe and Lachmann (1994), "Although each partner does not influence the other in equal measure or necessarily in like manner, both actively contribute to the regulation of the exchange" (134). This process has also been named "synchronization" (Stern, 1971, 1977) and "contingent responsivity" (Schore, 2003).

All the same, with their greater socioemotional sophistication, caregivers act as "psychobiological regulators" (Sroufe, 1997) for the infant, carefully and caringly gauging the infant's somatic/affective condition in the interaction. The caregiver discerns from the infant's cues what is tolerable and what is intolerable, when down-regulation is necessitated to quell or up-regulation is invited to enkindle. Empathic attunement is at the heart of this process, with the caregiver cycling in and out of being affected by and affecting the infant. Empathy presupposes a measure of differentiated relatedness, where the emotional boundaries between caregiver and infant, although permeable, do not become habitually dissolved. At some basic level, the infant's feelings are the infant's feelings, and the caregiver's feelings are the caregiver's feelings.

Tronick's (1989) model of caregiver-infant regulatory interaction is generally considered to be groundbreaking. He proposed that in the normal course of events, caregiver and infant recurringly shift in and out of mutually coordinated positive emotional states, to miscoordinated negative emotional states that are quickly recovered from. Asynchronous emotional exchanges, or "interactive errors," that lead to infant distress, although unavoidable, need to be promptly remedied by the caregiver, enabling restoration of synchronous positive emotional states. This salutary pattern is reflected in the following example.

Six-month-old Molly signals a readiness for added pleasurable stimulation with an inviting smile, sustained eye contact, and repetitive foot wiggling, feeding off of her mother's excitement when the mother gratifies with a wide-faced smile of her own. Her mother then ups the affectivity in the interaction more than a notch by shaking a rattle while smiling. Molly shows that the level of stimulation she is being confronted with is overwhelming by tensing up, averting her gaze, and whimpering. Swept up in her initial excitement, the mother, not to be deterred, attempts to force eye contact and shakes the rattle closer to Molly's face, hoping that Molly will reengage in the formerly mutually pleasurable exchange. Whimpering turns to crying and Molly clenches her arms closer to her body. Realizing that Molly is overcome with emotion, the mother quickly alters her approach and begins to soothe Molly, picking her up, rocking her in her arms, and softly saying, "There, there, my baby girl. Mommy got too excited and you are upset." The mother sustains this soothing approach until Molly is fully calmed. Content, Molly begins to visually scan the floor below and fixes her gaze on some colored foam blocks. Attuned to Molly's dawning interest in the blocks, her mother lowers her to within reach of them. Molly sits up and rocks back and forth in delight, tightly squeezing one of the blocks. The mother picks up a block and begins squeezing it at the same tempo as Molly. Molly squeals with delight.

Troublesome caregiver-infant sequences involve asynchronous interactions that incite prolonged negative emotionality, combined with caregiver misinterpretation of or disregard for the infant's cues for remedial attention (Tronick, 1989). In the above example, this might amount to Molly's mother persisting in her efforts to shake the rattle, bringing it closer and closer to Molly's face, pressuring for eye contact, while ignoring Molly's signals for reduced stimulation of this type. The mother might then disapprove of Molly's resultant loud flailing and crying and place her in her crib to "cry it out."

During infancy, a preponderance of asynchronous exchanges without speedy external provision of care that restores emotional equilibrium can forestall emotional development, causing the child to develop susceptibilities to underregulate or overregulate his or her emotions. Heightened affective states, whether positive (i.e., joy and euphoria) or negative (i.e., fury and distress) then retain a potential to disorganize the child and bring about desperate coping strategies. The disorganizing effects of heightened affective states can be seen in young children who are susceptible to tantrums, reckless behavior, and frenzied displays of excitement. Desperate coping strategies can take the form of emotional blunting, routine avoidance of emotionally charged interpersonal situations, and louder and more insistent expressions of distress to cue caregivers as to needed remedial attention. Belsky (1999) has referred to the latter as a "last ditch effort" on the part of the child to secure restorative care.

Toddlerhood

Autonomy

Toddlers are keenly invested in exercising their fast evolving fine and gross motor abilities to explore their surroundings and take an active role in their own self-care. Relatively helpless in relation to their own self-care as infants, at the mercy of caregivers to provide needed relief by correctly deciphering bodily discomforts, they can now show a measure of competence at moving around and gratifying their own needs. In fact, the fury that toddlers show in relation to wanting control over what happens to their bodies—whether it be what they are fed, how they are fed, what clothes they wear, when they are to use the toilet, and the like—may stem from wanting to disassociate themselves from the relative helplessness endured as infants with respect to what happened to and in their bodies. The same applies to their freedom of movement. Toddlers' spirited bouts to maneuver their own bodies in search of novel experiences in nearby places and spaces is perhaps due, in part, to inefficacy associated with being passive voyeurs as infants, precariously dependent on caregivers to be attuned to signals for needed repositioning of their bodies to better access novel sights, sounds, and tactile stimulation.

During the toddler years children have a propensity to want control over objects in their environment that they derive pleasure from. Toys are not just generic objects but sources of sensori-motor delight. Control over what toys they desire to play with, when and for how long, represents an urgent bid to govern sources of stimulation and pleasure that toys provide. Put differently, possessiveness with toys, refusal to share them, and forceful attempts to wrest them back from others, in light of formative autonomous processes, are unrefined attempts by the young preschooler to exert control over when, how, and for how long novel stimulation and pleasure will be experienced.

Self-Efficacy and Frustration Tolerance

Toddlerhood is a critically important period for emergent self-efficacy, or a developing sense of mastery, and the fortification of frustration tolerance. Countless challenges await the child on a daily basis that tax, enfeeble, or embolden his or her powers of frustration tolerance depending, in part, on the nature of caregiving received. Generally speaking, assisted self-mastery that honors the child's fledgling independent capabilities instills in him or her a more proactive, success-engendering orientation to everyday challenges. Whether the challenge be a linguistic one, where the child labors to communicate needs and wants, involves adequate eye-hand coordination to self-feed, or bodily repositioning to self-dress, parenting interventions that dial into the right measure of support to render a task self-achievable represent the standard to repeatedly aim for.

Parental gauging of how much support a child needs to achieve task mastery is partly related to the amount of frustration the child manifests. When the child's level of frustration is high, the task at hand may need to be reconfigured to allow for success with mild to moderate exertion. Hence, a father might pull a sweater with a maddeningly tight opening over his son's head but encourage him to put his own arms in the sleeves. Or, a mother might make a stepstool available for her son to climb on the toilet after the son grunts and groans that he is too tired to move his body onto the toilet by himself.

Disallowing a toddler to suddenly abort a task he or she cannot immediately master, nonintrusively redirecting him or her back to the task, playfully making it enticing, restructuring it to make it newly achievable with some effort, all embolden persistence, focused effort, goal-directedness, and frustration tolerance in the child. The sense of satisfaction in assistedly seeing the task through to completion can be its own reward, with positive affectivity surrounding the accomplishment being embellished by the caregiver's manifested delight. Abundant sequences of this sort bolster the toddler's sense of self-efficacy and generalized frustration tolerance.

Of course fatigue, inability, reduced motivation or desire, and overzealous parental re-directing can all lead a child to discontinue an activity or a task, or fail at it, culminating in varying levels of distress. As always, when there is marked distress the regulatory efforts of caregivers will have to be greater to establish a measure of emotional equilibrium.

Too much assistance afforded the child too frequently when he or she is eminently able to complete everyday tasks with mild, moderate, or no help can lead to intrinsic passivity, task-avoidance, or volatile expressions of frustration in situations that require self-reliance. Likewise, when there is a chronic pattern of caregivers anticipating and gratifying a child's needs without patient and caring verbal prompting in line with the child's linguistic and gestural proficiencies, the child can generalize expectations of "magical knowing" to other situations and become markedly distressed when others fail to automatically divine and meet his or her needs and wants.

Handling and Mishandling of Expansive Positive Mood States

While exercising their motoric exploratory competencies toddlers are often filled with euphoria vis-à-vis successful achievements. Toddlerhood brings with it a sense of omnipotence as to what can be accomplished. The thrill of standing upright, being able to engage in unassisted walking, then to run and climb with relative ease can all be intoxicating, leaving the child feeling as if there were no bounds to his or her brilliance. Expansive affective states such as joy and euphoria are felt more fervently as the child extends his or her kinesthetic reach and propels him or herself into the environment. Caregiver responses that ensure optimal regulation, in part, center on affirming the child's sense of exhibitionistic pride: "What a good runner you are! How did my little girl learn to run so fast? Mommy is so proud of you." Sharing in the child's sense of pride and joy during exhibitionistic moments helps render such viscerally felt affects more manageable, counteracts the potential for disorganization, and enkindles and concretizes feelings of efficaciousness and aliveness in the child. Along these lines, Kohut (1977) writes on how sensitive handling of the toddlers "grandiose-exhibitionistic needs" is one route to vitalization of the self.

Toddlers whose animated displays of prowess are consistently met with indifference, disregard, or belittlement on the part of caregivers, can be susceptible to up-regulating their exhibitionism and validation-seeking. They may be given to protracted performance episodes marked by insistent, demanding, theatrical behaviors to desperately elicit needed acknowledgment. A vicious cycle then gets set in motion where the child's shrill and insistent ways of seeking affirmation of displayed abilities are experienced as off-putting by caregivers, reactions that in turn cause the child to resort to even wilder antics to secure needed validation. Over time the frustration inherent in being routinely deprived of needed caregiver recognition during poignant exhibitionistic moments can render the child's overall recognition-seeking strategies more negativistic and hostile.

Failure, Shame, and Rage

Needless to say, during toddlerhood the child's imagined abilities often outpace what he or she is actually capable of and failure experiences abound. Performance failures, especially on tasks that the child affixes special value to, or that peers seem to easily negotiate, can result in rapid onset of a deflated mood, acute agitation, or rage. In these narcissistically injurious moments the child is flooded with primitive feelings of shame and rage, which can have profound fragmenting and debilitating effects. Archaic shame visits the toddler with an insufferable sense of feeling "all bad," incompetent, or defective. Sartre (1956) evocatively likens shame to an "emotional hemorrhage." This captures the degree of danger and incapacitation children undergo when ashamed. Much down-regulatory caregiving is necessary if the toddler is to bounce back from shame episodes. Sustained expressions of empathy for the child's wounded self-pride that have a soothing and restorative effect become essential (i.e., "You fell off the monkey bars when you really wanted to get to the other side all by yourself. Now you are feeling so bad about yourself. I'm so sorry this happened. . . . Let daddy know when you are ready for a hug to help you feel better"). Compassionately delivered statements that help the child modify their grandiose self-representations are also pivotal ("You're still a fine runner even though John beat you to the water fountain. John is older than you, has longer legs, and is hard to beat at running! But, let's not forget that you learned to cross the monkey bars on your own before him!). Gradually and incrementally the child internalizes these empathic offerings and adjusted appraisals and they form the experiential substrate for his or her own positive/realistic self-talk vis-à-vis performance failures, potentiating greater self-regulation of shame.

Rage, rather than shame, can burst forth when there are insults to the child's sense of omnipotence, bringing about an affective focus on others, or the object world. Rage can instantaneously induce feelings of power and control, counteracting those of weakness and powerlessness catalyzed by failed mastery. The child may externalize blame for his own unsuccessful efforts and aggressively lash out at others. When failures occur in attempts to manipulate objects or transact play activities, destructive behavior may be perpetrated by the child to obliterate the object, or spoil the activity that has painfully exposed the child to his or her incompetence. Once again, active caregiving is necessary to assist the toddler with toning down the intensity of his or her dissatisfaction, attenuate the length of time spent in negative mood states, and co-foster a readiness to transition into a more positively valenced mood state. Down-regulating interventions can take the form of physically restraining the child while "talking him or her down"; calmly but assuredly imposing a time-out, with the stipulation that anger be talked out afterward; or empathizing with the child, yet offering a verbal example of a modulated expression of anger (i.e., "It is so very, very frustrating when things don't work out well. Yeh, I can see that you are so angry. But it is not okay to hit. You could say something like, 'I hate it when

I can't make the ball go in the basket' using your angry voice"). Full recovery is predicated on following the child's cue as to when his or her negative mood state has subsided and there is a readiness to transition into a positive one (i.e., "I guess you are almost over being mad. Do you want to play a game with me other than the basketball game?).

Compliance and Noncompliance

The affective tenor imbuing a caregiver's directions and requests has ramifications for whether or not toddlers will react with compliance, defiance, or indifference. There is a greater likelihood of adherence to directions and requests when caregivers discern from the toddler's outward expressions whether he or she is overstimulated or understimulated by the interaction, with caregivers toning their affectivity up or down accordingly. What appears on the surface as noncompliance, or "not listening," on the toddler's part, upon closer scrutiny periodically is the child tuning the caregiver out in a desperate bid to cope with a level of arousal in the moment that is beyond him or her. Ignoring, tuning out, and becoming noncommunicative sometimes can be the toddler equivalent of the infant's averted gaze when overstimulated. Likewise, toddlers may tune out their caregivers if there is too little emotional intensity underlying verbal requests and directions, indicating to the child that the caregiver does not "mean business."

There can be rapid de-differentiation of toddlers' self-other boundaries in emotion-filled compliance-seeking interactions. Therefore, in cases where caregivers are perpetually reactive, meeting anger with anger, there is strong potential for such compliance-seeking interactions to devolve into episodes of mutual negativity and resentment, eventuating in the toddler becoming obstinate and intractable, or fearfully compliant.

Differentiated Emotional Responsiveness

A caregiver's empathic mirroring of the child's differentiated emotions with sufficient frequency, especially during heightened affective moments, helps anchor the child in his or her own self-experience, rendering feeling states containable and decipherable. The permeability of self-other boundaries throughout early childhood can result in the child becoming easily infused with the affectivity of those in his or her presence. A persistent and enduring pattern of elevated anxiety in response to the child's anxiety, overexcitement vis-à-vis the child's excitability, meeting anger with anger, or being overcome with sadness when the child is sad, can lead to the child overcontrolling or undercontrolling his or her own feelings in affectively charged situations. This can be manifested in children learning to blunt their emotions, avoiding and denying them for fear that others will be overwhelmed by them. It can also take the form of children becoming "intensity junkies," seeking out conflict or opportunities for unbridled expressions of excitement in their emotional lives, creating self-regulation problems that can negatively impact their social dealings with peers.

Symbolizing and Verbally Communicating Affective Experience

At its most generative, symbolization of affective experience throughout toddlerhood via the most common modalities of language and play is a highly interactive process, whereby caregivers act as translators and mediators of the child's inner experiences and imaginative productions, giving them form and dimensionality, helping concretize them and increasing their intelligibility.

The caregiver's differentiated, yet attuned, stance in relation to the child's inner life potentiates the child's capacity to represent his or her own inner life to him or herself. Fonagy (2001) refers to this as the beginnings of mentalization: "Children learn to represent internal experiences because these experiences are first made real by another's recognition of them" (95). In short, toddler's inchoate capacities to reflect on their own inner experiences are inextricably linked to caregiver's effectiveness in making these inner experiences recognizable to them. Diffuse feeling states gradually become coherent and identifiable through the imprint of the other, anchoring the child in his or her self-experience. Children thereby acquire a personal knowledge of emotions and their communicability, which can be used to generate plausible understandings of other's feelings.

Children as young as two are capable of discerning from facial expressions and naming global emotions such as sadness and happiness (Michalson and Lewis, 1985), but they may need active input from caregivers to be versatile in linguistically representing more physiologically proximal emotions like fear and surprise, as well as blended emotions. Likewise, if children's nonrefined attempts at verbalizing feelings are to steadily evolve into rich representational forms of affective expression that do justice to the temporal and intensive features of emotions, there has to be much linguistic modeling, and sensitive rewording and rephrasing on the part of caregivers.

During late toddlerhood and beyond, symbolic play can become a powerful mechanism for the child to concretize, integrate, and organize affective states, displacing feelings, wishes, and intentions onto play objects and fantasy characters. Maturation in affect regulation can be seen in the symbolic play of children who can capably use toys and play materials as representational forms to convey textured meaning about themselves, important others, and their experiential worlds. Throwing themselves into symbolic play they are able to displace potentially threatening feeling states onto play figures and fictional characters, thereby affording them with mastery over and deeper processing of such feeling states.

Yet, not all emotional learning occurs at the level of symbolic or semantic representation. Much "implicit relational knowing" (Lyons-Ruth, 1998) is prereflective and takes place outside of conscious awareness. For instance, the procedural knowledge involved in such endeavors as resolving a conflict or showing a desire to play entails rapid, largely subliminal, processing of complex intersubjectively mediated experiences. Language may help articulate and clarify implicit relational knowledge, but it is not able to be fully encapsulated with words and may even have its own nonlinguistic representational system (Beebe and Lachman, 1994).

The Father's Unique Role

Father-child relations theory and research points to the influential contribution of fathers during toddlerhood separation-individuation processes. In negotiating countervailing needs for oneness with and separation from the maternal figure, the father's active involvement can be essential to help the child manage accompanying separation anxiety, expansive mood states, engulfment fears, dysphoria, and rage reactions.

During early toddlerhood the father's active involvement helps galvanize the child's emerging interest in the other-than-mother world, while the mother is often looked to for "emotional refueling" and respite (Edward, Ruskin, and Turrini, 1991). Fathers' active play style may be uniquely suited to toddlers' needs to exercise their newfound exploratory and motoric competencies. Much research substantiates fathers' penchant for engaging in rough-and-tumble, excitable, vigorous play with young children, compared with mothers' more "quiet," "low-key" style of play (Lewis and Lamb, 2003). Accessibility to a paternal playmate can act as a stimulus for individuation from the primary maternal figure, allowing exploratory excitement to override separation anxiety. Moreover, arguably the child who is availed with a steady stream of high energy, arousing, kinesthetically challenging play experiences, juxtaposed with occasions for soothing and calming once the play has "gone too far," is well-positioned to acquire ways of regulating emotional highs and lows.

Developmental gains during what Mahler (Mahler, Pine, and Bergman, 1975) labeled the *rapprochement* subphase of separation-individuation may also be predicated on paternal input. The hallmark of the rapprochement subphase is the paradoxical interplay between the thrill of newfound motor capacities that fuel feelings of omnipotence and expansiveness, and the anxiety and distress the toddler experiences upon becoming aware of his or her status as separate. Crude assertions of independence in the form of defiant gestures feature prominently in the child's behavior. He or she oscillates between aggressive flights from the primary maternal figure and dysphoric awareness of his or her separateness from the maternal figure. Anger and grief have to be reckoned with as the toddler faces the central developmental task of this subphase: to "integrate his magnificence with his vulnerability" (Johnson, 1987, 41) or similarly, to "relinquish omnipotence in favor of competence" (Morrison, 1986, 9). Theorists and researchers underscore the father's significance for the child during this period as a person who can facilitate a grief process and aid in diminishing the potentially fragmenting effects of aggressive reactions.

During the rapprochement subphase reliance on mother for soothing and comfort can elicit engulfment fears and dissolution of emerging independence. The father can act as a grief-facilitating object who can render the toddler's painful disillusionment more manageable by virtue of the fact that his presence is less evocative of ambivalence, engulfment, or desertion (Edward, Ruskin, and Turrini, 1991). As Greenspan (1982) notes, the availability of the father as an alternative "base of security" can abet the grief process: "Father may be seen intermittently as second best to the primary object the youngster is relinquishing; yet to have second best available to modify the intensity of the mourning may make mourning possible at this age level" (136).

Winnicott (1944) maintained that the two-parent child is profited by having one parent to love while the other is being hated. Where there is paternal absence or unavailability, especially if there is a dearth of alternative attachment figures, the risks inherent in showing displeasure at mother can be immense. Directing developmentally expectable fury toward a mother who is simultaneously desperately needed, but whose care might be evocative of engulfment and subversion of independence, is to run the risk psychically of destroying an all-too-needed emotional lifeline.

In short, during toddlerhood fathers' active play style and emotional availability have important ramifications for incipient skills at managing excitement, grief, anxiety, and rage as separation-individuation processes unfold.

Social Referencing

From the first year of life on, young children learn about how to express emotions through social referencing. They are predisposed to take cues from those around them as to what, how, and when to display emotion. As such, if children are to learn to master a full range of emotions and modulate their expression of them depending on what the situation allows or demands, their social worlds need to provide ample exposure to parents, guardians, family members, and peers who are adept in these areas.

Sleep and Self-Control

Predictable routines and schedules have an organizing effect on young children and too much change can compromise children's maturing regulatory capacities. This is especially true with respect to sleep routines. Sleep irregularities in young children have been associated with mood fluctuations, forgetfulness, and reduced executive functioning—planning, organizing, suppressing impulses, and remaining mentally alert (Sadeh, Raviv, and Gruber, 2000). Indeed, it is perplexing why scarce attention is paid to impaired sleep as a cause of emotional lability, forgetfulness, and problematic executive functioning, rather than, or in combination with ADHD, given that the co-prevalence of ADHD and sleep impairments can be as high as 50 percent (Allen, Singer, Brow, and Salam, 1992).

Fatigue and sleep problems are often a covert, overlooked cause of diminished self-control in children, which is surprising given that the acquisition of an optimal sleep-wakefulness cycle in infancy is a primary indicator of "early biobehavioral organization and adaptation" (Sadeh, Raviv, and Gruber, 2000, 291). Many parents underestimate the existence of sleep problems and their adverse effects. In one study of kindergartener's sleep habits it was found that the mean number of night awakenings observed by researchers was five times that assumed by parents and that all the parents in the study believed their children's sleep to be good or very good when, via objective measures, 41 percent of them exhibited fragmented sleep

(Tikotzky and Sadeh, 2001). Also, there appears to be durability to suboptimal sleep habits with perhaps as many as 84 percent of children showing the same disrupted sleep at age three as was evidenced in their infancy (Kataria, Swanson, and Trevathan, 1987).

Sleep problems and resultant poor self-control in children can stem from being raised in a disregulated, permissive household where fixed bedtimes are not upheld and there is a dearth of nighttime rituals that induce states of restfulness (Sadeh, Raviv, and Gruber, 2000). Some researchers takes it one step further to suggest that modern society creates sleep conditions that are unnatural from an evolutionary perspective, confronting children with anomalous temperatures, light and noise conditions, and nonavailability of co-sleeping arrangements (McKenna, 1993). At any rate, good sleep patterns in young children are an interactive achievement, much dependent on caregivers' effectiveness at keeping bedtime rituals consistent and inducing states of restfulness.

Preschool Pedagogy

Despite a growing consensus among educators endorsing the need for learning experiences that embolden self-regulation of emotion at the preschool level, pedagogical approaches that effectively inculcate this are scant. The vast majority of kindergarten teachers view children's readiness to enter the school system in terms of their adeptness at expressing and overcoming negative emotions, refraining from acting disruptively, and being curious, enthusiastic, and sensitive to other's feelings, rather than in terms of acquiring proto-academic skills such as the ability to count to twenty, recite the alphabet, or adroitly hold and use a pencil (Lewit and Baker, 1995). Yet, didactic, directive, instructionally based curricula that tend to overregulate children's emotions predominate, eclipsing those that emphasize the sort of experiential, process-oriented, emotionally facilitative approaches that capitalize on preschoolers' naturally occurring affectively charged interpersonal exchanges. Needless to say, it is the latter that cultivates accelerated emotional mastery. This state of affairs is alarming given that intensive opportunity for fostering emotional competency in pre-school settings is critically important to augment favorable experiences or compensate for unfavorable ones occurring in the home environment. At the risk of asserting the obvious, the responsibility for building children's emotion skills is, in part, a societal one, and extends beyond the domain of the family, or parent-child relationship.

Gnaulati and North (2006) outline preschool teaching practices that offer promise in advancing young children's emotional development. Expectable, spontaneously occurring conflicts between preschoolers are viewed as unique opportunities for social and emotional learning that ought to be seen as integral to, rather than deviating from, a meaningful curriculum. When children are in conflict and teachers intervene to facilitate its working through, children are personally grounded in a learning experience that has immediacy and poignancy. They directly experience what it is like to be in conflict, to be understood, to have a felt sense that actions have interpersonal consequences, and to feel genuine desire to reconcile. It is one thing to be "taught" the "moral lesson" that children avoid those who hit, or to read about the bear who is lonely because his hitting other bears results in him being an outcast. It is another thing to directly experience being ostracized by a classmate for acting aggressively and for this classmate to communicate this as the cause. The latter is less abstract, has more personal relevance, and may lead to more potent socioemotional learning.

"Keeping the peace" by "leaping in" and fixing preschoolers' conflicts, issuing directives, and expecting speedy compliance with adult commands are often commonplace strategies used by adults in preschool settings (e.g., "The two of you need to stop arguing and get back to playing cooperatively. Here, Juan, you have one car and George, you have the other"). When routinely employed, such directiveness can thwart opportunities for children to identify, express, and master strong emotions underlying interpersonal conflicts and short-circuit processes by which children learn self-initiated ways of arriving at resolutions. This is notwithstanding how the *process* leading to effective conflict resolution, in essence, is part of the solution: Tolerating being in close physical proximity while an interpersonal conflict is brewing, regulating one's own feelings and responding to those of others, listening and being listened to, experimenting with "feeling words," are only a few examples of the valuable socioemotional competencies children learn in the process of making peace—competencies that serve them well in negotiating future disagreements.

Gnaulati and North (2006) offer ingredients of a pedagogical style that helps foster and consolidate self-regulatory skills in preschoolers:

• Aptitude at modeling optimal emotion regulation, or being calm and reassuring in the face of preschoolers' intense displays of distress, euphoria, agitation, or fury.

- Knowing when to "up-regulate" the intensity of interventions to energize and enliven children, and when to "down-regulate" to help children feel calm and contained.
- Teacher effectiveness in a "floating" role, or being vigilant and mobile in regard to intervening in interpersonal conflicts that arise between preschoolers.
- Prompt down-regulatory interventions when children communicate unmanageable distress.
- Maintenance of clear emotional boundaries so as to avoid any pattern of overidentifying with children's negative emotions, becoming personally distressed.
- Effectiveness in affirming children in moments when they enthusiastically exhibit mastery of a task that they seek recognition for.
- Adeptness at judging the degree of involvement necessary to assist preschoolers with arriving at mutually tolerable resolutions to conflicts.
- Skill at demonstrating genuine empathy with children of varying ethnicities and personality dispositions across a range of emotional states.
- Adeptness at judging the degree of involvement necessary to assist preschoolers with arriving at mutually tolerable resolutions to conflicts.
- Knowledge of children's emotional development; in particular the importance of
- rudimentary displays of autonomy, the acquisition of emotion regulation, empathy fostering, shame-based aggression, and the role of guilt in engendering reparation after conflicts, all of which are salient during the preschool years.

School-Age Years

During the school-age years established patterns of emotional arousal and de-arousal constructed during infancy and toddlerhood become further modified and consolidated. When development is on track, there is less reliance on caregivers and others to down-regulate or up-regulate the intensity of emotions consonant with situational demands. Peer norms as to acceptable and unacceptable forms of emotional expression become powerful regulatory motivators. Self-monitoring to establish and maintain affiliative peer connections takes on heightened significance. Entering the school system, the child encounters evaluative experiences heretofore unencountered, whether in the form of social evaluation by peers, or academic evaluation by teachers. Self-control, frustration tolerance, task persistence, and maintenance of organized behavior in the face of excitement or distress become preconditions for smooth academic functioning and peer socialization.

School-age children can learn to modulate and modify their emotional expressions in the face of parent's and guardian's sincere and genuine reactions to their behavior. In a balanced fashion, sincerely and genuinely communicating hurt feelings when the child acts hurtfully, annoyance when he or she is clearly defiant, and so forth, enables the child to learn that he or she lives in a world where actions have reactions. Overall love for the child may be unconditional, but acceptance of the child's behavior may be highly conditional. A father might refuse to talk to a child who is screaming loudly, letting that child know that he will be available to talk once the child is able to use a quiet voice. The child learns that screaming loudly is not an effective way to hold his or her father's attention. In short, the genuine, expectable, nonoverwhelming reactions of parents help the child cultivate more socially sensitive ways of communicating feelings, an important dimension of emotion regulation.

Play

The importance of play in enhancing affect-regulation capacities during the school-age years cannot be overestimated. As already mentioned, symbolic play functions as a primary vehicle for higher-order processing of feelings. Toys and play objects offer representational means to familiarize the child with a range of emotional expressions in nonthreatening ways. Displacing potentially dangerous affects onto objects and fictional characters provides a certain psychic distance, allowing for safer and more thorough emotional processing.

Pretend play is one avenue for the child to work out the frustrations inherent in having to adapt to the constraints of reality. Social and academic evaluative experiences can painfully confront the child with personal limitations that engender shame, disappointment, distress, and rejection. Identification with superheroes and action figures can elevate a child's mood and sense of self-importance in the face of ego deflation. Play that pleasurably engrosses the child can be a palliative distraction from painful affects. Routines, responsibilities, and overregulation of behavior required for manageable classrooms can exact an emotional price on the child and be compensated for with access to energetic free-play experiences that offer emotional release. In our achievement-oriented culture, where children are increasingly overscheduled with homework and extracurricular activities, play experiences that spontaneously and organically evolve, at a pace befitting the open-ended imaginative scenarios that might be unfolding, may be viewed by caregivers and teachers as nonproductive and frivolous. Yet, such play experiences can be emotionally restorative for the child, helping him or her unwind subsequent to the effortful cognition and behavioral controls associated with the school day. Accordingly, it should come as no surprise that there is empirical evidence substantiating the benefits of recess for schoolchildren: post-recess children are less restless and show longer attention spans than pre-recess or no-recess children (Pellegrini, Huberty, and Jones, 1995).

As anthropologists have pointed out, there is also a *practice* component to pretend play. As children imaginatively and repetitively try on and try out roles and modes of expression, they are expanding and consolidating their repertoire of social and emotional skills (Caillois, 2001). Repetition and mastery go hand in hand. Replaying the same games, or reenacting the same activities, builds in the sort of control, predictability, and familiarity to play experiences that children might need to strengthen and assimilate the role identifications and variegated emotions embodied in these play experiences. In pretending to be sad, mad, or glad the child obtains practice being sad, mad, or glad.

Age-regressed pretend play avails the child with opportunities to revisit, integrate, and master archaic emotional states. Age-advanced pretend play offers occasions for experimentation with more mature role actualization, and subtle, nuanced, complex forms of emotional expressiveness. For the eight-year-old girl to make-believe she is going to the prom, driving a car, or calling a prospective boyfriend, is to psychologically prepare for what is up ahead. Playful anticipation of and experimentation with future roles can inculcate the socioemotional skills embedded in these roles.

Kinesthetically vigorous play can be important to test and fortify the child's capacities to maintain organized behavior in the face of high arousal. This is especially true if this vigorous play takes place in open spaces, where greater freedom of movement can elicit emotional expansiveness, and in a social milieu, requiring a degree of self-other monitoring. It is lamentable that as active play spaces for adults are on the increase in American culture (mountain biking trails, golf courses, gyms, climbing walls, etc.) those available to children are on the decrease. Furthermore, over the past forty years the play of the average American child has gone from being predominantly active, social, and outdoors, to sedentary, nonsocial, and indoors (Elkind, 1994). This transition is predominantly due to a decline in safe play locations (especially in inner cities), parental perceptions of societal danger, litigious behavior of parents leading to schools, parks, and other child-service organizations scrutinizing what types of social behavior, play spaces, and play structures can minimize any potential for harm and be legally defensible, and increased television viewing and use of computer games (De-Grandpre, 1999; Glassner, 1999). One social commenter has intriguingly proposed that reduced opportunities for active play parallel the burgeoning rates of ADHD in American culture, and that the former may, in part, account for the latter (Panksepp, 1998).

PARENT-CHILD ATTACHMENT

Bowlby (1969, 1973) conceived of parent-infant attachment as a transactional system wherein newborns are biogenetically primed to use emotional communications to elicit care from parents in survival-promoting ways. Indeed, implicit in attachment theory is the notion that affective experience is at its very core communicative and serves important interpersonal functions, one of the most basic being to signal danger in ways that impel close proximity on the part of primary caregivers. From an evolutionary perspective, the survival value of swiftly enacted, close, parent-infant contact cannot be understated. In primordial habitats where lurking predators or catastrophic climatic and environmental events posed imminent danger, children who were most adept at conveying alarm in ways that induced parental nearness maximized their chances of survival. Therefore, compliments of our bioevolutionary inheritance, in times of pointed distress children are apt to resort to whatever modes of emotional expression effect physical proximity on the part of select attachment figures. In some parent-child dyads a normal cry or modulated expression of distress by the infant is enough to make a parent appear; in others, the infant learns that a needed parent presents him or herself only subsequent to loud, protracted crying. There are also those parent-child dyads where the infant begets contact through subduing his or her affectivity, appearing accommodating and non-demanding. These learned proximity-engendering strategies that offer the infant leverage within a given parent-child dyad form the basis of the child's "internal working models" of attachment, or generalized tacit knowledge of how to emotionally communicate to preserve relationships (Bowlby, 1969, 1973).

Yet, Fonagy (2001) clarifies that it is not parental proximity per se but the experience of security that assumes primary motivational significance as the needed transactional outcome during times of distress. This is an important distinction because a felt sense of security on the child's part does not always entail physical closeness with a parent. Children's developmental and situation-specific needs govern whether immediate or delayed caregiver responses are called for, or whether reassuring contact be brought to bear through proximal (i.e., positioning oneself close by, physical holding and comforting), or distal (i.e., gaze and vocal exchanges) channels.

In fact, as children leave infancy and enter the toddler years, what they need from parents to embolden a sense of security undergoes change. Caregiving that supports their emerging autonomy while allowing for continued connectedness becomes salient. Having a parent as a "secure base" available for emotional sustenance during periodic check-ins while exercising his or her exploratory competence mitigates separation anxiety in the child, increases his or her comfort level with expansive emotional states (excitement, joy, euphoria), and inspires curiosity and novelty seeking. Likewise, having a parent who promptly responds during moments of acute need, whether due to fleeting infusions of separation anxiety, or bodily injuries, frees the child up to take risks and more carefreely explore, confident in the knowledge that remedial care is ready-at-hand. "Confident expectation" (Fonagy, 2001) that autonomous gestures will largely be supported against a backdrop of reliable access to restorative experiences during moments of acute need, in essence, is emblematic of the child's achievement of secure attachment (Ainsworth, Blehar, Waters, and Wall, 1978). Secure attachment involves a sort of psychological immunization against any susceptibility to states of intolerable frustration or disorganizing emotional arousal, given the child's internalized expectation of restorative support.

The emotional lives of insecurely attached children take on a different coloration. In the case of avoidant children, recurrent parental indifference to and rejection of his or her needs for soothing interactions leads to pre-emptive and inordinate dampening of emotions. The child overregulates his or her feelings because to fully experience and express them in a climate of parental unavailability is to court psychological danger. Without confident expectation in the caregiver's timely restorative intervention, a stylistic preference for emotional suppression becomes a way to keep from being overaroused and destabilized. Appearing nonneedy and unaffected may also represent an adaptive attachment strategy to keep a minimally engaged parent involved. Refraining from placing emotional demands on a caregiver who finds this unacceptable may be what keeps that caregiver invested in being attached. Yet, there are adverse intra- and interpersonal consequences to these avoidant tendencies. The child's range of affect necessarily becomes constricted and outward expression of emotion foreshortened. Detachment from his or her own inner feelings disallows the child experiential inroads to identify and empathize with others. Hence, avoidant children have been found to be less empathic with peers and at greater risk to victimize them than securely attached children (Sroufe, 1997; Suess, Grossman, and Sroufe, 1992). Social interaction in general may be viewed as aversive and unrewarding because it threatens to stimulate archaic needs and feeling states that have been foreclosed.

Overregulation of feelings can have deleterious physiological and cognitive effects. Subtle signs of stress in avoidant children have been noted in their cortisol levels and heart rates (Fox and Card, 1999). Also, screening out and guarding against emotion can exact a price on the child's developing attentional capacities. Internal resources that might be used to become fully engrossed in a task and bring it to completion are otherwise used to subliminally scan, screen out, and evade sources of emotional stimulation.

Whereas the adaptive challenge for the avoidant child is one of inevitable caregiver unavailability, that confronting the insecurely attached ambivalent/resistant child is inconsistent caregiver availability. The seeming capriciousness of the caregiver's availability and nonavailability keeps the child in a high state of vigilance and tension. Fearing being left alone and unprotected in a moment of acute need, the child is mobilized to keep tabs on the caregiver's whereabouts, and to extract the maximum amount of nurturance possible when it is made available to him or her. Provision of comforting may frequently center on the parent's need to give rather than the child's need to receive. The child's risk taking and environmental exploration may at times be encouraged, at other times discouraged, ill anchored to his or her cues regarding what is attainable or unattainable.

Up-regulation of emotion, or a proneness to accentuate one's agitation and anguish, becomes adaptive insofar as it dramatically and unambiguously communicates need states to a parent who may be intermittently off-cue, self-focused, or preoccupied. Up-regulation of emotion can also be an attachment-preserving strategy to prolong contact with a parent whose involvement is momentarily available but nonlasting. Unable to count on interactions that are lasting and restorative, the ambivalent/resistant child may be given to distrust or incompletely absorb the caregiver's comforting and supportive gestures. Suffice to say, the child with this attachment style lives with a high degree of anxiety and frustration, afflicted with sensitivities to feeling abandoned, rejected, and misunderstood that can be carried into peer relations. The physiological signs of stress are more apparent with ambivalent/resistant children than with avoidant children (Fox and Card, 1999), and deficits in self-regulation can often be manifested as low frustration tolerance, problems with attention and concentration, and thought processes that are tangential and unfocused (Cassidy, 1994).

The child with a disorganized attachment style has learned no fixed pattern of eliciting caregiver involvement (Main and Hesse, 1990). In situations requiring that he or she alert caregivers to needs for closeness and safety, bizarre and unusual behavior can emanate from the child. He or she might hide, freeze, appear dissociated and emotionally vacant, or behave uncontrollably. These extremes in behavior and emotion dysregulation take place in an attachment context where parents are prone to engage in frightening or frightened behavior. On the one hand, hostile and terrifying behavior displayed by parents floods and destabilizes the child. At other times, parents may be so frightened and immobilized by the child's behavior that they are rendered ineffectual as figures who can provide comfort and containment.

Evidence suggests that insecurely attached children, including those who fit the criteria for disorganized attachment, are more aggression prone than securely attached children. Attachment-based explanations for this center on how aggressivity in children is the outgrowth of normally expressed attachment needs for proximity and security being habitually met with parental indifference, rejection, incomplete satisfaction, hostility, or timidity. In a similar vein, chronic thwarting of or inconsistent responsiveness to autonomous gestures are also thought to produce aggressivity in children.

TEMPERAMENT, NEUROBIOLOGY, AND REGULATORY CAPACITIES

Chess and Thomas (1996) as well as others (Buss and Plomin, 1984; Kagan, 1989) argue that children's unique ways of regulating emotion, to a greater or lesser degree, reflect their constitutionally given temperament. Genetic and biological factors are thought to largely govern children's preponderant ways of experiencing emotions, their intensity and duration, and the type of coping mechanisms children acquire.

Chess and Thomas (1996) distinguish three overarching modes of temperament. The "easy" infant exhibits an overall positive mood and recovers quickly when distressed, adapts well to novel situations and unfamiliar people, and settles into regular sleep and feeding schedules. The "difficult" infant's expressions of distress tend to be intense and prolonged, change and novelty engender stress, and consistent sleep and feeding schedules are hard to implement. The "slow-to-warm" infant is predisposed to initial withdrawal and fear and needs repeated, relatively nonpressured exposure to new situations and people to allow for adaptability.

Kagan and colleagues (1989) offer a temperament model that generally parallels that of Chess and Thomas. Their work focuses on extreme inhibition in children and the temperamental fearfulness that gives rise to it. Emotionally inhibited children show a greater sensitivity to and prolonged recovery from stress, are prone to emotional withdrawal, are less likely to initiate vocal exchanges with strangers, and maintain close proximity to caregivers in unfamiliar surroundings. Kagan (1989) maintains that inhibited children are slower to adapt in novel situations due to: "greater arousal of the sympathetic and hypothalamic-pituitary-adrenal axis following challenge and unfamiliarity" (4).

At the disinhibition end of the spectrum, children's aggressiveness and disruptive behavior may reflect a biological susceptibility to elevated dopaminergic activity caused by excessive stimulation in the amygdala (Haber and Fudge, 1997). Also, a biologically based diminished sensitivity to fear and stress has been implicated in risk taking, novelty seeking, and disruptive behaviors in children (Raine, 1997).

However, neuroscientific findings increasingly call into question the notion of temperament as a composite of stable inherited traits rooted in neurobiological predispositions and minimally mutable through social experience. Schore (2003) has compiled a remarkable body of brain research data and synthesized it with existing knowledge of early attachment processes to propose that growth in the neurological substrates associated with young children's incipient emotional styles is highly experience dependent. In particular, he links emotion regulation capacities to postnatal maturation of the orbitofrontal cortex, brain growth that he proffers is inextricably linked to the quality of early caregiver-infant attachment processes.

In Schore's model, positively emotionally valenced face-to-face interactions and synchronized vocalizations that occur in caregiver-infant exchanges offer critically important sustenance for the right-hemispheric orbitofrontal cortex, in part through the activation of dopamine and endogenous opiates. The orbitofrontal cortex is a brain location where cortical and subcortical structures meet, and where *external* visual and auditory information is processed in conjunction with *internal* somatic stimuli. Interconnections with the limbic system enable the orbitofrontal cortex to play a role in reward-excitatory and aversive-inhibitory arousal mechanisms.

Schore (2003) asserts that favorable, early, caregiver-infant attachment patterns are crucial for right-brain development, which matures before the verbal-linguistic left brain and is largely responsible for children's empathy skills, perception of emotions, mental processing of nonverbal communications, and encoding of implicit memories that potentiate relational expectations.

Schore's work lends credence to a model of brain development that accounts for the complex interplay between early interpersonal experiences and infant neurobiology, making it untenable to discount or negate the contribution of environmental factors in children's formation of affect-regulation capacities. In the words of Bradley (2000), "Both neurobiological and experiential factors are capable of inducing changes in the individual's experience of affect and in his or her capacity to respond to the affective demands of the situation" (133).

2

ADHD: THE ROLE OF EMOTIONAL DYSREGULATION, NARCISSISTIC VULNERABILITY, AND ATTACHMENT CONCERNS

Mainstream conceptualizations of ADHD account for relevant symptoms largely in terms of neurocognitive deficits. Core symptoms of the disorder, whether it be the hyperactivity/impulsivity variant (i.e., motorically driven, problems waiting one's turn, excessive talking, fidgetiness), or the inattentive one (i.e., distractibility, listening failures, forgetfulness, premature discontinuance of mentally challenging tasks) are thought to stem from neurological impairments and the faulty cognitive processing they produce. For instance, Barkley (2006) proposes that ADHD children are afflicted with impoverished executive functioning: Marked difficulties with retaining and mentally manipulating information contained in short-term memory (nonverbal working memory), using self-talk and internalized speech to guide actions (verbal working memory), and processing information in complex ways before initiating action (reconstitution).

Although Barkley (1999) honors the role of self-regulation of emotional arousal as a feature of ADHD, this is accorded a relatively minor role in his overall model and is framed strictly along cognitive-behavioral lines, predicated on inflexible perceptions of emotionally laden events or failures to act on the environment to reduce anger, frustration, anxiety, boredom, and other negative affective states.

Yet, there is a burgeoning literature indicating that for a sizeable number of ADHD children emotional dysregulation and its harmful interpersonal effects are a fundamental dimension of the disorder, in many cases conducive to its most detrimental outcomes. When compared with their non-ADHD counterparts, ADHD children often show diminished emotional control when performing tasks of a competitive nature with peers (Mangione, 2003), demonstrate trouble managing their emotional reactions in situations requiring accommodation to parental demands (Melnick and Hinshaw, 2000), have greater difficulty accurately deciphering and labeling emotions (Norvilitis, Casey, Brooklier, and Bonello, 2000), exhibit elevated frustration levels, even during seemingly positive social interactions (Bonello, 1998), tend to become fixated on expecting others to react with anger and shame in interpersonal exchanges (Siegel, 1997), and are less empathic in their dealings with peers (Losoya, 1995). All in all, the reduced sociability ensuing from many ADHD children's problematic emotional regulation has been well documented and may shed light on why some authors have advanced the notion of ADHD being a "social disability" (Greene, Biederman, Faraone, and Ouellette, 1996) or a "social learning disability" (Henker and Whalen, 1999).

Moreover, emotional dysregulation has a bearing not only on the interpersonal difficulties associated with the disorder, but on its constitutive diagnostic symptoms. Arguably, narrow construal of ADHD as a neurocognitive disorder has obscured the role of affective processes in attention difficulties, overactivity, and compromised impulse control. For instance, there is much to be learned about how a predisposition to shame and other somatically charged emotions can lead to disorganized thinking and behaving (Nathanson, 1997; Schore, 2003), and how hyperactivity sometimes masks the persistence of unmet needs for kinesthetic competence to be witnessed and affirmed by caregivers (Gnaulati, 1999).

Another intriguing, yet largely overlooked, area of investigation is the overlap between ADHD symptoms and archaic emotional expressions shown by narcissistically vulnerable children. There are those ADHD children for whom tendencies to avoid or abort tasks requiring effortful output arise due to omnipotent expectations, where immediate mastery of tasks is presupposed. They believe they can succeed at tasks without application and engrossment, only to appear agitated and distractible, implode in shame, or explode in anger, when their grandiose performance expectations fail to square with the realities of the situation. Trial and error learning situations foment impatience since ego fragility precludes an acceptance of error making. It is tempting to wonder if such dynamics point to a proto-personality or self-disorder, rather than ADHD per se, or some combination of the two.

Furthermore, confounds between ADHD symptoms and attachment-related difficulties are only beginning to be explored in the literature. To the observer who is well versed in attachment theory, many ADHD symptoms seem to mimic attachment-maintaining operations acquired by insecurely attached children. For instance, disruptive behavior can reflect the child's

crystallized way of seeking satisfaction of attachment needs from a preoccupied or inconsistently available primary caregiver, inclinations that get
generalized to other relationships and social situations. As is illustrated below, there is also a surprising degree of overlap between accepted forms of
insecure attachment (avoidant, ambivalent/resistant, and disorganized)
(Ainsworth, Blehar, Waters, and Wall, 1978; Main and Hesse, 1990) and
many core ADHD symptoms and allied socioemotional deficits.

Consequently, in this chapter, I offer an overarching framework for
conceptualizing the core symptoms of ADHD and related socioemotional
difficulties that emphasizes the role of affective processes and represents an
alternative to mainstream neurocognitive approaches, extrapolating from
contemporary psychoanalytic developmental psychology (Fonagy, 2001;
Kohut, 1977; 1985), affect-regulation theory (Schore, 2003; Sroufe, 1997),
the attachment paradigm (Cassidy and Shaver, 1999; Slade, 1994), and functionalist accounts of emotional development in children (Denham, 1998;
Saarni, 1999).

DISORGANIZING EFFECTS
OF VISCERALLY FELT EMOTIONS

Many ADHD children show markedly compromised abilities to maintain
organized thought and behavior in the face of heightened affectivity. Somatically arousing emotional states such as elation, excitement, acute anxiety, shame, rage, and disgust are especially challenging for them to down-
regulate. Such viscerally felt affects are a challenge to contain and articulate,
thereby propelling the child to act in ways that appear out of control, haphazard, and foolish. These children may spiritedly exert themselves to give
motor expression to or achieve a modicum of emotional release from their
overarousal. Affect flooding can impede and incapacitate cognitive processing, aggravating difficulties closely following rules in games, reading subtle
social cues, remembering information, listening to directions, or the like.
Of relevance here is Johnson and Magaro's (1987) research showing how
heightened distress and expansive mood states can disrupt mental functioning, learning, and memory processes.

Indeed, ADHD phenomena such as motor restlessness, inattention,
forgetfulness, cognitive disorganization, and poor mental alertness to the
task at hand can be fallout from the child having to perpetually deploy psychological resources to avoid, manage, and recover from implosive and explosive episodes.

LISTENING AND COMPLYING

Key symptoms of ADHD are an enduring pattern of appearing to not listen when directly addressed and demonstrable problems following through with plans and complying with requests. Although the DSM IV requires that these symptoms not be primarily due to oppositionality for them to be applicable (American Psychiatric Association, 1994), clinically it is often impossible to tease out when these symptoms are psychologically motivated, an outgrowth of the child's neurological equipment, indicative of an inattentive cognitive style, some combination of all three, or differentially germane depending on the interpersonal context or mental task. To complicate matters, sometimes problems with listening, following through, and complying can denote covert, rather than overt forms of oppositionality. The same applies to ADHD symptoms such as forgetfulness and disorganized work habits. The child may be opposing, asserting autonomy with, or individuating from caregivers in a more subdued, indirect manner. It is always instructive to entertain the possibility that problems listening, "zoning out," and acting in accordance with adult requests can sometimes be reducible to none other than a pernicious case of garden variety passive-aggressiveness!

When assessing and treating attention problems, it is important to be mindful that the act of paying attention is as much an interpersonal event as it an intrapersonal one. Failures and successes in securing a child's attention, ensuring follow-through with requests, and assisting with engrossment in a task can hinge on the degree to which the communicator is experienced by the child as an impinging, authoritative, or negligible presence. A susceptibility to "tuning out" or appearing unfocused may indicate emotional shutdown, a means to protect oneself from overstimulation when the other's utterances are suffused with a level of affect that is too insistent or unsettling. Of relevance here are research findings suggesting that parental intrusiveness, seductiveness, and overstimulation predicts distractibility in children (to a greater degree than temperamental or biological factors) (Carlson, Jacobvitz, and Sroufe, 1995). Sometimes a vicious cycle can unfold when frustration sets in and the communicator up-regulates his or her feelings due to not being listened to or complied with, only to find the child becoming more emotionally remote and inattentive, not so much out of anger as from being overwhelmed.

Similarly, problems listening and accommodating to a caregiver's directions and requests can be due to a long-standing pattern of the affective tone of such communications being insufficiently strong to persuasively alert the child as to the need for responsiveness and compliance. Simply put, the child's attention has routinely not been "commanded."

EMOTIONAL REACTIVITY
AND FAULTY SELF-OTHER DIFFERENTIATION

Perhaps the greatest challenge for the ADHD child is to delay reacting to a precipitating event, especially in emotionally evocative interpersonal exchanges. Holding back from emoting on impulse, and thoughtfully processing feelings before acting on them, are phenomena not often observed by clinicians working with this population, which has also been corroborated in the empirical literature (Mangione, 2003; Melnick and Hinshaw, 2000).

Intensive work with these children, especially in lively group and unstructured play contexts, can reveal how their emotional reactivity in many cases stems from a susceptibility to rapid de-differentiation in self-other boundaries. Evidence of fragile self-boundaries can be seen in their quickness to become infused with and feed off others' emotions. They may also provoke others to share their affects and affectivity, or seek to invoke complimentary feelings in others. They often match and exceed the feeling states of children and adults in their immediate milieu, especially vis-à-vis negatively valenced emotions and expressions of excitement. Anger conveyed by others in their presence can be experienced as an inducement to become incensed with anger of their own. Excitement conveyed by others in their presence can be experienced as an inducement to show unbridled excitement of their own. In situations where there is much emotional stimulation, their permeable boundaries can leave them feeling engulfed, causing them to become disorganized in their behavior, or prone to "zone out" or "blank out." Closing themselves off emotionally may be a necessary protective down-regulatory gesture, but it leaves them ill-disposed to be present to others in their moments of excitement, joy, happiness, anger, and other poignant social expressions. Conceivably, it may be poor affective self-other differentiation that best explains some ADHD children's ill-timed, off-cue, awkward, intrusive, out-of-context social behaviors (Henker and Whalen, 1999).

The strength or weakness of the ADHD child's self-boundaries determines the degree to which he or she negotiates the feelings of others in ways that inspire empathic concern or beget personal distress reactions. In acts of empathy, the boundary between self and other is preserved and the child can identify with another's distress, anger, or excitement, be *sensitized to it*, without becoming *oversensitized or desensitized by it*. Contrastingly, personal distress reactions occur when there is a rapid de-differentiation of self-other boundaries and the child is inundated by another's emotionality (Eisenberg et al., 1989). The behavior of some ADHD children that alternates between impulsive aggression, tantrums, sudden flight reactions, and social nonresponsiveness can thus be seen through the lens of poor self-other differentiation and a resultant susceptibility to personal distress reactions.

Furthermore, a fruitful area of discourse involves how reduced empathy skills in subpopulations of ADHD children (Losoya, 1995) are linked to concomitant aggressiveness and social friction. Concern for others and feeling connected to them can be an antidote to ruthless displays of aggression. Where there is empathy, there is an identification with the other's suffering, a sense that to some degree the other's suffering is one's own. The emotional pain in the other caused by the infliction of harm resonates back to the aggressor via empathic connection, acting as a deterrent against prolonged or overreactive aggression. Likewise, an aptness to feel emotionally bonded with others, albeit in boundaried ways, is a countervailing force against protracted conflict. Empathy can quicken the desire to restore affiliative ties that have been spoiled through conflict.

The parent-child relationship is one crucible for the acquisition or exacerbation of emotional reactivity, personal distress reactions, poor self-other boundaries, and empathy erosion often seen in children who seem diagnosable with ADHD. Parents who match anger with anger, frustration with frustration, and anxiety with anxiety can undermine a child's emerging self-regulatory capacities. Eisenberg and colleagues (1999) propose that a major bidirectional pathway to overarousal, emotional negativity, and externalizing behaviors in children is chronic exposure to a parenting style marked by criticism, minimizing, and quickness to become distressed. Direct empirical links between negative-reactive parenting practices and ADHD have been noted (Johnston, 1996; Taylor, Chadwick, Heptinstall, and Danckaerts, 1996). Furthermore, the expressed emotion construct, originally applied to family stress variables in the relapse rates of schizophrenics, has been extended to the study of families with ADHD children and has shown how parental criticism, reduced warmth, and overreactivity predicts a poor ADHD prognosis. In fact, these authors contend that expressed emotion is not always a consequence of how vexing it can be to raise an ADHD child but can be a distinguishable characteristic of the parent. Astute clinicians know that sometimes a child's reactivity and negativity is an artifact of similar traits in parents, and that the most productive way to proceed is to treat the parent-child relationship, or the parent.

DIFFICULTIES MODULATING
THE INTENSITY AND DURATION OF EMOTIONS

Social difficulties encountered by ADHD children frequently reflect under-developed capacities for toning down or amplifying the intensity of feelings congruous with what an interpersonal situation permits. In other words, they may struggle to bring the intensity of their emotional communications in line with their social goals. Often these children overrely on amplified expression of emotion as a means to achieve social goals, such as angrily usurping a leadership role in peer interactions or exuberantly stepping to the front of the line, unable to contain the anticipatory excitement and frustration aroused by waiting one's turn.

Self-recovery from emotional episodes can seem insurmountable as the ADHD child gets stuck feeling angry or exhibiting unbridled excitement, even with ample restorative care. Attempts by parents or teachers to redirect them, or pacify them when they are in a heightened state of emotional arousal, can be futile, the situation devolving into one of mutual exasperation.

A stylistic pattern of underregulation of affect may best explain symptoms of hyperactivity. Motor restlessness and impulsivity behaviorally signify the child restlessly struggling in vain to assuage a variety of feelings of fluctuating intensity. The fact that the struggle is all the more formidable, and less fixable, in social settings simply attests to the myriad emotional triggers that come into play in group contexts. Classrooms can be treacherous for the emotionally under-regulated child due to abundant sources of emotional stimulation combined with expectations to be sedentary, self-collected, and cerebral in school.

Predispositions to overregulate affect may best account for symptoms of inattention. The child's conscious and preconscious mental resources may be consumed guarding against being overwhelmed by emotions that are diffusely experienced. Isolating, blunting, or dissociating emotional experience takes mental effort, whether these self-protective operations occur unconsciously, preconsciously, or consciously. The same applies when the child is caught up in prereflectively and reflectively scanning the environment for stimuli that might elicit diffuse emotions that cannot be adequately internally managed. Sometimes children's distractibility and difficulties screening out extraneous stimuli represent overt and covert scanning for signs of emotional danger in their immediate surround. This can be something as imperceptible as rapid subliminal processing of an interpersonal situation to ensure that a high-pitched voice be ignored, for fear that it overstimulates. Or, something as perceptible as impulsively, yet consciously, walking out of the classroom to avoid being overly rattled by the emotional tenor in the room during a spirited group activity, at the same time oblivious to the reasons why. Such mental operations to ensure emotional self-protection can have monopolizing effects in the cognitive sphere and forestall capacities to become engrossed in and complete tasks. It is always a curiosity when parents and teachers seem surprised by the ADHD child's more resolute concentration in one-on-one situations. It may simply be that the emotional triggers in group situations are more numerous than in one-on-one situations, such that in the latter the child can relax his or her need for emotionally self-protective mental operations.

UNDERDEVELOPED REPRESENTATIONAL MODES OF REGULATING AFFECT

The ability to represent emotional experiences linguistically, or via symbolic play, in coherent, organized, detailed, and nuanced ways is a developmental achievement often ill-acquired by ADHD children. They commonly show inadequate psychic distance from emotions to be able to speak about them and are more likely to have an enactive style of emotional communication. They seem propelled to "act out" how and what they feel more so than "think out" or "think through" how and what they feel. Deficiencies, gaps, and inconsistencies abound in reflecting on and verbally articulating inner experiences. Likewise, profound difficulties often exist in accurately decoding other's feelings, thoughts, wishes, and motives.

Problems using the "signal function" (Piaget, 1962) of language to identify, integrate, and elaborate feeling states render them less meaningful, and therefore less manageable for many ADHD children. These failures at the level of linguistic representation of affect may explain why many ADHD children commonly experience emotions as diffuse forces, poorly differentiated from their somatic underpinnings, fueling a reduced sense of self-control (Losoya, 1995). After all, steady improvement in putting words to feelings over time is one major route to setting soma and psyche apart, and gaining a sense of emotional mastery and personal agency (Fonagy, 2001).

A foreshortened vocabulary for capturing the transitory nature of feelings and difficulties communicating a range of affect are two prominent areas of underdeveloped emotional literacy in ADHD children. As for the latter, such children frequently evince a restricted range of affect, becoming fixated on negatively valenced emotions such as anger, frustration, and shame (Siegal, 1997) while being constricted in their communicative fluency within this cluster of negatively valenced emotions. Hence, we may encounter an ADHD who is frustration prone, while simultaneously limited in his or her means for expressing it (i.e., hitting, breaking things, yelling, agitatedly running around). Reduced socioemotional aptitude in ADHD children can also take the form of an overreliance on totalistic words and phrases to capture feeling reactions (i.e., "You are a mean person and I hate you"; "Why am I such a sad and stupid person?").

Play is often void of its symbolic function for ADHD children. They tend to be limited to play that is action-oriented, high-energy, and seemingly nonsymbolic, using toys and materials more to physically enact scenarios than as representational tools to convey textured meaning about themselves, important others, and their experiential worlds. Abstracting themselves from the immediacy of their play, to reflect on it, sort out who is feeling or thinking what, and determine why this is so, seems to be dimly achievable.

Not uncommonly, there is an absence of the capacity for pretend play. Often what pretend play that does exist is perseverative, disjointed, or lacks richness and dimensionality. For many ADHD children, ill-formed capacities for pretend play deprive them of the displacement function that it affords, including higher-order means to regulate affect. "Putting" feelings, thoughts, wishes, and motives "into" toy figures and fantasy characters allows for safer, more industrious processing of these mental states.

In the last analysis, what Fonagy (2001) has to say about borderline mental states may equally apply to certain ADHD children: "As a consequence of the lack of flexibility of the representational system for mental states, the individual does not have the capacity to evoke psychic experiences in any other way than enactment and provocation. Even relatively simple and common subjective states such as worry and concern cannot be experienced except through creating them in another person" (177). Disorganized, disruptive, out-of-control behavior may induce in the therapist feelings of panic, outrage, acute anxiety, or barely containable excitement that actually reflect the inner life of the ADHD child, affects that are poorly representable in a linguistic, symbolic, self-locused way by the child.

COMPROMISED AUTONOMY
AND LOW FRUSTRATION TOLERANCE

Mental and kinesthetic tasks that pose to be arduous are often avoided or terminated midstream by ADHD children. As is taken up below, sometimes this speaks to coexisting, or overriding, narcissistic vulnerabilities and omnipotent attitudes, leading to tasks being dodged chiefly because they painfully confront the child with personal limitations. Another explanation for low frustration tolerance can be an enduring and cumulative pattern by caregivers, reinforced by the child's educational experiences, of failing to structure tasks that allow for success with moderate levels of effort, what Vygotsky (1978) refers to as "scaffolding." An early history of caregivers providing inordinate help when children are well able to accomplish tasks independently with mild, moderate, or no assistance can create dulled initiative-taking behavior, reduced self-efficacy, task avoidance, or fits of anger and frustration when expected to work in a self-directed fashion. The same applies with children whose formative years were replete with home and pre-school experiences in which they were expected to complete everyday tasks in a hyper-independent fashion, without due consideration to degrees of intervention required to ensure task mastery.

Less-than-optimal early childhood socialization habits that inculcate focused attention and task mastery, against a backdrop of respect for the child's autonomy, can also be one pathway to poor frustration tolerance. Carefully preventing the young child from abandoning tasks uneasily triumphed at, nonintrusively redirecting him or her back to tasks, rendering them enticing, reconfiguring them to maximize their achievability with mild to moderate effort, all cultivate a success-engendering attitude and enhanced frustration tolerance in the young child. The sense of satisfaction gained from assisted achievement can be intrinsically rewarding, with boosts of positive affectivity imbuing the achievement stemming from the caregiver's or educator's overt praise. Deprivations in these ways of socially constructing self-efficacy, with an eye toward the child's autonomy needs, can bring about compromised task mastery and frustration tolerance in children of the sort that raises suspicion of ADHD.

As a side note, some caregivers and educators can unwittingly aggravate ADHD children's low frustration tolerance by chronically expecting them to complete schoolwork in content domains that fall outside of their aptitudes, at a pace that is unrealistic, and in a manner that is experienced by the child as an assault to his or her autonomy, eventuating in a climate

of mounting bidirectional upset. Worrisome levels of low frustration tolerance can also be produced in an otherwise "normal" child this way.

HYPERACTIVITY AND PROTRACTED EXHIBITIONISM

In everyday language, hyperactive children are frequently observed "clowning," "horse playing," "goofing off," "acting silly," or "showing off." Many
clinicians are apt to view these as immature attention-seeking behaviors
warranting elimination. However, when viewed from a self-psychological
perspective, sometimes the antics of children in the throes of hyperactivity
can be meaningfully understood in terms of archaic exhibitionistic tendencies, the sensitive handling of which has important ramifications for the development of self-esteem. This is not to say that hyperactivity in children
can be uniformly conceived of in psychogenic or developmental terms.

Self-psychologists propose that the seeds of self-assuredness reside in
optimal caregiver empathic attunement to "grandiose-exhibitionistic" needs
that come into prominence during toddlerhood and persist in varying degrees throughout childhood (Kohut, 1977). The child brims with a sense of
pride and omnipotence as he or she displays newly acquired psychomotor
capacities, turning to caregivers for confirmation of his or her brilliance.
Overtly communicated appreciation and joy by caregivers during these moments of exhibitionistic pride become part of the child's self-experience
and set the foundation for a sense of aliveness and self-worth.

Nevertheless, disappointments are inevitable. Children cannot always
be impeccable in their demonstrations of prowess and caregivers cannot always be exquisitely attuned. The child who has experienced sufficient affirmation of his or her exhibitionistic displays when faced with failure will
be able to internally summon forth such experiences to soothe any emotional pain and ease his or her wounded pride. Failures can also be constructively tackled and learned from if caregivers are available with empathic
communications that aid restoration of self-esteem, while modifying
grandiose self-images.

Problems arise when the child's enthusiastic demonstrations are met
with either a pattern of outright rejection, indifference, or overindulgence by
caregivers. A "more demanding, insistent exhibitionism" (Miller, 1996, 45)
surfaces and holds sway. It is precisely this type of exhibitionism, the clamor-
ing to be seen, heard, and responded to in confirmatory ways, that sometimes
explains hyperactive behavior in children. This dynamic is one where the
child protractedly up-regulates the intensity of his or her affectivity during

displays of competencies to yield desperately needed affirmation or steal prideful recognition from caregivers. The frustration resulting from chronic deprivation of needed caregiver affirmation, or from others repeatedly failing to match a caregiver's characteristic vainglorious appraisals during important exhibitionistic moments, can engender recognition-seeking behaviors that degenerate into negative theatrics over time. These dynamics sometimes underlie generic manifestations of hyperactivity.

SHAME, AGGRESSION, AND REDUCED SOCIOEMOTIONAL COMPETENCE

The prevalence of aggression in ADHD children has been widely documented (Whalen and Henker, 1998; Wheeler and Carlson, 1994). Propensities to become embroiled in peer conflicts, to vociferously blame others when confronted with the unpleasant consequences of actions, to carry roughhousing too far, and to misinterpret others' actions as malicious and deserving of retaliatory aggression, are aspects of many ADHD children's clinical profile. The frequent co-occurrence of hyperactivity and conduct problems has even led some commentators to proffer that they are both subtypes of an overarching disruptive behavior disorder (Trites and Laprade, 1983). Indeed, the combativeness shown by many ADHD children may be the pivotal source of their diminished sociability, since aggressive children are prime targets for peer rejection (Landau and Moore, 1991).

In the clinical and research literature, the preponderance of nonpharmacological strategies offered to reduce aggression in ADHD children tends to be cognitive-behavioral in nature. Interventions derived from Meichenbaum's (1975) stress inoculation approach appear to have gained ascendancy. Children are taught to interrupt the chain of automatic thoughts presumed to justify aggressive responses, question the evidence meriting the perceived need to go on the counterattack, and rehearse more adaptive ways of giving voice to anger and frustration. However, the overriding emphasis on the role of cognition in precipitating and preventing aggressive reactions has tended to drown out the contribution of emotion. Of relevance here are shame experiences.

To feel ashamed is to suddenly and painfully have one's "basic flaws" exposed for all to see (Gorsuch, 1990). There is a debilitating sense that one is "all bad," defective, or unworthy of love. The subjective experience of being flooded with shame renders a person disorganized and helpless. There may be a distressing awareness of the fragility of one's self-esteem, whereby others have the power to suddenly and massively alter one's self-experience for the worse, or in self-psychology nomenclature, inflict "narcissistic injury" (Kohut, 1977).

A frequently employed emotion-regulation strategy is to convert shame into rage, to dominate and seek revenge against the person perceived to have provoked the shame. Wurmser (1981) aptly names this dynamic as "turning the tables" and Kohut (1985) encapsulates it as a manifestation of "narcissistic rage," where revenge is a dire ploy to undo damage to the enfeebled self. In the act of converting shame into rage the person is desperate to reinstate a sense of control and dominance in the face of emotional danger through attacking others and provoking feelings of shame in them. As Lansky (1992) points out, "The disorganization and helplessness are induced in others rather than experienced by the violent person himself" (149). However, although such shame-deflecting tactics temporarily alleviate feelings of disorganization and impotence, they ultimately sour the individual's relations with others and increase feelings of alienation (Nathanson, 1992).

ADHD children may be especially susceptible to shame and ways of managing it that cause interpersonal problems. Possible early difficulties with fine and gross-motor coordination, coexisting learning disabilities, and dependence on medication use to maintain self control can leave them feeling defective or fundamentally impaired in some way. Parents, teachers, and peers are inclined to view the ADHD child's impulsive behavior as willfully enacted, proof of immaturity or moral turpitude, with the resultant negative social feedback instilling in him or her a sense of "inner badness." Moreover, it is not uncommon for hyperactive children to be teased and ridiculed by classmates for not being able to complete schoolwork in a timely manner, or for producing messy, disorganized, inferior work. In addition, classmates may be amused and entertained by the ADHD child's "clowning" but have little interest in befriending him or her.

Another socially disabling way of regulating painful feelings of shame in subpopulations of ADHD involves the externalization of blame. Many ADHD children have been shown to "deny responsibility for negative social events" (Hoza et al., 1993, 284) and to attribute hostile intent to peers during social mishaps and minor provocations (Murphy, Pelham, and Lang, 1992). Commonly cited explanations for such phenomena tend to center on the faulty social cognitions of ADHD children; in particular, their impulsive style of interpreting social cues or proneness to judge peers based on an incomplete assessment of evidentiary social information (Whalen and Henker, 1998).

Nevertheless, a fuller explanation for many ADHD children's tendencies to externalize blame and overattribute hostile intent to others needs to account for the role of shame and narcissistic vulnerability. Oftentimes, these children resort to externalizing blame in the context of being reproached for having acted offensively. Their quickness to implicate and accuse others, deflecting negative attention away from themselves, may actually indicate shame-proneness and problems with self-esteem regulation. Overcome by shame, they experience a collapse in the distinction between being perceived as having acted badly, and being perceived as "all bad." To confess to some misdeed is akin to submitting that one is an unlikable person. To "own up" is to run the risk of feeling that one is worthy of being disowned. In essence, externalization of blame signals that the child cannot tolerate the feelings of inner badness associated with being at fault. Projecting blame outward is seen as the only means available to reinstate feelings of likability and self-worth.

Needless to say, shame can disable important ego functions and leave the child void of internal access to positive self-images and attributes. As is elucidated later in the book, if attempts to foster responsibility-taking behavior in ADHD children are to bear fruit, it is incumbent on the therapist to confront misbehavior while simultaneously conveying overall acceptance of the child. Tangible reminders of the child's strong points need to be spelled out if he or she is to countenance even reasonable criticism and learn from it. Shame-inducing experiences are usually rapidly banished from consciousness, reducing their potential to be learned from. Facing a child with his or her misdeed, in a backdrop of positive recognition, bolsters the likelihood that thoughts, feelings, and mental imagery pertaining to the misdeed will be retained in conscious awareness long enough to be complexly processed and learned from. Ultimately, these are the conditions that enable the child to answer to the negative consequences of his or her actions with less defensiveness, which also paves the way for reduced social friction.

NARCISSISTIC VULNERABILITY AND ADHD SYMPTOMS

As mentioned above, sometimes the avoidance and premature discontinuance of tasks requiring effortful attention, which is one of the hallmarks of ADHD, can be more comprehensively accounted for in terms of the sense of omnipotence shown by narcissistically vulnerable children. Tasks that offer sparse promise of immediate mastery threaten to challenge their grandiose self-images and are abstained from or abruptly discontinued. The same applies to tasks that do not fall within their narrow domains of accelerated aptitude, whether on the face of it such aptitudes seem substantive or not. Along these lines, it can be quite revealing when a child engages in a pattern of "exhibitionistic off-task behavior" in the context of certain games, activities, or schoolwork. Expertly twirling a pencil instead of completing a math assignment or suddenly aborting a game of chess and insisting on kicking a soccer ball around may represent the narcissistically vulnerable child's way of gravitating toward a skill or activity that readily elevates his or her self-esteem in the face of one that has a high potential for shame-inducing failure.

Problems managing feelings associated with winning and losing also sometimes masquerade as ADHD symptoms. I have in mind here those children who frequently become elated in theatrical, disorganized ways upon winning a game, proudly proclaiming their brilliance, and speedily wanting to change games as if to "rest on their laurels." Upon losing, these same children become shamefully deflated, markedly agitated, or jump from game to game until they hit on one that has a greater chance for victory.

Similarly, narcissistically vulnerable children may have considerable difficulty being "one of the gang" in classroom settings, adhering to rules and routines geared toward maximum learning for groups of students. They may desperately need or feel entitled ("soft edged" versus "hard edged" narcissism) to be treated with special attention and to have their unique needs and preferences accommodated. ADHD-type symptoms such as blurting out answers, interrupting, refusing to wait one's turn, and talking ceaselessly can be emblematic of how narcissistically needy, as distinct from impulsive, a child is. Being ignored or chastised in such pointed moments of need can be narcissistically injurious, the resultant shame or rage leading to disruptive, unfocused, and off-task behavior—other noteworthy ADHD-type symptoms.

ATTACHMENT-RELATED
CONCERNS AND ADHD SYMPTOMS

A small body of literature is emerging establishing parallels between ADHD symptoms and attachment-related difficulties. These linkages often seen in the consulting room with ADHD children are gradually being empirically explored by academics (Allen, 2001; Clarke et al., 2002; DeKlyen, 1996; Lyons-Ruth, Zoll, Connell, and Grunebaum, 1989). Inquiry into whether or not certain variants of ADHD can be subsumed under pathological or problematic attachment predispositions is still uncharted territory. Likewise, the extent to which a preexisting ADHD condition might be aggravated by the diminished quality of a child's attachment with primary caregivers remains a relatively underinvestigated topic. Typical forms of disruptive behavior associated with ADHD such as whining, lack of compliance, and negative attention seeking can denote an insecurely attached child who implicitly knows that such behavior is necessary to elicit proximity and involvement on the part of caregivers. Put differently, embellishing, amplifying, and prolonging negative feelings and behaviors has crystallized as an attachment-preserving strategy designed to elicit prompt involvement from primary caregivers who are inconsistent in their physical and emotional availability. Up-regulation of feelings is depended on not only to elicit prompt care, but to force its continuance once received. The seeming capriciousness of when and for how long a primary caregiver is available keeps the child poised to ramp up his or her feelings, communicating a desperate need for prompt and lasting involvement. The "internal working model" embodied by the child is one in which feelings need to be stoked up, or behavior needs to reach a peak of agitation before a caregiver will physically and emotionally present him or herself and stay available. Brisch (2002) evocatively refers to this dynamic as follows: "The fear that an attachment need will not be formed, or that a developing relationship will be lost, leads via the experience of unassuaged attachment needs to a massive activation of attachment behavior and even to a battle for attachment. Because past experiences have led the child to expect rejection from the attachment figure, a desire for attachment may be primarily expressed by aggressive means" (69).

Naturally, the interpersonal exchanges that transpire when a parent is forced to respond to a child because of the extent of his or her unruliness will be negatively tinged and mutually unpleasant. However, the child's underlying anxiety over the nonproximity and noninvolvement of essential caregivers is temporarily lessened. This may explain the not uncommon scenario that occurs when a professionally busy, preoccupied caregiver is livid over being called into the principal's office because of his or her son's disruptive classroom behavior, only to find the child surprisingly unconcerned. There is wisdom in the old adage, "negative attention is better than no attention at all."

Nonetheless, not all attachment-maintaining, up-regulatory strategies take on aggressive features. There are those children for whom revving up melodramatic, silly, clowning behaviors becomes the preferred interpersonal mechanism to solicit needed individualized involvement from important attachment figures. On this note, I am perpetually struck by the number of children in my practice whose attachment sensitivity is such that they tune out and academically underachieve with teachers whom they wish treated them with warmth and high regard, but who do not. Conveyed disinterest and academic underachievement become misguided attempts to make the teacher take notice.

In general, for those cases of ADHD where impulsive-aggressive behavior is a component, examination of past and present caregiver-child attachment patterns may be necessary. As outlined in the previous chapter, aggressivity can stem from formative and enduring attachment experiences in which children's efforts to elicit proximity and emotional security from parents are persistently met with rejection, hostility, timidity, or inconsistent satiation. Repeated thwarting of and irregular support for children's emergent autonomous capabilities can also result in aggressivity.

Symptoms of inattention, such as forgetfulness, distractibility, and problems sustaining focused attention sometimes reflect a learned pattern of preserving an attachment to a caregiver who is overrelied upon for anxiety-abatement, direction, and organizational input. Symptom amelioration or deterioration unfolds based on the predictability of a primary caregiver's availability and active involvement. This can be a chronic problematic parent-child attachment sequence that mimics a long-standing ADHD condition. The child may even meet the criteria for ADHD-Inattentive Type. However, he or she may become asymptomatic with intensive parent work aimed at reducing the capriciousness of parental availability and building greater self-reliance in the child.

Moreover, compromised abilities to mentally invest in tasks, attend and concentrate, catch and correct output errors, and remember visual and auditory information can indicate an avoidant attachment orientation in which a general vigilance against emotion overworks the child's mental resources.

The socioemotional deficits exhibited by insecurely attached children often resemble those of ADHD children. The avoidant child's restricted range and blunted expression of emotion subverts his or her ability to identify with and negotiate other's emotions. There are limitations to how he or she assimilates emotionally laden social feedback. Therefore, initiating and ending social interactions may be ill-timed, off-cue, abrupt, and awkward. Empathic behavior enabling others' pain to be vicariously felt, respected, and understood is severely curtailed. This can lead the child to underestimate harm caused to peers during conflictual exchanges and sap motivation to engage in reparative gestures.

The ambivalent/resistant child's characteristic high anxiety, amped up displays of emotion, and sensitivity to rejection can impede sociability. His or her overzealousness to be liked and more enmeshed style of relating may be overstimulating and off-putting to peers. In an urgent bid for relational mastery the child may reject a peer in anticipation of being rejected by him or her, only to be flooded with regret afterward and be oversolicitous in winning back friendship. Strong needs for anxiety reduction can leave the child self-focused and inconsistently capable of showing empathy. Consequently, the child may oscillate between underestimating and overestimating the effects he or she has on others.

To the untrained eye, behaviors associated with a disorganized attachment style may be easily collapsed into a severe case of ADHD. The child can be extreme and erratic in his or her behavior, alternating between dissociation and motionlessness to frenetic displays of aggression and agitation. A proneness to panic exists and is dealt with through sudden flight reactions or freezing responses. At the other end of the emotional continuum, the child is susceptible to explosive displays of anger and acting menacingly or assaultively, even vis-à-vis minor provocations.

ADHD-type symptoms such as excessive talking and interrupting can even belie underlying attachment concerns. A habit of picking up the tempo of one's speech, especially in the context of lulls in the dialogue signaling "verbal separations," talking endlessly, showing marked dysfluency in speech prosody, "talking over," or interrupting with insistence in the presence of needed attachment figures can be subtle ways to elicit proximity and ensure prolonged contact. When these phenomena are frequent occurrences they can reflect an attachment-maintaining style, rather than impulsivity, per se.

Beginnings and endings of psychotherapy sessions with ADHD children are occasions for coexistent or overriding attachment-related concerns to crop up. There may be reluctance to separate from parents and enter the playroom when sessions commence. Disorganizing levels of anxiety and excitement over remobilizing an attachment to an idealized therapist may ensue. Then again, disruptive behavior may prevail in a bid to impart distance in the relationship with the therapist, who is a nonparental figure, and as such, felt to be threatening. As sessions wind down the child might up-regulate his or her behavior, acting recklessly, making messes, insisting on finishing games or activities, dragging out or launching into discussions-qua-monologues, refusing to leave, all as a means to prolong contact with an idealized therapist, or manage anxiety over the shifting of attachment needs back over to the caregiver awaiting them.

In the last analysis, it behooves clinicians to assess the quality of children's attachment with primary caregivers when ADHD is suspected. Attachment concerns often overlap, exacerbate, or even subsume ADHD symptoms, such that for psychotherapy to be effective it must incorporate a focus on parent-child attachment remediation and overall family cohesion. Frequently, attachment concerns seem innocuous, subtle, and not readily identifiable. We forget how attachment-sensitive children are and how separations from primary caregivers that are sudden, unexpected, prolonged, or random can have a disorganizing effect throughout childhood. This has societal and lifestyle implications. Even psychologically stable children who are subjected to a pattern of insufficient or erratic contact with parents, especially in the context of life transitions (i.e., geographical moves, school changes, divorce), can become destabilized. Normal career, educational, and extended family obligations can render primary caregivers overtaxed and insufficiently available to children in ways that have disorganizing effects on them. Sleep, appetite, impulse control, and attentional capacities can all suffer. Parsimony dictates that as clinicians we assess and intervene at the level of parent-child attachment to determine whether or how ADHD symptoms are an artifact of underlying problematic parent-child attachment processes.

3

PARTICIPATORY PLAY THERAPY

T raditional play therapy finds the therapist adopting more of an observational than a participatory stance, awaiting the child's inevitable
gravitation toward symbolic play. The high-water mark is for the therapist to
subdue his or her subjectivity and maintain a nondirective attitude, thereby
permitting unconscious material that is troubling for the child to be given
unobstructed and full expression in the play. It is believed that there is a direct correspondence between what occurs in the play and what exists in a
precomposed state in the child's unconscious. Emphasis is placed on the content of the child's play and interpretations that can be offered regarding its
representational significance. Thus, we find pioneers in the field likening the
child's play to dreams adult patients bring to the consulting room, the therapeutic task being to divine who play figures really represent in the child's
life, or what play themes reveal about unresolved traumas and conflicts, forbidden feelings and desires. Play analysis then finds its corollary in dream
analysis, the work at hand being to help the child decipher the latent meaning in the manifest play content. The child's ego is strengthened through insight into linkages between what is contained in the play and what it really
means. Additionally, sometimes ego strength can be garnered from self-
initiated, quasi-solitary play experiences that allow for uninhibited displays
of emotion, or playful working out of underlying conflicts, with the therapist being ancillary to the process. Erikson (1999) captures this supposed self-
curative aspect of play as follows: "The most obvious condition is that the
child has the toys and the adult for himself, and that sibling rivalry, parental
nagging, or any kind of sudden interruption does not disturb the unfolding
of the play intentions, whatever they may be. For to 'play it out' is the most
natural self-healing measure childhood affords" (475).

On the one hand, the implication is that the child is tacitly aware of what needs to be worked out in the play and is capable of self-amelioration if just provided with the proper conditions and given license to play. The child's supposed "instinct of mastery" (Waelder, 1999) guarantees that toys and play materials will be used to actively re-create unsettling life experiences that the child was passively subjected to, in a manner that renders them more assimilable. On the other hand, it is assumed that the child has at his or her disposal the inner potential for self-recovery from regressive expressions in the play. This reflects a sort of "cathartic bias" in traditional play therapy, where it is presupposed that strong emotions are "neutralized" through their very expression, without any measurable contribution by the therapist. Ample opportunities to vent through play somehow inoculate the child against disturbed and disturbing emotionality, it is proposed. Modulation of affect, according to this model, is strictly an intrapsychic achievement.

Needless to say, traditional play therapy is ill-suited for ADHD children, whose play activities tend to be more "concrete" than "symbolic," propelling themselves into interpersonal enactments with the therapist with whom they want to "play for real" rather than "just pretend." They may provoke actual involvement on the part of the therapist lest their behavior become disorganized, disruptive, or destructive. Self-recovery from intense display of emotion often seems unreachable. Typically, their play is "person" versus "object" mediated (e.g., preferring to wrestle with the therapist rather than with action figures). They are liable to experience interpretations as unwanted intrusions into their active play scenarios (e.g., "I'm waiting, I'm waiting, would you quit talking and take your turn on the chess board"), as inducements to act (e.g., "I can see that you are so mad at me you are worried you might hit me"), or simply as perplexing. Indeed, to expect an ADHD child to engage in low-key, object-mediated, talk-heavy play is tantamount to requiring that they be cured as a precondition for therapy.

Furthermore, undue attention paid to play content and its interpretation obscures the emotion-regulating, self-organizing, and attachment-promoting benefits afforded by the play process itself. Winnicott (1971) himself was disconcerted by an exclusive focus on the referential dimensions of play: "I seem to see in the psychoanalytic literature the lack of a useful statement on the subject of play. . . . The psychoanalyst has been too busy using play content to look at the playing child, and to write about playing as a thing in itself" (40). The process of playing, with the direct involvement of the therapist, can remedially address underdeveloped emotive capacities in ADHD children. Active participation of the therapist is pivotal if he or she is to effectively join with or engage these children, evoke a greater range and intensity of affects, and facilitate the acquisition of enhanced emotion regulation. Optimal emotion regulation is not a preformed capacity of the child awaiting "holding," "mirroring," "containing," or "mutative interpretations" for it to emerge and take hold in the child's personality structure. As we shall see, progressive emotional mastery in the child is relationally/intersubjectively learned and predicated on the therapist's judicious use of his or her subjectivity.

As therapists we forget how playing with children in ways that show keen attention to their developmental needs potentiates our value as attachment figures, awakening idealizations and associated expansive and deflationary mood states that need careful monitoring and management. The therapist who has become special to the child can also be a source of identification, someone whose style of communicating in the play may resonate with the child, creating pathways for the overt and covert procurement of finessed social and emotional competencies. Receptivity to feedback, mentoring, and oversight are also enhanced when the therapist is predominantly perceived as a valued attachment figure.

Of greater import to our discussion is how play therapy models have incompletely absorbed the juggernaut of postmodern thought in psychology and been slow to incorporate the wealth of findings from infant research, in ways that have relevance for working with ADHD children. Postmodernist notions highlighting the essential indivisibility of subject and object, and of the reciprocal influence inherent in all interpersonal exchanges, make neutrality, observation without participation, and nondirectiveness, all specious methodologies. The idea of an active therapist is lent epistemological legitimacy, since he or she cannot *not* act, with respect to the clinical situation. This carries weight regarding work with ADHD children since the reserved and constricted behavior constitutive of the therapist's supposed neutrality and nondirectiveness can undermine effective therapy, precluding the therapist from engaging ADHD children commensurate with their heightened activity level and fluctuating affectivity, and nullifying the therapist's use of his or her authentic subjectivity in ways that might optimally arouse, de-arouse, and organize the child.

Nowhere is the permeability between self and other more evident than in the world of emotions. Along these lines, Mitchell (2000) reasoned that "Affect is contagious, and on the deepest level, affective states are often transpersonal. Intense affects like anxiety, sexual excitement, rage, depression, and euphoria tend to generate corresponding affects in others" (61). Relationists propose that emotions are not distinct properties of individuals that are meaningfully communicated and understood independent of whatever social contexts that give rise to them, but intersubjectively engendered, managed, and comprehended. This has salience for emotion-centered child therapy, since what feelings are shared, when, how, and for what reason will depend in large part on the active participation of the therapist.

Moreover, a participatory, relational approach may be in order for action-oriented children insofar as their provocations and impulsive actions are not conceived of as counterproductive and tangential to the real work of therapy, but as enactments that are integral to the process of redoing and undoing seemingly inflexible and problematic styles of relating. For instance, the ADHD child might expect, yet simultaneously fear, that the therapist will become reactive, exasperated, or immobilized when his recurring automatic inclination is to abort one game in favor of another, leaving the office in a shambles. However, in disallowing this, redirecting the child back to an unfinished game, all the while caringly voicing his or her subjective reactions in ways that refocus and soothe the child, the therapist contributes to the child unlearning a problematic impulsive style of relating. This more active, socializing therapeutic stance does not circumvent the need for interpretation. When the interaction is more conducive to reflection or tempered processing of feelings, the therapist can explore with the child fears around expected reactions from the therapist, and hopes for wished ones.

A more participatory role for the therapist is also substantiated by infant research findings and innovations in psychoanalytic developmental psychology. Good-enough therapy has elements of good-enough early caregiving, inasmuch as we view therapy as a milieu in which corrective developmental experiences occur. The therapist draws knowledge from the intersubjective field within which he or she is embedded with the client, and uses it to configure and reconfigure his or her degree of involvement. Emotional synchrony and empathic attunement are central to ascertain from the client's cues when up-regulatory or down-regulatory interactions are necessary to dampen or draw out feelings. Sensitivity to modifying nonverbal forms of communication, such as eye contact, speech prosody, and proximal versus distal body positioning, in concert with the client's varying needs and what the interaction permits, take on significance. Finally, as we see in the pages below, an active therapeutic stance is instrumental to gauge how much assistance children need to build frustration tolerance while pursuing effortful tasks and to overcome the narcissistic vulnerabilities that underlie exhibitionistic displays, grandiose self-images, or shame/rage cycles.

It is lamentable that play therapy is often sidelined as an effective treatment modality with ADHD children. Their action-orientedness, as well as their problems with mental representation and internal manipulation of information, leads to them being viewed as poor candidates for play therapy. However, this has less to do with the intractable nature of the cognitive and emotional vulnerabilities of ADHD children than with the way play therapy historically has been devised. We need to question the basic method utilized, rather than attempt to shoehorn the child to it or deem the child ill-suited to the method.

In this chapter, I outline the ingredients of a participatory play therapy model, elaborating on and adding to the ideas contained above, along the way dispelling the belief that ADHD children are ill-served by play therapy. A more participatory style of working with ADHD children allows for their symptoms to be brought out into the open and constructively worked on in an *in vivo* fashion. This coincides with Barkley's (2006) position that for treatments to work with this client population they have to reach the child at a "point of performance," or when the child is in the throngs of a symptom. Put in more relational terms, this is when the child and other are both co-subjected to and co-subjects of the symptom and its remediation.

NEUTRALITY, EMPATHY, AND AUTHENTIC RELATEDNESS

Neutrality as a therapeutic stance is one of the mainstays of classical psychoanalysis, as well as its variants, the Kleinian and ego-psychological approaches. It centers on the analyst conscientiously refraining from acceding to the client's demands, needs, or wishes, being thoughtfully detached, and nontendentious. Neutrality is thought to be the sine qua non of bringing the client to see how his projections onto the therapist reveal the inner workings of his or her own mind, not the analyst's. In other words, if the analyst is to unerringly represent the client's inner dynamics to him or her, the analyst needs to step back, reserve all judgment, and mobilize his or her powers of objectivity. That way when the client confuses the analyst for a rejecting or seductive father, say, the true source of the perceptions can be accurately interpreted (transference interpretation). The client can then reconnect to painful childhood memories, talk them through, and gain psychic relief. If the analyst steps outside of this neutral attitude and provides advice, affection, or censure, avenues for remembering and working through painful childhood memories are foreclosed. Countertransference, or the analyst's own unresolved personal conflicts, is believed to govern such gratifying actions, and needs to be kept in check, since it threatens to compromise the analyst's objectivity. This method when generalized to play therapy entails the analyst striving for neutrality not only when he or she is the object of the child's attention, but also when toys or dramatic play scenarios captivate the child's interest.

Neutrality as a therapeutic stance is rife with epistemological problems too many to cover in this brief section. Mitchell (1993, 1997, 2000) and others (Stolorow, Atwood, and Orange, 2002; Stolorow and Atwood, 1992), drawing upon postmodern theory, accentuate the impossibility of the therapist ever removing him or herself from the interactional field since the investigating subject is always inextricably linked to the investigated object. The therapist's own subjectivity is always a part of any objectivity he or she proffers. As such, interpretations can never in any pure sense be renderings of the contents of the client's mind without, to a greater or lesser degree, reflecting also the contents of the therapist's mind. The therapist can never empty out the contents of his or her own mind, to make room for the contents of the client's mind, as neutrality would seem to suggest.

Epistemological problems aside, the behaviors constitutive of a neutral therapeutic stance, silence, quasi-emotional indifference, disengaged reflectiveness, and the like render treatment with ADHD children ineffectual. Extrapolating from Wineman's (1957) idea on working with aggressive children, ADHD children are often "sublimation deaf," seemingly disinterested in using toy play to mediate feelings, or onto which to displace conflicts, instead pressing for tangible involvement on the part of the therapist. All children, let alone those with ADHD, need confirmatory experiences to concretize and consolidate basic feelings and perceptions. Keeping a child in a state of uncertainty or indifference as to what the therapist thinks and feels can be mystifying, invalidating, and counterproductively disorganizing. As contended by Wachtel (1987), even in adult therapy, "an atmosphere of safety is not cultivated by an ambiguous, non-gratifying stance" (181). A related idea is contained in the "still face" experiments of infant researchers wherein infants were found to become agitated when their gestures for responsiveness from caregivers were met with nonresponsiveness. We are all to some degree unnerved—infants, children, and adults alike—when in our encounters with others pointed displays of emotion are met with imperviousness.

A neutral therapeutic attitude can also bring about its own set of iatrogenic effects with the ADHD child. To remain passive in the face of the child's overanimatedness or outright provocativeness, only to find him or her becoming frenzied or belligerent, is not necessarily evidence of how trenchant the child's ADHD is, but may speak to an iatrogenic effect—a treatment-induced aggravation of symptoms. It is important to remind ourselves that when neutrality and abstinence are practiced in their most or-thodox forms the therapist is essentially dehumanizing him or herself, leav-ing the door open for ruthless attacks by the client. Aggression can be ex-pressed in its most primitive form, without regard for harm caused, when there are few experiential bridges to the other's subjectivity. Therefore, when ADHD children's actions have become unmanageable in the play what they often need is a counteraction, not a disengaged interpretation.

Empathy has come to rival, if not replace, neutrality as the preferred observational stance the more self-psychology has gained a foothold in psy-choanalysis. Kohut (1977) wrote of using empathy as a technique whereby the therapist can deduce what the client is feeling through "vicarious intro-spection," or through bracketing his or her own internal feeling states and being moved by the client's separate feeling states. Stark (1999) describes this as the therapist "decentering from her own experiences, entering into the patient's experience, and taking it on as if it were her own" (46). Being able to ascertain the client's differentiated affects through vicarious intro-spection supposedly allows the therapist to adequately mirror and affirm them for the client. Empathizing with the client's feelings is a way to affirm them, not necessarily confirm them. The difference is a subtle one. The therapist might affirm the client's sadness or gladness without really person-ally sharing in these affects or being moved in personal ways that draw him or her more into the relationship. Stark (1999) alludes to another dimen-sion of this *affirmation without confirmation* hypothesis in illustrating how the validation process in self-psychology might provide the client "recognition that she really wishes she could be special to the therapist, not that she is in fact special" (70). Consequently, empathy can be a postured way of being with clients, a way of being inauthentic, a more palatable way to detach.

Moreover, close scrutiny reveals how at a conceptual level empathy suffers from the same epistemological problems as neutrality; namely, a pre-supposition that self and other, or minds, are essentially divisible. There is the misguided belief in self-psychology that the therapist can function as a self in relation to the client as a distinguishable other. If in a more ortho-dox psychoanalytic approach neutrality can be thought of as dispassionate detachment, in self-psychology empathy is a sort of compassionate detach-ment. The problem is the same, the essential achievability of detachment.

Frank (1999) astutely points to some other pitfalls associated with an em-pathic approach. Unswerving attunement to the client's "internal life" can de-flect from the therapist's self-mindfulness and undercut awareness of feelings elicited in him or her by the client, experiential data that might be used for important therapeutic purposes. Valuable opportunities for providing direct feedback and honest disclosures that enliven and enrich the treatment can also be foreclosed when empathy is the sole therapeutic frame. In clinical work with ADHD children, being able to source one's own personal reactions and offer direct feedback in assimilable ways are crucial in assisting the child to build interpersonal awareness.

From a relational perspective, authenticity as a way to engage and understand the client encapsulates the spirit of neutrality and empathy as therapeutic methods—even-mindedness, disciplined exploration, sensitivity, concern for the client's experience—yet omits the questionable epistemological baggage—the presumed divisibility of self and other, or of minds. As defined by Stark (1999), authentic relatedness with the client involves the therapist "remaining centered within her own experience, allowing the patient's experience to enter into her, and taking on the patient's experience as her own" (46). Being moved by a client and relating accordingly is not consonant with removing oneself from one's own experience. The therapist always perceives the client from within his or her own vantage point. "Mutual influence" (Aron, 1996) is inescapable in the relationship, as client and therapist co-evoke reactions in each other. This is not to say that the therapist should avoid the task of trying to bracket his or her subjectivity, or attain some semblance of objectivity. Differentiated relatedness remains an important avenue for the client to obtain confirmation of feeling states and ground the client in his or her own self-experience. The therapist's differentiated relatedness, or nonreactive recognition of the child's feelings, assists the emotionally reactive child with procuring a more emotionally responsive interpersonal style since it recurringly gives him or her pause to distinguish his or her own feelings, recognize them, and think about them before acting on them.

Authentic relatedness is also a safeguard against the artificiality and lack of intimacy that can imbue an acerbic neutral therapeutic attitude, or a postured empathic one. The therapist's genuine concern for the child (and the ADHD child is no exception) is a prerequisite for meaningful therapy. A stilted way of relating is not conducive to trust building and playfulness. Spontaneity, humor, physical contact, judicious self-disclosure, open expressions of positive regard, and even anger all have a place in child work. The latter was not lost on Spiegel (1989), who wrote: "The therapist's never showing anger is just as much an error as his becoming angry at everything" (113). Winnicott (1992) was also privy to the idea that a negative reaction can have a more humanizing effect than no reaction at all when the client is acting offensively. As child therapists we would do well to remind ourselves of the old adage that the opposite of love is not hate, but indifference. When we adopt a sterile or postured stance in the name of professionalism we risk confronting the child with a level of imperviousness that can leave him or her feeling unseen and unheard, compounding any sense of despair or nihilism already felt.

Yet, we might ask ourselves: How is it possible to preserve good technique and remain authentic as therapists? Or, to paraphrase Frank (1999), to be authentic while still being strategic? Or, yet again, to be authentically professional or professionally authentic? The answers to these questions lie in the therapist's own integrated selfhood, lived capacities for synergizing spontaneity and intentionality, organic blending of roles, and facility at personalizing his or her clinical knowledge. Somehow our humanity has to imbue our technique and cloak our professionalism if we are to be of therapeutic benefit.

Forbearance and genuine commitment are called for in therapy with children who externalize since the relational pull is often a negatively valenced one. The child may be inured to the consequences of his or her actions and blandly expect criticism, rejection, or dismissiveness. Any lingering hopes that this will not be the case, and that the therapist will respond in ways dissimilar to ingrained negative expectations, may be dashed in the child. Such hopes may need to be temporarily carried by the therapist him or herself.

To assist the ADHD child with maintaining organization and goal-directedness in the play, command his or her attention when there is undue distractibility, and transition out of intense displays of excitement or agitation, all require the therapist to be emotionally present and capable of acting caringly and carefully. The therapist needs to be poised and sensitized to the child's needs for prompting, containment, and redirection as they become interpersonally engendered.

At bottom, having an encounter with a real person who responds to him or her in real ways can be the optimal therapeutic undercurrent that the ADHD child needs to appreciate the mutuality in relationships. This can be as basic as waiting one's turn, speaking and listening, sharing, assisting with cleanup, and all the verbal and nonverbal negotiations of these processes that occur. Essentially, what the ADHD child needs of the therapist is for him or her to be, not so much a "real object" as a real subject, which might involve the therapist not objecting to being objectified, or needed in certain ways.

PARTICIPANT OBSERVATION
AND OBSERVANT PARTICIPATION

Interpersonalists at odds with the orthodox view of transference in psychoanalysis used the concept of participant observer to substantiate their critique

(Sullivan, 1953). Originally advanced by anthropologists to highlight how the behavior of another cannot be meaningfully understood independent of the observer studying it, interpersonalists seized upon the concept of participant observer to claim that the therapist's actual here-and-now presence has a bearing on how the client perceives him or her. They refuted the belief that the therapist could be a "blank screen," completely innocent of the client's attributions. Granted, the client may fixate on some facet of the therapist's personhood and remain ignorant of other facets, based on the client's relationship history and what he or she has come to expect from people. But the client does not transferentially fabricate; that is, project onto the therapist attributions that are invalid in terms of the therapist's current behavior yet valid concerning important people from the client's past, as presupposed in Freudian psychoanalysis.

In short, for the first interpersonalists transference entailed the client being guilty of a sort of motivated exaggeration, or oversight, but not outright distortion. Transference to them became less a medium to activate and understand past hurts and disappointments in relation to outside figures, and more a medium for in vivo learning about relational expectancies and needs as they unfold in the therapeutic exchange. The legacy has endured within the interpersonal tradition to think of transference as an admixture of realistic and unrealistic perceptions, who the therapist is in actuality and who the client needs him to be. In the vernacular of contemporary relational approaches, the therapist is both an objective subject for the client and a subjective object, as relational interchanges are lived out.

In practice, the original interpersonalists tended to emphasize their observational role. The task at hand was to be vigilant for and withstand the client's press to replicate problematic relationship expectations. Detaching oneself and issuing "objective" interpretations as to how the client sets himself up to be rejected, treated with indifference, and so forth, was the proper procedure. Needs for affection were not to be gratified, nor fears of rejection countered, but interpreted. Breaking the cycle of undesirable self-fulfilling relationship prophesies through insight was the noble aim, a variation of the Freudian tenet that self-understanding and rational insight bring relief and transformation.

It took a new generation of interpersonalists to flesh out and rework problems inherent in the idea that the therapist can act as a differentiated observer, imparting objective interpretations; as if observation was not a type of participation, and objective interpretations could be unmoored from subjective experience: "The analyst's point of view, even if arrived at through rational, self-reflective observation, cannot be separated from his forms of participation. Observation is never neutral. Observation is always contextual, based on assumptions, values, construction of experience" (Mitchell, 1997, 87). The step from viewing observation as a type of participation, to examining the role of the therapist's overall active contribution, and how it hinders or enhances the client's growth processes, became a short one.

Hence, we find contemporary relationists making reference to the therapist using his or her authentic subjectivity, or status as a "real object," to occasion new relationship experiences for the client. Providing insight into perseverative relationship tendencies is now viewed as a foreshortened therapeutic aim, just part of the overall process in which the therapist introduces his or her personhood into the relationship in ways that facilitate the redoing and undoing of the client's fixed, unsatisfactory ways of being in the world. As an authentic subject, willing to express personal reactions that have been interpersonally evoked, the therapist risks becoming in actuality an old-bad object for the client, wherein problematic relationship predispositions become replicated in the here-and-now therapy situation. The client lures the therapist into interpersonal dramas that, although familiar, are unsettling, and the therapist is complicitous via his or her naturally occurring reactions. However, when therapy is operating well, the therapist is not entirely ensnared, is able to recover his or her objectivity, and may respond as a new good object in ways that open up possibilities for the client to experience old hurts in new ways and acquire modes of being that are more interpersonally efficacious.

Countertransference in this model is not conceived of as "noise in the system," or personal reactions that automatically compromise the therapist's objective appraisals of the client, but as encompassing the totality of the therapist's reactions to the client. Relational definitions of countertransference stress its potential to generate important information regarding the client's "object world" (Aron, 1996). Put differently, the therapist can use countertransferential reactions to tap into greater awareness of how the client typically affects and is affected by others in his or her life.

A more participatory, interpersonal style of therapy shows promise in clinical work with ADHD children. It may even make engagement with ADHD children possible, given their propensity for action and press for interaction. The rich interpersonal exchanges nested in the play process itself become the crucible for therapeutic change in the child. In vivo social and emotional deficits such as the misreading of social cues, provocation of negative reactions, externalization of blame, sudden abortion of effortful tasks, and their interpersonal effects can be productively worked with, as a core rather than auxiliary dimension of treatment. Furthermore, insight-oriented work is inherently alienating for ADHD children, since being expected to abstract themselves from the ongoing flow of the play and reflect on their actions in any routine fashion may exceed their capabilities. This is not to say that insights anchored in the ongoing flow of here-and-now therapist-child communications cannot be poignant, believable, and assimilable. The distinction is contained in Lomas's (1987) assertion that "A considered statement designed to increase insight will have a different meaning from a spontaneous response that may incidentally increase insight" (56).

In the last analysis, in relationally oriented psychotherapy with ADHD children there are risks inherent in positioning oneself as either too much of an "observer," or too much of a "participant." In the former, there can be "failures of engagement" (Stark, 1999) where the therapist's nonresponsiveness and discomfort with participating in active play can constrict and stagnate the treatment, foreclosing opportunities to help the child commensurate with his or her level of emotionality and action-orientedness. In the latter, there can be "failures in containment" (Stark, 1999) where the therapist becomes overly involved in the play and unduly agitated or immobilized, with reverberating disorganizing effects on the child. The artistry in working with ADHD children resides in the therapist navigating the dialectic between participatory observation and observant participation.

THE UNCONSCIOUS RECONSIDERED

The imprint of Freud's conceptualization of the unconscious retains a certain appeal in the psychodynamic play therapy tradition. For many therapists, the mainstay of child work continues to be decoding *the specific unconscious meaning* embedded in the child's play, particularly repetitive play episodes. There is a readiness to see play scenarios as discreet referents to unconscious memories, fantasies, wishes, or needs—psychic events occurring inside the child that have been banished from conscious awareness. Put differently, disturbing, preformed psychic events are actively expelled from consciousness. In play, just as in dreams, these disturbing unconscious items are symbolically disguised to offer a measure of emotional distance. Ferreting out the distinctive unconscious event a given play scenario represents, in a way that allows for its avowal by the child, with psychic relief, is believed to constitute the work of therapy. In more technical terms, this amounts to the child obtaining insight, or pointed awareness of the true source of his or her disquietude. Relief comes from the "binding effects" of an interpretation, in bringing a piece of experience within the domain of the ego, availing the child with a more hardy explanation for a confusing behavior or upsetting feeling. Relief also comes from "the lifting of repression," the child no longer needs to work at staying unaware of painful psychological experiences. There is mental labor involved in disguising, falsifying, distorting, and avoiding.

Over the past few decades, a host of psychoanalytic commentators influenced by postmodern thought have challenged Freud's modernist account of the unconscious mind as a repository of precomposed psychic contents awaiting discovery through veridical interpretations. Stern (1997) has written persuasively on the unconscious as "unformulated experience." He asserts that unconscious experience is really experience that is yet to undergo a process of articulation. He takes issue with the notion that experiences start out as conscious, attain a certain coherence, then are rendered unconscious, retaining their original coherence. Rather, he proposes that all experience is essentially indeterminate until it is articulated, whether through reflection, symbolic action, or language. Indeed, the very process of explicating unformulated experience not only contributes to its outward expression but its inherent meaning. Put differently, unformulated or unconscious experience does not have a predetermined meaning that can be discovered and uncovered, rather it has diffuse meaning that is fleshed out and created in the communication process.

To state the obvious, in the context of play therapy the process of articulating unformulated experience occurs interactionally, whether with the therapist or play materials. In the words of Richard Rorty, the American pragmatist philosopher, there is no "God's-eye point of view" or "view from nowhere" (Guignon and Hiley, 2003) whereby the therapist is positioned to offer objective interpretations of preexisting unconscious psychic events that are intact and discoverable, symbolically embedded in the child's play. Rather, the therapist is necessarily limited to *plausible* interpretations of the child's play that are warranted by, at the very least, the here-and-now interaction, knowledge of the client's past and current family situation, and the therapist's clinical knowledge base, accumulated life experience, and own defensive organization. Moreover, these plausible interpretations themselves add a coherence and intelligibility to the client's experiences that is not preexistent. Whatever significance the therapist makes of the client's verbalizations and actions has an essential bearing on the client's own explanatory attributions.

There is still the question as to why children would be motivated to keep experiences unformulated, or unconscious. From a Freudian vantage point, it is the disturbed nature of the unconscious content and its disturbing internal effects that motivates repression in children. Stern (1997), on the other hand, intimates that it is the effort involved in actively articulating unformulated experiences that is aversive and therefore conducive to avoidance. "What if the natural tendency is for experience to remain outside awareness? What if action and effort are required, not to keep experience out of consciousness, but to bring it in? What if conscious experience is not so much stifling the uproarious beach ball as it is like lifting a rock from the bottom and hauling it to the surface?" (85). This idea has implications for child work. A more active stance on the part of the therapist is imperative to prompt initiative taking and perseverance in the child as he or she strives to communicate and rework diffuse experiences. Whether the struggle is one of the client finding suitable words to capture a vague feeling or seemingly contradictory feelings, deciding on a game or play sequence that appears to have unique expressive potential, or persisting with a playful interaction that challenges the client's need for interpersonal distance or closeness, the therapist's offerings may stoke the client's motivation to remain engaged in the articulation process. If the play is stagnating, or the child's play themes seem disjointed and incomplete, it may have less to do with avoidance of painful unconscious feelings and thoughts unfolding in the play, and more to do with the therapist's failure to stimulate play conditions conducive to expressive consolidation of ill-defined feeling states, needs, wishes, or fantasies.

For Freud, the impetus for repression is rooted in intrapsychic events. Troubling thoughts and feelings are actively kept from consciousness because they are unacceptable to the individual. This reflects Freud's monadic view of the mind and belief that psychic development is largely an internal achievement, with inner resistances needing to be overcome in order for unconscious experiences to be rendered conscious. Countering this, Stern (1997) and other theorists propose an interpersonal/intersubjective framework for understanding unconscious experiences and their motivated disavowal. Stolorow and Atwood (1992) delineate three interrelated dimensions of the unconscious. The *prereflective unconscious* constitutes overarching ways of organizing experiences based on psychic structure internalized from early infant-caregiver interactions before the advent of conscious memory. This might manifest itself in a child who appears characterologically immune to states of excitement or exuberance due to an affect-regulation style acquired through failures in early parent-infant dyadic exchanges that obstructed the child's capacities to contain and recover from heightened positive mood states. The *dynamic unconscious* refers to emotional experiences that are denied and avoided because of a learned expectancy that their outward expression would jeopardize needed attachments to important caregivers. There is an ingrained fear that overt expression of covert thoughts and feelings will have imminent retraumatizing effects. This might apply to the child who dreads showing homoerotic feelings because his father's religiosity disallowed for such expressions and thereby threatened significant withdrawal of love, or outright rejection. The *unvalidated unconscious* has as its focus those experiences that remain fractured and easily dissolvable because they failed to meet with the kind of caregiver responsiveness, assurance, and affirmation necessary to cognitively crystallize them. Stern (1997) conjectures that this is the kind of experience that remains unconscious "because it does not receive the interpersonal imprimatur it would need to be cognized" (60). Void of ready access to caregivers capable of providing attuned recognition, a range of feeling states may remain vague and poorly distinguished from their physiological underpinnings, experienced by the child as impersonal forces that wash over him or her, with disorganizing effects. Without the necessary "interpersonal imprimatur" to anchor the child in his or her own self-experience, the child may be unsure of what he or she is feeling, thinking, or intending, and be gullible or too open to suggestion. It stands to reason that a decidedly neutral stance by the therapist who refrains from offering confirmation of a client's emergent experiences can contribute to his or her confusion, self-doubt, or emotional wavering.

From an interpersonal perspective, the client cannot be his or her own source of self-assuredness in any fundamental way when it comes to the articulation of unformulated experiences. The accessibility of the therapist's "subjective" confirmatory input, albeit from within the client's self-experience and vantage point, is what activates and maintains the client's willingness to pursue the not uncommonly arduous process of explicating diffuse experiences. Likewise, if the client is to overcome tendencies to deny and avoid fuller expression of certain feeling states, forbidden wishes, fantasies, or such, there needs to be a measure of confidence derived from interactions with the therapist that to do so will not recurringly lead to a dangerous replication of their childhood traumatic effects.

RETHINKING THE INTERPRETIVE PROCESS

In contemporary psychoanalysis, much ink has been spent attempting to ascertain whether objectivity in any meaningful sense can be achieved when commenting on a client's inner experiences, what constitutes the truth value of an interpretation, and what about the interpretive process is therapeutic. The influx of hermeneutical and constructivist thought into the field has cast doubt on the achievability of interpretative objectivity in the classical sense. There is greater affinity for seeing an inextricable link between the therapist as investigatory subject and the client as investigated subject, as well as for underscoring the impossibility of the therapist ever responding from outside his or her subjectivity or observing without participating in any fundamental sense. Questions arise as to whether our interpretations can ever be dislodged from our clinical knowledge base, or favored and favorite ways of conceptualizing client behavior, or for that matter be uninfluenced by our accumulated life experience. Perhaps it is more epistemologically sound to think of interpretations as offerings from our own subjectivity that have salience and applicability for the client insofar as we maintain affective resonance and attentive involvement with him or her.

"Warranted assertibility" (Guignon and Hiley, 2003) or "plausibility" (Mitchell, 1993) obtain relevance when assessing the accuracy of interpretations: What experiential data from here-and-now therapist-client interactions justify an interpretation? What extensions from this experiential data can be made regarding the client's past, present, and anticipated family situation? What aspects of the client's nonverbal behavior complement or fail to complement his or her verbal disclosures? What clinical paradigm is most elucidating given this particular client, with his or her unique set of life dilemmas? Is there plausible deniability, whereby the client's disconfirmation of part or all of the therapist's interpretation seems believable? These questions and more enter the picture. Additionally, interpretations have to "fit" for the client in order to be transformative, not in the sense of them being objectively true, so much as personally convincing, helping to coalesce and crystallize diffuse experiences in new, believable, and assimilable ways.

Mitchell (1997) claims that interpretations are relational, more so than informational, events. The very act of offering a salient interpretation conveys to the client that his or her experience and behavior are potentially intelligible, which can have a restorative effect in and of itself. Interpretations also have an organizational function. Being in the presence of a therapist who is emotionally attuned and poised to tease out meaning, clarify, speculate, reiterate, elaborate, and so forth, enables the client to become rooted in his or her own subjectivity and achieve greater versatility expressing a range of experiences more coherently and cogently. A tolerance for ambiguity can be incrementally acquired as the client entertains differing interpretations, reflectively sifting through the experiential evidence to authenticate or decline them.

A focus on interpretations as objective statements or restatements of psychic events occurring in the mind of the client has obscured the overt and covert ways in which they actually shape clients' emergent verbal repertoires and attempts at meaning making. When clients experience interpretations as directives, admonitions, or injunctions to act, they are thought to be distorting the therapist's neutral communications. However, it is arguable that all interpretations to varying degrees are both *descriptive* and *prescriptive*. The degree to which they are more descriptive than prescriptive, or vice versa, has to take into consideration not only the informative elements of an interpretation but its performative elements—what is said, when it is said, and how it is said. A therapist who shifts in his chair, nervously coughs, and haltingly utters, "When you run out of the house during a conflict with your brother, you are escaping in a way that you wished you could have done so many times when your parents argued bitterly before they got divorced" may unwittingly be ascribing meaning and prescribing action. For instance, he may be communicating at a basic level that taking flight during conflicts solves little and offering an appealing cognitive frame for understanding a heretofore inexplicable compulsion; namely, that the child's flight reactions stem from having had to endure painful parental arguments. The child might convey this insight in explanations given to others for his or her behavior: "I hate conflicts. My mom and dad used to argue all the time and I'd rather run off than be stuck in a bad argument with my brother."

Interpretations can also indirectly serve as model verbal expressions. For instance, the interpretation, "You hold back from crying because if you start you are worried that you are so sad about so many things that you will never stop crying," implicitly offers up a verbal model for use by the child to communicate his or her upset under similar circumstances. Later that month the child might say to a trusted teacher, "Today is one of those days when I feel like I could cry forever." Indeed, an understudied area of psychoanalytic psychotherapy is the manner in which interpretations bring emotional relief to clients because they tacitly offer lexical and gestural expressions for clients to pattern their own communicative creations after. The fact that interpretive objectivity is unachievable ought not to have paralyzing effects on the therapist. Rather pragmatic choice of words knowing the client's life situation, within a backdrop of authentic relatedness, is what enables interpretations to be personally meaningful for the client and conducive to efficacious communication.

Enactments by the therapist can also have interpretive effects, expand-ing the client's facility at aligning actions with underlying wishes. I have in mind here impromptu gestures on the part of the therapist where precon-scious processing of interpersonal information culminates in a communica-tive act, not consciously intended to impart meaning to the child, although having that effect. Imagine an action sequence between child and therapist where the child grunts loudly and roughly squeezes the therapist as a way of greeting him at the beginning of a session. The therapist returns the grunt, although less loudly, and squeezes the child back, less roughly. The therapist follows this up with an affectionate sound, followed by a gentle hug. In an implicit way the therapist is conveying to the child meaning about the interpersonal effects of his or her roughness and the possibility of a different kind of physical contact that is in line with the child's underly-ing wishes. Arguably, for some children, some of the time, the sort of ac-tion sequence described would lead to more potent insight than an inter-pretation to the effect of: "You really want to give me a gentle hug but you are worried that since boys are not supposed to like gentle hugs this might make you look girly." This is not to say that this interpretation in concert with the mutual enactment described does not have its place.

Interpretations can also be effectively supplied indirectly, through stay-ing in rather than stepping out of the play, and conveying meaning through verbal metaphor. This might take the form of speaking through or for play characters in ways that have personal relevance for the child but do not con-front him or her directly with the concrete source of the problem. A play therapy scenario will be instructive here. Take the child client whose beloved pet cat is fatally run over by a car and who stifles her grief because the loss is so upsetting. During a session while playing with puppets she suddenly throws a lion puppet across the room out of sight and blithely states, "that lion just bit the dust." The therapist, discerning that there is something being communicated in this action that has a bearing on the lost pet, speaks through a horse puppet about how it feels to have his best "pup-pet lion friend" suddenly and unexpectedly die. "I feel so sad about my lion friend dying. I can't bear it. It all happened so fast. I really loved my lion friend and life will not be the same without him." The girl picks up a rac-coon puppet and comforts the horse puppet. "There, there, horsey, it will be okay. Losing a good friend is awful, it makes you want to cry, and cry and cry." The therapist then has the horse puppet cry and say: "It's hard to let your sad feelings out when something terrible happens. But I know now that I can do it and feel better." Working metaphorically in this way to en-gender meaning making and arrive at insights can be effective with children in that it offers them a measure of psychological distance from the distress induced by addressing a life problem head on. Staying in "pretend mode" allows the child the illusion that the problem and its solution do not really pertain to them, when they preconsciously or consciously know otherwise. Spiegel (1989) goes so far as to propose that interpretive work in treatment with children can be handled entirely at the level of metaphor and still yield potent insights.

Interpretive work can be especially challenging with ADHD children. Reflecting back feelings or interpreting motives when the child is acting in an unruly or belligerent manner can be tantamount to a failure in containment, sometimes unwittingly replicating expectations of permissiveness in the child's relationships with important caregivers. When the child is in a state of high arousal, cognitively oriented interpretations that require ample mental processing to be assimilated are ineffectual. The therapist and his or her interpretations may be ignored outright, or the interpretations may result in pseudo-insights where the child parrots an intellectualized understanding of his or her symptoms, although the problem behaviors persist. Furthermore, an interpretation of a motive or intent is often experienced by the ADHD child as an invitation or inducement to act. One might want to duck and cover after uttering to the child, "You look so angry right now that you are worried you might hit me." Additionally, interpretations are frequently experienced by ADHD children as impingements to the play, and their negative reactions (e.g., "Can you just play?" and "Do you have to talk?") often speak less to any resistance kicked up by an interpretation that "hits the mark," than to annoyance at having to temporarily forgo the organizing effects derived from the play process itself. Not uncommonly, children will indulge the therapist's interpretive cleverness and endure the emotional awkwardness and confusion that results from its oddness as a tradeoff for being provided with the undivided attention of a sensitive adult. In this regard, children often improve in therapy not because of our interpretations, but in spite of them.

Yet, ADHD children's enactive style of communicating does not automatically foreclose a role for interpretation in therapy. The performative dimensions of the interpretive process take on added significance with this client population. Speech prosody, melodic tone, strength or weakness of voice tone, presence or absence of physical touch, gaze prolongation or discontinuance, proximal versus distal placement in relation to the child, can all make or break whether a child is able to digest an interpretation. In short, how information is communicated based on the emotional tenor of the interactive moment potentiates the use a child can make of that information.

Sometimes singing an interpretation on cue is what captures a child's attention (e.g., "Johnny doesn't like to lose, like to lose, like to lose, Johnny doesn't like to lose because it makes him feel so small and weak"). Likewise, there are those moments when touch, close proximity to the child, and softly spoken words help the child countenance an interpretation, as when the therapist places an arm around the child and gently whispers words in his or her ear. Nevertheless, for some ADHD children the process of rendering underlying feelings and fantasies coherent may only be possible if turned into a spirited activity, as in the case of playing a multiple choice game with answers to the question, "I am most mad at my teacher because . . ." being written using a variety of colors on a white-eraser board.

The organizational advantages of the interpretive process with ADHD children cannot be overstated. Tracking and labeling feelings, offering phraseology to choose from, establishing links between action sequences in the play, proffering what might happen next in a play scenario, and generally staying engaged and attentive to maintain coherence in the child's communications and disclosures are fundamentally valuable. As mentioned earlier, Slade (1994) maintains that this type of therapeutic involvement is vital for self-fragmented children to steadily build the capacity to symbolize, or represent and cognitively rework, inner experiences more intricately.

A "tentative approach" to interpreting can also build a tolerance for ambiguity in ADHD children whose problems with active working memory and impulsive decision making leave them susceptible to incomplete information processing and arriving at conclusions prematurely. Phrasing interpretations suggestively, speculating out loud why the child might be feeling a certain way based on experiential evidence, and juxtaposing various interpretive options, can mobilize underdeveloped self-reflective and evidentiary reasoning processes, as well as assist with greater tolerance for ambiguity. The mere offering of an interpretation or question aimed at defining more complex motives for a client's stated wish or desire, rather than its hasty concrete gratification, can effect greater delay of gratification. Undoubtedly, for ADHD children, the epiphanous quality of an insight, with acute understanding and emotional upwelling, is less characteristic of good therapy than the psychological organizing effects of an interpretive process that instills experientially grounded self-reflection.

The effectiveness and utility of an interpretation with ADHD children not only resides in how and when the interpretation is spoken, but in its wording. As indicated above, interpretations can covertly represent model verbal expressions for children to draw from when communicating experiences under similar interpersonal conditions. An interpretation along the lines of, "You are ignoring me and that makes me wonder if you are angry with me for ending our session without letting you know how much time was left," can indirectly offer linguistic choices for a child when he or she faces similar upset over an abrupt transition: "Dad, you changed the TV channel without asking me. I'm angry with you and feel like ignoring you."

The ADHD child may be predisposed to more adequately metabolize the meaning of interpretations framed in an experience-near, than an experience-distant, "depth psychological" way, since the objectification of experience required by the latter may be too cognitively taxing for the child. Verbal statements by the therapist that assist the child with sourcing, clarifying, and labeling perceived causes to feelings, aligning intentions with actions, or fleshing out feelings, thoughts, and fantasies, can be more readily heard and integrated when the data from which they are derived are grounded in here-and-now therapist-client interactions. This is not to say that there cannot be a depth psychological component to interpretative work where primitive urges percolate and are recognized. Indeed, communication and mastery of basic aggressive urges may be especially important in clinical work with ADHD children. Regressive content can be interpreted based on the child's behavioral demonstrations and conveyed fantasies in the here and now, rather than on presumed archaic infant fantasies stored in the child's mind. Along these lines, in the context of a heated pretend sword fight the therapist might interpret, "I can see that you want to kill me off, gobble up all my power, and leave me for dead."

As an aside, it is ironic, to say the least, that many of us in our formative training in child work were exhorted not to be derailed, or "lose the scent," if children react with indifference or confusion to our accurate interpretations. Because of their cognitive immaturity and natural inclination to deny even miniscule amounts of anxiety, we were taught, children would shun accurate interpretations of their inner conflicts, motives, fantasies, and feelings. However, we were reminded not to be dismayed, that the child's unconscious would hear our accurate interpretations and know them to be true. Furthermore, we would be well advised to abandon any reliance on the child's verbal acceptance of an interpretation to authenticate it. Rather, watching for subtle and not-so-subtle shifts in the play subsequent to an interpretation would provide evidence as to its correctness or incorrectness. It was disconcerting, then intellectually inspiring for me, when I routinely found my child clients, especially the action-oriented ones, reacting with grudging tolerance, indifference, irritation, bewilderment, or polite acceptance to my best attempts at "depth psychological" interpretations, and when looking for confirmatory or disconfirmatory evidence in shifts in the play subsequent to interpretations, I felt like I was in a veritable hall of mirrors with a multitude of justifiable interpretations diverging in all directions! A relational/hermeneutical approach to interpretation has its merits in anticipating the hall-of-mirror effect operating when interpreting children's play, because there is no presumed ready-made index for uncovering meaning; on the contrary, the meaning of human behavior can be eminently ambiguous and the very act of coalescing data to form an interpretation stands as a creative act. Undoubtedly, children's negative reactions to our interpretations can sometimes simply reflect reactions to us as people, or to our stylistic ways of delivering information, that need examination.

KNOWING THAT AND KNOWING HOW

One of the most piercing criticisms of psychoanalytic psychotherapy pertains to its reliance on insight as the primary medium for personal transformation. Existentially and relationally oriented analysts have always been uneasy about this. They contend that insights have to be constituted in action for them to be valid and efficacious. There has to be congruence between what the client believes about him or herself, and how this aligns with his or her actual way of being-in-the-world. Anything short of this is self-deception. Additionally, they argue that it is problematic to assume that insight impels behavior change. *Knowing that* one avoids mentally arduous schoolwork out of a fear of rivaling a father who was an academic overachiever can be a useful bit of self-knowledge. Nevertheless, there is no guarantee that this insight alone will enable the client to *know how* to engage in mentally arduous schoolwork.

Children with ADHD are especially hampered when it comes to converting self-knowledge and social knowledge into action. An abundance of research has shown that these children are as cognizant of the rules of social engagement as other children, yet have greater difficulty executing them (Barkley, 2006). In other words, their *procedural knowledge* is out of step with their *declarative knowledge*. Knowing how to patiently listen, see a task through to completion, or wait one's turn, often eludes them. Knowing that they will be more socially successful if they patiently listen, see a task through to completion, or wait one's turn, does not. It is unlikely that knowing the reasons behind these deficits will suffice in remedying this discrepancy.

Needless to say, effective treatment with ADHD children must embolden their social know-how, or socially relevant procedural knowledge. Insight does have its place. Take the child who insists on repeatedly tossing darts at a dart board, seemingly indifferent to the therapist having a turn. The therapist might interpret that the client is so eager to show her wonderful dart-throwing skills that she forgets that the therapist even exists. He might add sensitively that perhaps the client gets a great deal of satisfaction from exhibiting her dart-throwing skills, so much so that she gets absorbed in the activity and becomes unaware of what is happening around her. The child might humorously acknowledge that indeed she does derive a great deal of satisfaction from having her dart-throwing skills witnessed and does become very caught up in the activity. The therapist moves to build upon this realization by surmising that perhaps this happens in other arenas, where she so desperately wants her friends to see and acknowledge her that she has trouble seeing and acknowledging them. He might even elaborate by linking it up to the client's family situation, and how when her sister was born somehow she felt that everything about her sister seemed magical in the eyes of her parents, while her attributes and creations faded in appeal. If the client is receptive, after admitting her own pain over this, the therapist could conjecture that her bad feelings when she feels overlooked by her parents might resemble the bad feelings her friends have when she overlooks them. Palpably connecting her own feelings with those of her friends around the issue of being ignored may enable the client to identify with her friends and propel future efforts to honor and pay attention to friends.

To sum up, insights that arise out of here-and-now therapist-client play scenarios are suffused with emotion and are generalizable to the client's everyday life situation and can enhance the client's social know-how. This is in contradistinction to insights that remain intellectualized, unmoored from the immediacy of the interactive affective moment, and are bathed in archaic imagery and cryptic phraseology, which have limited socioemotional utility.

At the same time, much basic interpersonal learning occurs outside of conscious awareness and need not be made explicit to be of benefit. Lyons-Ruth (1998) labels this type of interpersonal learning "implicit relational knowing." In the context of therapy, implicit relational knowing refers to the rapid subliminal processing of intersubjectively communicated information that transpires in therapist-client interactions. It is at the level of implicit relational knowing that many of the client's rudimentary emotion-regulation dispositions are enacted and potentially expanded. The child's proficiency at prolonging or foreshortening affects, dampening or amplifying them, and animating or de-animating them with nonverbal gestures is furthered as child and therapist synergistically feed off each other's emotions in coordinated ways during active play scenarios. The therapist's gestural spontaneity is important here, for it embodies his or her broader range of affective cues, expanded array of embodied emotional expressions, and more sophisticated speech prosody, all of which can be tacitly noted by the child and incorporated into his or her repertoire of personalized expressions.

ENACTMENT: VICE OR VIRTUE?

Historically, enactments have been viewed as a sort of vice in therapy, where the client acts out an unconscious conflict in ways that obviate insight into it. It usually takes the form of the client unconsciously inducing the therapist to step into a role, or adopt an attitude, to satisfy underlying wishes of the client's for defensive reasons (Chused, 1998). For example, a child who is overly friendly with her therapist, eager to take direction and answer questions, who covertly tries to muster a kindly response in the therapist, could be masking a fear that the therapist, like her grandfather, will be bent on persecuting her. If the therapist actually responds in a kindly manner, the child is spared of having to face and gain insight into the warded-off fear and persecutory memories. This is an enactment that morphs into what is considered a transference cure, where therapist and client troublesomely bypass the recovery of unconscious meaning that saturates the interplay. Enactments suggest that behavior has lost its symbolic meaning for the client and insofar as the therapist responds concretely and nonanalytically he or she is complicitous in keeping the symbolic meaning lost. Enactment through this conceptual lens is an amnestic endeavor, serving to forget, not remember; act, not reflect and talk, and it is ultimately antithetical to insight.

A more benign view of enactment is that it is a nascent way of gaining insight into behavior. Enacting an unconscious conflict may be the only psychological means at a client's disposal to remember it. In this regard, Ekstein (1966) considers enactment to be a type of "experimental recollection." In the above example, the child may sense her unease as she is overly friendly with the therapist, apprehend that her friendliness feels too forced, and entertain the therapist's inquiry into her unease, eventually uncovering painful persecutory memories. Accordingly, enactment is seen as an inroad to discovering precomposed memories that exist in the client's unconscious.

Through a relational/intersubjective lens the aforementioned definitions of enactment contain a variety of questionable assumptions, not the least of which is the cleavage between thought and action, as well as speaking and doing, with the presumption that talk is meaningful whereas action is nonmeaningful. This belies the fact that actions are communicative and imbued with intentionality. Also, talking is never just a mentalistic phenomenon. Talking cannot be divorced from the bodily expressions accompanying it and the interactive contexts, real or imagined, in which it occurs when we try to divine its meaning. As such, arguably, if psychotherapy is to be truly efficacious the talking cure has to be "transformed into a cure through action, interaction and enactment, in which what is talked about is enacted and what is enacted must be talked about" (Aron, 1996, 192).

Traditional accounts of enactment presuppose that conscious insight into an action is imperative for it to be meaningful. However, there is much meaningful communicative behavior transacted within and between people that occurs below the threshold of conscious awareness. For instance, facial expressions and voice tone convey something about a person's intentions and are often instantaneously processed and reacted to with varying degrees of awareness. First impressions may be lasting, as the saying goes, usually because they are discerning, even though they may never undergo earnest cognitive inspection. Ultimately, it is conceivable that the most potent social and emotional learning that fuels self-transformation occurs at an experiential level, incorporating preconscious as well as conscious processing of interpersonal exchanges. Such experiential learning draws from the intersubjective field in which people interact, giving it personal poignancy and social-communicative relevance.

Viewing enactments as nascent strivings by the client to discover precomposed troubling memories residing in his or her unconscious is also dubious. Enactments may be more accurately thought of not as pathways to elucidating discreet unconscious contents that underlie behavior, but as embodied ways of expressing diffusely formulated experiences that press for enhanced articulation in the therapist-client interaction. It is worth noting that memories are often state dependent and interpersonally evoked, so much so that their activation in therapy may speak to experiential ingredients, however imperceptible, in the here-and-now therapist-client interaction that are reminiscent of the past. As such, enactment leading to memory recovery is an interpersonal affair. It is an interpersonal affair not only in stirring up client memories, but in the affects and meanings that the client in the interaction with the therapist attributes to them.

In play therapy, since the child gives him or herself over more fully to action than reflection, play may be indistinguishable from enactment. This is especially true of play that is person-mediated, more so than object-mediated. While playing with the therapist the child necessarily elicits responses, induces role adoption, and provokes reactions. These phenomena are unavoidable and inherent in the work of playing. Whether play enactments serve ameliorative ends or defensive ones is entirely dependent upon how they are handled or mishandled in the therapist-client relationship.

One form of enactment comprises the child demonstrating a problematic relationship predisposition during and around play interactions with the therapist. In object-relational terms, the child induces the therapist to act consonant with how an old-bad object acts, tacitly expecting familiar, although noxious, interpersonal outcomes. This is reflected in the child who orders the therapist around, rifles through his desk drawers without permission, and insists on cheating to win at checkers, covertly expecting the therapist to be too intimidated to assert his boundaries, similar to how the child's father permissively gives license to his entitled behavior. The therapist may be momentarily drawn into this drama, fearing the child's blustery reactions if challenged, and may shrink from asserting what his sensibilities tell him are normal personal boundaries to assert. The therapist's countertransferential fear may override access to his clinical knowledge about the child; namely, that the child was brought in for treatment due to a vicious cycle of bossiness with parents, their exasperation causing them to withdraw, eventuating in heightened negativity on the child's part to secure some parental contact. Insofar as the therapist's countertransferential fear dominates the interaction, this borders on a failed enactment.

Any number of actions on the therapist's part can lead to it being a successful enactment. The therapist can make an interpretation to the child linking up what is occurring in the here and now with what occurs at home, and its undesirable interpersonal consequences. The therapist can also respond with an enactment of his or her own, asserting his personal boundaries caringly, yet firmly, followed by an interpretation of the sort indicated. Then again the therapist could respond with a playful interpretive enactment where he acts in ways that covertly impart the same meaning as the interpretation: "Bill, here, let me open my desk drawers for you, and be sure to go through everything without asking my permission while I sit in the corner frightened to intervene. And, when I'm done feeling frightened, I'll just ignore you. I know you'll hate that and want to get back at me." In the clinical scenario provided, what differentiates a successful from an unsuccessful enactment is the degree to which the child's relationship expectation, namely, that the therapist will be intimidated and withdraw, is understood and to some degree meaningfully countered in lived ways during the session.

Pressuring the therapist to meet developmental needs is another form of enactment common in child therapy. This can be as primal as pulling for physiognomic mimicry, or the therapist sensing in the intersubjective field that the child thrives on shifts in eye contact and facial expressions that simultaneously match and compliment, or build on his or her own. Accompanying needs for vocal mimicry may also exist, where the client responds to a dense and varying interplay of vocal tones, rhythms, and sounds around linguistic expressions in the play. Mutual gestural mimicry sometimes enters therapeutic interactions where the therapist and client, playfully and synergistically, exchange intention-rich, emotion-rich gestures with the therapist's more sophisticated array of expressions having identificatory significance for the client. Needs of the client's warranting a response from the therapist can also center on moment-to-moment verbal tracking, matching, amplifying, and confirmation of emotions. The therapist may also feel a relational pull to provide confirmatory responses to a host of exhibitionistic displays of the child's, such as kinesthetic-bodily feats, exemplary gamesmanship, or demonstrations of mental swiftness.

The child's insistence that certain play scenarios be duplicated across sessions can speak to the strength of developmental needs operating and precedents set by optimal play conditions for their satisfaction. Repetitive play can also have a practice component, availing the child with predictable opportunities to articulate, rework, and consolidate diffuse experiences. However, well-choreographed play that the child gravitates toward time and time again can also serve defensive ends, reflecting his or her fear to move into alternative modes of expression and relational attitudes.

Myriad developmental phenomena infuse children's play actions that pull for confirmatory, challenging, and organizing responses on the therapist's part. Sometimes what is fittingly called for is the therapist's straightforward meeting of a need. Sometimes it is talking with the client about a need that exists. Sometimes it is both. In the last analysis, when it comes to client play enactments that are developmentally salient, what leads to successful outcomes pivots on the therapist determining if and when something extra needs to occur in the intersubjective field between therapist and client to move the child beyond fixation on a developmental need.

Play that is tilted in a person-mediated, sociodramatic direction inherently involves mutual enactment. For this play modality to transpire, let alone be beneficial, the therapist is necessarily drawn into meeting the child's enactment with one of his or her own. The therapist playfully assumes the roles he is assigned, invites the child to assume complementary or noncomplementary roles, sometimes leads, sometimes follows, relative to the tenor of the play interaction and what it supports. The therapist does not need to stand back and wait for insight before he or she can act insightfully. Spontaneous responses to the child can reflect rapid preconscious processing of intersubjective information that, when lived out, can send the play in meaningful directions. After all, it is possible to be both spontaneous and strategic. When person-mediated play therapy is working best, play activities unfold imbued with bits and pieces of the child's and the therapist's subjectivities, each party co-initiating and co-orchestrating the play in the moment-to-moment interaction culminating in the child acquiring expanded relational and emotional options. Mutual enactments only become vices when the therapist is recurringly lured into the play in ways that overpower his or her capacity to make prereflective and reflective judgments, perpetuating the child's existent relational and developmental vulnerabilities.

AFFECTS, AFFECTIVITY, AND MUTUAL REGULATION

In participatory play therapy the relationship is the crucible within which the child's affects and affectivity co-mingle with those of the therapist in ways that have expressive, elaborative, organizing, and consolidating benefits for the child.

This said, before proceeding let me reacquaint the reader with the relational presupposition that affects are not distinct and impermeable properties of individuals that can be unearthed in therapy with proper technique. They are not proto-lucid experiences awaiting elucidation through accurate mirroring. Rather, they are only meaningfully expressed and comprehended in the interpersonal contexts in which they are embedded and out of which they arise. As such, when we speak of assisting the child with processing emotional reactions in therapy, it is erroneous to think of this as an operation in which the child's preformed emotions are clarified and liberated, with relative immunity from the therapist's lived presence. It is more accurate to think of this endeavor in terms of the child's emotional experiences being coexpressed, coformed, and coconsolidated in the intersubjective field with the therapist.

Furthermore, when we speak of assisting the child with processing emotions, the aim is not just to enhance the child's competency at differentiating and linguistically expressing them but also to attend to his or her stylistic ways of intra and interpersonally managing them. These cut across the temporal, intensive, and sociocommunicative dimensions of emotion and are phenomenologically identifiable in how quickly or slowly emotional experiences emerge for the child, as well as the pace at which they are recovered from; how ardently or quietly they are expressed; the child's aptitude at modifying his or her outward expression of emotions in the actualization of an interpersonal goal; and how the child copes with others' emotional displays. As we discovered in chapter 2, dysfluencies in these areas can explain the core symptoms of ADHD, as well as the social impediments surrounding it.

More often than not, the child's style of handling emotions can be best addressed when there is an emphasis on the play process itself, rather than its content. In the midst of a person-mediated, dramatic play scenario, oftentimes what is germane is not *what* the child is excited, angry, or frustrated about, as much as *that* he or she is acting excitedly, angrily, or frustratingly, and *how*. The content of the child's play and deliberation over its possible symbolic meaning recede into the background, as the therapist reflectively and prereflectively attends to the child's in vivo, emotion-laden enactments and responds with those of his or her own in ways that meet and challenge the child's affect-regulation style. Citing reasons for the child's emotional reactions predicated on experiential data from the here-and-now interaction, or pertinent knowledge of the client and his or her life situation, might be one aspect of this process. However, attempts to source causes for reactions may be sidestepped altogether if they threaten to obstruct other expressive possibilities rooted in the emotionally charged mutual play enactment.

Dramatic, enactive, person-mediated play outshines sedentary, talk-heavy, object-mediated play in its emotion regulation potential for the child in a variety of ways. The range and intensity of feelings that are aroused are likely to be greater, as well as the opportunities for identification with the therapist's physiognomic, gestural, and vocal embodiment of affects. Its free-flowing, kinesthetically vigorous essence surely affords superior advantages to test and expand the child's ability to stay organized in the face of high arousal, of special import with ADHD children. For example, it is one thing for a boy to pretend play an oedipal dynamic with toy knights, sitting on the office floor, putting words in the mouths of the toy knights under prompting by the male therapist. It is an entirely different affair for a boy to gravitate toward dramatically enacting an oedipal battle with the male therapist, swords and shields being hurled every which way, bodies clashing, faces grimacing, voices grunting, with insults, flattery, and fears all being verbally exchanged, eventuating in the child pretending to slaughter and disembowel the therapist!

In the case of dramatic role play there is safety for the child in inhabiting a role because it is "just pretend." This can free up therapist and child alike to try on and try out a wide array of emotions and their expressions,

from the regressive to the highly evolved. Sometimes the therapist's spontaneous enactment of a more regressive display of emotion in the role that he
finds him or herself in covertly communicates to the child that such expressions are allowable. This is a useful lesson with overregulated children,
who shun emotional experiences for fear of their disorganizing effects.
With emotionally underregulated children, the therapist's tactful in-role expressions often are beneficially modular. Not uncommonly, in dramatic role
play, character assignment, who is supposed to impersonate whom, is often
a highly intersubjective phenomenon, initiated within and governed by the
interaction. Such is the case when a therapist, sensing boredom in a child
who has exhausted the role of superhero, announces that she wants to be
the superhero, edging the child in the direction of an inferior persona. Insofar as the child is receptive, he or she conveys to the therapist a readiness
to assume a subordinate role and countenance the disquieting emotional experiences it threatens to arouse—fear, anxiety, smallness, and defenselessness. Of course, role allocation can often be a clear-cut decision under
command of the child. The characters the child insists on playing no doubt
reveal something about the child's own affective life, the types of feelings he
or she is ready to contend with, in what way, and when combined with
outside knowledge of the child, why.

As dramatic play enactments unfold, therapist and child take their cues
from each other as to the brevity or prolongation, amplification or quelling
of emotional expression the interaction supports. This is at base an intersubjective, mutually regulative process. The emotionally charged interaction
dictates what emotions are tapped and what manner of expression they
might take. The therapist cycles in and out of affecting and being affected
by the child, calibrating from the child's verbal and nonverbal cues what is
emotionally tolerable and what is not. However, to paraphrase Aron (1996),
mutual influence should not be confused with mutual contribution. There
may be inherent mutual influence in the way emotions unfold, crystallize,
and are handled in active play sequences, but primary regulatory steward-
ship ultimately lies with the therapist. It is the therapist who strives to gauge
when down-regulatory or up-regulatory interactions are necessary to maintain the child's optimal expression, organization, and consolidation of emotions. In concert with the child, it is the therapist's charge to help the child
test his or her readiness to dwell in negatively and positively valenced emotional states that have become insufferable, find a way to modulate their expression, and transition out of them. Additionally, it is the therapist who
labors to ascertain when the emotional risks taken in the play indicate compromised objectivity on his or her part, or challenges for expanded subjec-

tivity on the child's part, or when the therapist's edginess reaches beyond the edges of what the child can emotionally make use of.

DEMYSTIFYING EGO-FUNCTIONS ATTAINMENT

Emotional mastery falls under the rubric of what in psychoanalytic psychology is referred to as *ego functions*. Frustration tolerance, tailoring one's emotional reactions in proportion to the precipitating social event, higher-order verbal and symbolic articulation of feelings, tactful suppression of emotion, recovery from emotional outbursts, knowing when a more amplified expression of feelings might be more interpersonally efficacious, and so forth, all fall under the domain of the ego. Since one of the premises of this book is that deficiencies in and ill-acquired development of such ego functions are at the heart of the ADHD condition, it behooves us to demystify how ego functions are attained in child therapy. I say demystify because a close inspection of the literature in this area reveals much conceptual dishevelment.

Proponents of traditional play therapy view more sophisticated ways of processing and communicating emotion as a natural outgrowth of rationality being reinstated into the intrapsychic system once strong feelings are discharged and neutralized in the play. In adult analysis this same phenomenon is supposed to be operating when the client recovers from a cathartic expression connected to a painful recollection. Kris (1952) referred to this as "regression in the service of the ego." Good regulation and rationality are believed to be internal properties of the child that are activated subsequent to the child being allowed a measure of regressive display of emotion. The underlying assumption is that as strong feelings are neutralized through their very expression in the play, then the child becomes a neutral or balanced person in general. These presuppositions can be traced back to Freud's quasineurological view of the mind in which mental processes worked like neurons, where a discharge of energy was necessary to restore the nerve to a state of equilibrium (Fancher, 1973).

From its inception, play therapy has been more concerned with the liberation than the modulation of emotion; or, more accurately put, with how the liberation of emotion automatically leads to its modulation. Ginott (1993) amusingly refers to this liberation process as taking the "lid off the id" (293). Klein's (1932) approach highlighted how play was the counterpart to free association in adult analysis, and that a laissez-faire method ensured that the child's affects were given free reign in the play.

"Often a toy is broken or when a child is more aggressive, attacks are made with a knife or scissors on the table or piece of wood; water or paint is splashed about; and the room generally becomes a battlefield. It is essential to enable the child to bring out his aggressiveness" (Klein, 1932, 120). One gets the impression reading Klein that children are endowed with the capacity to differentiate between fantasy and action, a capacity that is somehow sharpened—children being further able to have fantasies without acting on them—when provided with ample opportunities for regressive play. Presumably, the more the child intrinsically embraced fantasy as a mechanism to contain primitive affects, the better able he or she was to act civilly in the real world. Therefore, Klein was no more inclined to inhibit or redirect a child's play than she was to do likewise to an adult's telling of a fantasy or dream.

For all their differences with Klein, Anna Freud (1946) and other ego-psychologists shared her assumption that self-regulation was an emergent property of the child that was actualized in the play. In their structural model, ego strength resulted from a redistribution of energy and realignment of mental functions occurring in the child's internal dynamics. Painting a broad brushstroke to describe this model, forbidden feelings had come to control the child, albeit unconsciously, and making them conscious, through interpreting them in the play, ensured that the child could control them. More technically put, id impulses steadily come under the governance of the ego, the more they are brought to light in the play and concretized through interpretation. In a way, self-mastery resides in greater knowledge of id impulses, conscious awareness of their existence somehow being enough to promote self-control.

Anna Freud and her supporters also maintained that self-mastery was bolstered the more the child was able to use play therapy to work though traumas visited upon him or her. They proposed that life traumas disable the ego because they happen suddenly and unexpectedly, flooding the ego with feelings that exceed its synthesizing capacity. The child gravitates toward repetitive play scenarios reenacting the traumatic event, incrementally assimilating and making sense out it. This way, traumas that were passively suffered can be actively integrated. The same applies to feared catastrophic outcomes from destructive fantasies. In the play destructive fantasies that are passively endured are actively manifested and the child's ego is better able to distinguish that they do not have in real life the effects that they do in the child's imagination.

Another route to ego enhancement in this tradition is linguistic self-expression. For instance, Chethik (2000) states that "the process of verbalization modulates the raw affective drive components and helps a child order his instinctual life" (40). There has always been unease around the status of play-qua-play in analytic work with children and a penchant for tilting the treatment in the direction of talking. This is true partly because it becomes a complicated affair to reconcile one's playing role and one's professionalism to parents, mental health bureaucrats, and the public at large. There is, in my estimation, the erroneous belief that if talking is happening there is something productive occurring and that if play is the route to talking then it will be sanctioned. The reverse opens up a minefield. That is, if play predominates over talk very little that is therapeutically useful must be occurring. Notions of therapy as a "talking cure" have permeated our culture, no less in work with children. However, at this juncture I will not discuss the merits of playing over talking, or talking and playing with emotional immediacy in the here and now of therapy.

Of course, it would be foolish to abnegate a role for talking in child work. The interesting question is how different schools of thought view what is ego enhancing about the verbalization process. In the ego-psychological tradition the emphasis is on unearthing what are believed to be the child's pre-existing feeling states and giving them verbal shape and form. The therapist embodies a form of midwifery, prompting exploration of feelings, drawing them out, clarifying them, and mirroring them back. By contrast, relational approaches see the very clarification process itself as coconstructing what is verbalized and how it is verbalized. In some real way, when the therapist reiterates, clarifies, and mirrors back the child's feelings he or she is putting words in the child's mouth, words that might not have been there to begin with, but whose felt meaning was.

It should be evident by now that in ego-psychology the agent of emotional processing and synthesizing ("synthetic function of the ego") and of rational appraisal of emotions in line with social realities ("observing ego") is the pre-existent ego. Any notable contribution made by the therapist is of secondary significance. The interpretative process itself, the way it soothes and organizes the child, renders his or her experiences more intelligible, thereby communicable, or unwittingly provides verbal models to use to articulate dimly felt emotions, is overlooked. It would not be an overstatement to say that in ego-psychology the contribution made to the child's rationality by the therapist's actual participation is marginal. Indeed, interventions geared toward containing the play are viewed as peripheral to the real work of therapy—exploring and understanding the child's internal dynamics—and are not directly accounted for as influencing the child's acquisition of improved self-regulation. Along these lines, we encounter Chethik (2000) writing:

> If the child is using a crayon and he wants to tear off the wrapper, I might suggest that he just take off enough so that the end of the crayon is exposed and useful. Or if a "play karate chop" looks as though it can break one of the slats of the Lincoln Logs, I will caution him about the amount of force he can use. These small, continuous limits establish a boundary for most children. The child can play out and act out all sort of aggressive or sexual ideas, but the force of the play cannot damage or break things in reality. This is a relieving boundary for the child, when he is given permission to explore his internal life. (233)

In the psychoanalytic paradigm the actual participation of the therapist in the construction of ego functions in the child is taboo because it speaks to a level of directiveness usually considered unfriendly to an analytic way of working. Yet, with ADHD children, varying levels of active intervention in step with their demonstrated abilities may be what makes change possible. For instance, adequate recovery from emotional outbursts often requires down-regulatory intervention by the therapist. In its mildest form this can be the offering of an affirming interpretation (e.g., "John, I know that you hate losing. I wonder if you are still mad at me because I beat you at foosball last week"), a soothing empathic statement ("Mary, I can see that you are feeling frustrated"), a joke that fits with the emotional tenor of the moment, a suggestion that a different game be played, or a gentle pat on the back. In its extreme form this can be physical restraint, all the while "talking the child down" and releasing body parts as the child proves himself to be in control.

Likewise, if greater frustration tolerance and perseverance in the face of adversity are to be realized, the therapist's active input is crucial. Assistance commensurate with the child's demonstrated need and latent independent capacities may bring a task within reach of a successful outcome. The task can be as simple as carrying a box of toys from one side of the room to another, or as complicated as the child painstakingly stacking domino after domino on an uneven carpeted surface with every other one falling as quickly as it is positioned. In each case, insofar as the ADHD child motions to abort the task immediately or midstream, the therapist might have to noninvasively redirect him or her back to the task, offer words of encouragement, or restructure the task to make it achievable with moderate levels of effort.

Sensitive input from the therapist is imperative if ADHD children are to progress in symbolizing and more complexly processing inner thoughts and feelings. Slade (1994) zeros in on the unique needs of children whose personal narratives and play habits are disjointed and incoherent. She reasons that mere labeling of feelings and reactions, simple linking up of causes and effects in action sequences during the play, and generally intervening to keep verbal disclosures and playful dramas relatively organized are immensely helpful steps for such children. Indeed, she asserts that such steps are foundational if the child is to learn to represent inner experiences in complex ways and incrementally turn toward play that is more symbolic than enactive in nature.

The social-communicative dimensions of emotion have been largely neglected in the psychoanalytic play therapy literature, chiefly due to the preoccupation with viewing emotions as impersonal forces, or psychic energies. A fuller appreciation of the social-communicative dimensions of emotions in child treatment necessarily leads the therapist to incorporate a socialization role into his or her overall therapeutic style. Children, especially ADHD children, do not always intrinsically grasp that it is acceptable to suppress feelings for social diplomacy reasons or have fantasies that need not be enacted. Likewise, choice of words when communicating a feeling can be momentous and children may not have nuanced wording at their disposal. Not that the therapist need be didactic or imposing in offering alternative phraseology. Much headway can be made with ADHD children who habitually lock onto abrasive or offensive wording of negative feelings by playfully and suggestively offering smoother alternatives that still capture the inner nature of the feelings and their social intent. By offering rather than didactically prescribing such modular expressions, the child's autonomy is respected because suggestions can be face-savingly rejected in ways that prescriptions cannot. Of course, speech prosody, facial expressions, and other nonverbal gestures are factored into the communicative act. The tone of a verbalized suggestion can frame it as a prescription, and vice versa.

How feelings are conveyed also has a bearing on the child's interpersonal functioning. The ADHD child may be prone to habitual loud demonstrations of feelings and ill-attuned to their social effects. Using one's countertransference reactions as clues to how peers and other adults in the child's life may be impacted by his or her amplified emotional expressions, and disclosing them, can assist the child with developing social insight ("Francisco, I find myself wanting to step back and cover my ears when you use a loud voice with me. I wonder if any of your friends want to get out of your way when you use a loud voice?"). Countertransferential reactions can also be used to inform mutual enactments that have the same goal in mind. ([Therapist playfully saluting] "Yes, sir, sergeant Francisco. Or is it captain Francisco? I am at you command sir. Seriously, Francisco, when you use a bossy voice I get worried that you might lose friends and not know it is because they get tired of your bossy voice." It goes without saying that there are risks here in evoking guilt and shame in the child that would then need to occupy the therapist's attention.

In conclusion, there is something consequential to say about the idea that neutralization of emotion through discharge creates a child who is less emotive in his or her overall personality style, as implied in ego psychology. Emotional mastery has a social context. Stoking up feelings, or dampening them down, relative to one's interpersonal goals and the perceived thresholds of the dialogic other is the sign of an interpersonally versatile child. The neutral child, the child who is "above it all," may not be so interpersonally versatile.

LEARNING TO KNOW AND RELATE WELL TO OTHERS

How the self comes to know and relate to others has been a relatively neglected topic in psychoanalytic developmental psychology. For that matter, how the client learns to more incisively know and relate to others, as a treatment goal, rarely occupies hallowed status across psychotherapy models. This is far from being an arcane epistemological question as regards child work, especially with ADHD children. Constricted sociability of one sort or another is often the most pressing problem that ushers children into treatment. Underdeveloped capacities for sharing and cooperating, showing patience and sensitivity in social contexts, desirously accommodating to the needs and wishes of others, negotiating other's affects and affectivity, or crafting one's emotional communications to maximize the potential for their being met with acknowledgment or gratification, frequently underlie common symptoms.

It is not enough to propose, from either a developmental or a treatment standpoint, that individuation ensures emotional self-sufficiency and fortifies the client against inevitable interpersonal disappointments, or that others are useful so long as they are not acutely disappointing or frustrating. Neither is it enough to propose that self-understanding is the antidote for the projections, perceptual distortions, and displacements that create friction in the client's social world. Nor is it enough to propose that for individuals to operate well in social groups they need to have a moral sensibility, a judicious superego, not one that is merciless or lax. These ideas are at the heart of object-relational, self-psychological, and ego-psychological formulations of the self's normative dealings with others. Contemporary relationists eschew viewing the other simply as a relinquishable need-satisfying object, or someone whose difference becomes apparent when they fail to mirror or affirm the self. They do not see the other, strictly, as someone to be adapted to out of rational self-interest or moral obligation so much as they underscore how mature selfhood is predicated on a greater appreciation of the other's subjectivity and of the mutual influence inherent in relationships.

Benjamin (1988, 1995) is credited with the shrewd idea that emergent selfhood in infants requires a mutual recognition process in concert with the caregiver. At the most elementary level, in order for the infant's inchoate feelings to eventuate in a substantive self-experience there has to be confirmatory recognition from the caregiver-as-subject. Not only does what is "given back" have to fit sufficiently with what was "given out," in an emotionally attuned way, but it has to be given back in a way that the infant feels he or she is making a real impact on the caregiver. What makes the infant feel that he or she has made an impact is not only the synchrony in the exchange, but the elements of the caregiver's subjectivity that inject tolerable novelty and otherness into it. The infant recognizes the caregiver-as-other, while in the act of being recognized by him or her. Paradoxically, the infant finds him or herself in the caregiver, as well as learns the rudiments of intersubjective relatedness and mutuality. Building on this model, Benjamin (1988, 1995) asserts that fully developed selfhood involves the child steadily honing his or her awareness and acknowledgment of the caregiver's discernable subjectivity, of mother being a person in her own right, and of mutuality in relationships. This is in contradistinction to Winnicottian and Kohutian developmental conceptualizations of the child coming to know caregivers through empathic failures, whereby the presence of the caregiver is established through default—he or she fails to respond optimally and emerges as someone-other-than-self.

Benjamin's ideas have implications for a therapeutic stance with narcissistically vulnerable children whose presenting symptoms are ADHD-like. What therapeutic stance offers the most promise with children whose dominance needs override their ability to wait their turn, listen as well as talk, who are agitated when encountering social pressure from peers or adults to conform, and are confused or enraged when their obliviousness to social feedback results in them being ignored, rejected, or avoided? For therapy to be beneficial, grappling with someone else's needs and wishes, whether they match or differ from one's own, somehow has to become a psychological possibility for the child. An empathic stance, where the therapist tracks and affirms what is presumed to be the child's emergent self-experience, likely contributes to the child attaining greater self-cohesion and self-knowledge of personal needs and wishes, with overall calming effects. It likely activates the mental capacity for self-reflection and self-empathy insofar as the child is able to internalize aspects of the interaction. Failures in and restoration of empathic connectedness with the therapist may incrementally open the child up to the unavoidable existence of otherness. However, self-cohesion, self-knowledge, self-reflection, and an awareness of otherness may position the child to relate to others, but not necessarily *relate well.* The sort of interpersonal versatility rooted in an acceptance of others' needs and wishes that is a genuine transcendence of narcissistic tendencies requires more than consistent empathy from the therapist, although I suppose this depends on how empathy is defined.

Extending Benjamin's mutual recognition theory (1988, 1995) to the domain of child therapy, the therapist's otherness, the therapist's subjectivity, always to some degree infuses the tracking and affirming process we usually associate with empathy. Therefore, realistically speaking, empathic gestures aimed at grounding the child in his or her own self-experience always contain elements of the therapist's own subjectivity. When the child is empathized with, it is someone else seeing her, not just an extension of herself seeing her. If we think of empathic gestures in this more intersubjective way, we can begin to grasp how they necessarily introduce mutuality into the interaction, how they implicitly create occasions for the client to encounter bits and pieces of the therapist's own needs and wishes, even as he or she is being recognized by the therapist.

Undoubtedly, if the therapist's attempts to empathize with and recognize the narcissistically vulnerable child are frequently suffused with too much or too little of the therapist's otherness, problems can arise. Stolorow and Atwood (1992) have mapped out the "pathological accommodations" that can occur when the therapist's chronic misattunement to the client aggravates preexisting tendencies for the client to lose him or herself in others, compulsively seek to please, or become attachment phobic, factors that obviously undercut attainment of mutual relatedness. Yet, little has been written explicitly on how overconscientious control of the therapist's otherness in his or her communications with clients can forestall what Aron (1996) identifies as the client's ability to "reflect upon oneself . . . as an object of the wishes and intentions of others" (73). In short, the therapist's delivery of his or her subjectivity into his or her therapeutic actions in ways that are digestible for the client, but still contain novel, unfamiliar elements tied to the therapist's distinct personality, establishes the ground from which the client can view himself as an object of the therapist's interest.

Fuller sociability, where the child willingly entertains, or even fulfills, what he or she believes the therapist needs or wants from him or her is predicated on the therapist's actual otherness becoming increasingly more manageable for the child. This is as much an interactional achievement as an intrapsychic one. Indeed, a key aspect of therapy with the socially challenged child is for the therapist to know how to be a real person in ways that facilitate the child willingly reflecting on and accommodating to the perceived needs and wants of the therapist. It is tempting to call these sorts of accommodations on the part of the child "salutary accommodations," insofar as the desire to deal with the therapist on his or her own terms without loss of self reflects greater relational sophistication.

After all, "shifting sets" emotionally, cluing in to how the therapist might be feeling, without it having impinging and disorganizing effects, is a relational skill conducive to reciprocity and coexistence with others.

As nontherapeutic as it may sound to the average helping professional, true mutuality involves the child knowing how to convey his or her desire to accommodate to the needs, wishes, and wants of the therapist. On this note, it can be an enormous developmental and interpersonal achievement for a narcissistically vulnerable child to genuinely praise her therapist who has just beaten her at chess and gladly put the game away as requested by the therapist, who wants to sit back and savor his victory, when during the previous session the roles were reversed.

THE THERAPIST'S MENTORING ROLE

In one of Anna Freud's (1946) most influential texts on psychoanalysis with children, she issues a curious statement: "the analyst must succeed in putting himself in the place of the child's ego-ideal for the duration of the analysis" (45). It is made all the more curious by the fact that she is the one in the psychoanalytic tradition who exhorted the analyst to maintain a stance equidistant from the client's id, ego, and superego in clinical work. She, in the footsteps of her father, did appear to believe in the spirit of analytic abstinence—refraining from being tendentious in supporting the client's unrestrained, restrained, or overrestrained sides. However, a close reading of her literary contributions shows that in practice she was keenly aware of the need for the therapist to be more directly involved to maximize the chances that the child learn to view the therapist as a trustworthy figure, before and during the treatment. Unlike Klein, Anna Freud tried to remain mindful of the real life family, educational, and cultural contingencies bearing down on the child and of the unavoidable adaptations the child is forced to make on account of these.

What are we to make of the fact that it is the ego-ideal that Anna Freud singles out as the psychic structure worthy of the therapist's surrogacy? In psychoanalytic metapsychology the ego-ideal houses the ideals the ego has for itself. The ego-ideal is associated with the aspirational goals and exemplary self-images a person defines and pursues. It is a mental function that sustains motivation for the self to go beyond itself, striving for excellence and improving upon its accomplishments. The ego ideal is a psychic structure that is modeled after internalized images of cherished figures in a person's life and the value systems, ideas, and achievements that are emblematic of these cherished figures. These notions are the antecedents of Kohut's (1985) concept of the "idealized parental imago," or the psychic processes by which the self uses idealizations of others as identificatory pathways to personal enhancement and goal attainment.

Reich (1954) defined the ego ideal succinctly in terms of the self a person *desires to be*, as opposed to the self a person *ought to be*, the latter being associated with the superego.

It would appear that Anna Freud believed that the therapist must enduringly occupy a place of importance for the child at the level of human values, attributes, goals, and life commitments. Clearly, she was cognizant of the need for the therapist to establish him or herself as a credible figure in the child's life, perhaps even of a mentoring role that the therapist might personify in treatment.

The mentoring dimensions of child work are rarely emphasized, yet are weighty. The mere fact that the therapist engages in play with the child can fuel a strong attachment. Many children crave, yet fail to sufficiently obtain, occasions for play with adults. This can be markedly true of boys, especially paternally deprived boys. Add to the mix that it is active, person-mediated, participatory play that is being offered and the therapist's value to the child can be galvanized. This is no less the case with ADHD children who may be primed for kinesthetic, emotion-regulating play and who are wont to hold in high esteem a therapist who does not grow impatient with their heightened activity level and disorganized behaviors. The therapist's undivided attention, genuine regard, skill at playing, and facility at emotional engagement can arouse in the child genuine feelings of appreciation and admiration. Moreover, if we sidestep discourse on the defensive reasons for benign idealizations, the therapist remains a person who looks a certain way, comports him or herself a certain way, stocks the office with appealing toys, is generally on time for sessions, is courteous, and so forth, such that child clients may look to him or her as a role model in the way they might look to other available adults in their life as role models. Maybe even in a preferential way, because of the quality of what he or she relationally and emotionally provides.

Consequently, it should come as no surprise when on occasion the child may *desire* advisory input that is personalized and grounded in the therapist's intimate knowledge of the child's life situation. This is not to say that such desires are explicitly communicated. More commonly they are implicitly communicated, through perplexed looks that beg a response, or through a conveyed receptivity when the therapist motions to offer advisory input. When such desires for advisory input occur in therapy there may be benefit to exploring with the child what solutions he or she can self-generate. However, the child may also experience such explorative suggestions by the therapist as a sort of empathic failure, a missed moment on the therapist's part to respond to the child's genuine desire for advice from the very therapist whom he or she basically sees as a reliable, trustworthy, loyal person, who must have useful ideas because of his or her intimate knowledge of the child's life situation.

It should come as no surprise either when the child on occasion *desires* that the therapist intervene with a parent on his or her behalf. The therapist may detect that a reported conflict with a parent requires more than the usual processing of feelings and exceeds the child's ability to resolve alone with the parent. If a choice is made to intercede on the child's behalf, the potential for the encounter to have positive reverberating effects is maximized insofar as the therapist has built emotional capital with the child's parent, knows how to divulge sensitive information in nonthreatening ways to him or her, and is confident that any disclosures will not have detrimental effects for the child and that the problem is psychologically within the reach of the parent to constructively address.

It should be mentioned that the groundwork for the child being receptive to the therapist's mentoring role is predicated on the child's degree of self-other differentiation and precedents in the treatment, where the therapist has delivered his or her subjectivity into the relationship in ways that are welcomed by the child and not experienced as impinging. These factors pave the way for the child to desire advisory input without it seeming restrictive or demeaning.

Sometimes the therapist is able to offer words of wisdom or caution at opportune moments that, because of the therapist's credibility in the child's eyes, are well heeded. The therapist's utterances may have a moral flavor to them even though he or she is not ostensibly moralizing. Likewise, well-intended words of encouragement by the therapist arising out of a genuine exchange with the child can be convincing because of the significance that the therapist has taken on.

For children with ADHD, the mentoring component of treatment might entail sensitively discussing goals that are in alignment with his or her abilities, or practical matters that have a bearing on his or her lived vulnerabilities, such as how baseball might not be an optimal sport to pursue because of the amount of waiting around involved—better soccer where there is much running and opportunities to make kinesthetic mistakes; or, how switching over to word processing might help with the frustration incurred when writing by hand. Not that this advice should be discussed solely in the context of individual therapy with the child without extension to the domain of parent consultation. In general, it is more accurate to think of the therapist as the mentor of the treatment, more so than of the child per se, coordinating the child's care across school, home, and therapy milieus. Of course, what represent the most potent life lessons for children with ADHD are the myriad opportunities to identify with and model after the rich array of affectively suffused actions of the therapist, his or her self-differentiated ways of relating, and displays of genuine regard occurring in participatory play therapy, for in these identifications lie possibilities for such children to acquire the requisite socioemotional competencies that will serve them well in their social lives.

4

PARTICIPATORY
PLAY THERAPY IN ACTION

When initiating therapy with any child, no less the child ascribed an ADHD diagnosis, it is incumbent on the therapist to establish him or herself as a benevolent, approachable person who genuinely knows how to relate with children. Adopting a "neutral stance," or approaching the child in a stilted, formal way can unwittingly intensify the combination of resentment, fear, and confusion most children experience when brought in for therapy. We all know the old saw that children rarely elect therapy and typically are forced into it, setting the stage for active or passive resistance. Moreover, even novice therapists know to watch for the child confounding the world of psychotherapy and that of medicine, fearing that he or she is about to be subjected to a painful medical procedure. Less frequently discussed by mental health professionals is how perplexed the average child is by the whole idea of psychotherapy and why it is supposed to be of benefit, and how devoid he or she is of societal figures with whom to compare the therapist. Is the therapist like a medical doctor? A minister, priest, or rabbi? A school teacher? A school principal? A coach? A family friend?

Resentment, fear, and confusion may be pronounced in the child brought in for treatment of ADHD. He or she is more likely to have encountered a host of adults in positions of authority due to objectionable behavior and been lectured to and reprimanded. Why should the therapist be any different? Casual exposure to medicalized accounts of ADHD being a "brain disorder" can induce anxious fantasies in the child that any professional he or she is brought to see will tamper with his or her brain or perform some unsettling medical procedure. If any negative expectations, fears, and fantasies are to be explored, it is best to do so as a backdrop to their having been rendered improbable. What the therapist says, but more importantly how he or

91

she comports him or herself, can begin to convey the therapist's essential benevolence and quickly undo any phobic expectations.

Twelve-year-old George was undergoing a difficult year at the local Catholic school he attended. His teacher was convinced he was a wayward child whose corrupt character explained his fidgetiness, talking out of turn, forgetfulness, and frequent requests to go to the bathroom. She was determined to stamp these behaviors out and liberally used the classroom system of issuing a red card to George whenever he behaved impulsively. At the first session, George sat erect on the corner of the couch with his hands tightly clasped. I warmly and jokingly said: "George, you're sitting like I imagine kids sit in the principal's office when they are about to get lectured. I am no principal, and I'm certainly no teacher who is going to get on your case for being an energetic kid who has a hard time keeping his body still. If you keep sitting like that you had better start saving your allowance to pay for good massages." George smiled and went on to talk about how angry and confused he was that his teacher assumed him to be a bad kid who did bad things on purpose. He eagerly went along with my suggestion that we have this discussion while throwing a Nerf football to each other across the office.

Six months before being brought in for therapy, eleven-year-old Jasper had been psychiatrically hospitalized due to what appeared to be hallucinations. These were deemed to be an adverse side effect of the psychotropic medication he was on at the time and cleared up with a medication change. Several parent meetings were held before the first visit with Jasper. During these meetings, I sensed the parents needed reassurance that I would work collaboratively with them and treat their son humanely. They confessed their demoralization over Jasper being treated like a "Guinea pig" by various psychiatrists who had utilized a cornucopia of medications with him. It would have been their preference to avoid all contact with the mental health profession. Yet, Jasper's problems focusing at school, completing assignments, and adhering to limits at home without exploding continued unabated and his parents were desperate for help.

Within minutes of meeting Jasper he appeared restless and visually scanned the office, checking out the toys that were out in the open. I suggested that he look at my rubber sword collection, stored in the wicker chest in the corner. Jasper animatedly pulled out several swords, swishing them around in the air, saying "Cool, these are great." I arose, picked out a sword, and asked if he wanted to duel. Jasper seemed surprised, yet intrigued by my actions. As we, rather timidly at first, began the duel, with his parents watching on and laughing, I mentioned to Jasper that I was the sort of doctor who liked to help kids by playing with them. In time Jasper's exuberance got the better of him and he began roughly poking his father with the sword. I commented, "Jasper, I guess I am seeing with my own eyes one of the things you need help with. When you get excited sometimes you lose control and carry roughhousing too far."

As this example alludes, the formation of a positive alliance with parents typically precedes direct contact with the child. This topic is covered in detail in the next chapter. For now, suffice to say, even in cases where the parent is a major source of dissatisfaction and disappointment for the child, that parent is still a primary attachment figure, and most children will take their parents' lead as to how to feel toward the therapist at the basic level of emotional safety and danger.

The tendency to externalize blame for personal and interpersonal difficulties shown by many children diagnosable with ADHD precludes use of standard rationales for therapy that refer to the alleviation of emotional pain or the promotion of happiness (e.g., "I'm here to help you play and talk in ways that help you get your feelings out and make you happier"). Such children may consciously believe the source of their problems to be a domineering classmate, a boring teacher, a parent who favors a younger sibling, or the like, and view any emotional pain they may experience as secondary to this. Therefore, careful consideration has to be made to frame the rationale for therapy in ways that are not shame inducing and that sufficiently tap their conscious belief as to the source of their personal difficulties, while gently locating some causality with them. The high-water mark is to state problems in everyday language that children can grasp and that have general applicability, while still being grounded in actual events occurring inside or outside the office:

"When you couldn't use the foosball handles to do power shots you had a mad look on your face, you went all quiet, and suddenly wanted to play a different game. Now I know some things I can help you with: Getting better at using words to let people know how mad you feel when you cannot be brilliant at a game right away and realizing that you have to practice something over and over to get good at it. If you let your frustration take over it's going to be hard to ever get good at games, math, spelling, soccer, or other things that are important to you."

"I can see that you are enjoying this ring toss game too much! Look at you using baby talk and rolling around on the floor! Is this one reason why your friends stop playing with you, because you act all silly when you get excited? What a silly Billy you are being! Can we get back to this ring toss game, I was sooooooo liking it."

"I know I was being strict and used a strong voice when I said you needed to ask permission before looking through my toy cupboard. It can be a real pain having to deal with adults and their rules, especially when you are suddenly told to do something without prior warning, like when your dad suddenly tells you to turn off your PlayStation, without any advance notice. That's one reason I meet with your parents every week, to help them get into the habit of giving you notice before they want you to stop what you're doing. However, when you and I meet one thing I want to help you with is being aware of how ignoring adults when they tell you to do something can make them mad and make them raise their voice."

Many parents balk at the idea of play therapy, seeing it as trivial or unproductive, especially given our achievement-oriented, goal-driven culture. They may seem outwardly agreeable, yet silently unconvinced, when offered the explanation that play is the child counterpart to adult talk. It is not enough for the therapist to offer scripted or global rationales, and it does not bode well when the therapist assumes a resistance on the part of parents when such rationales are questioned or shunned.

In my estimation, the lion's share of the responsibility to justify the utility of play therapy to parents falls squarely with the therapist. This is no easy task, and it is made all the more demanding for the therapist who emphasizes the importance of the play process, since to the naïve observer this approach may seem especially frivolous.

When meeting with parents I sometimes make reference to how problem behaviors are best dealt with when exhibited in the here and now, and how active play can be essential to bring these behaviors out into the open, as when a child becomes mutely furious when losing at a game of darts or uncontrollably excited when winning. On occasion, I give descriptive examples to parents of play scenarios that could occur between me and their child based on the background information provided to me, and I speculate on what might be implicitly and explicitly accomplished. For example, I might explain how if the child and I were to engage in a mock sword battle, he or she would likely enter a state of aggressive arousal that might be challenging to internally manage. I might indicate how advantageous it would be for the child to maintain a focus on pretend rather than actual harm being inflicted, follow agreed-upon rules, engage in mutual cuing as to tolerable levels of aggression, playfully experiment with angry words, and give expression to primal fantasies. I might add that it may even take the child being in a state of aggressive arousal to prime him or her to talk about anger-inducing life experiences.

Sometimes doubting parents need to be permitted to sit in on initial sessions with the child and have the socioemotional work undergirding play interactions effectively unpacked for them during parent meetings for the whole concept of play therapy to be of appeal.

TOY SELECTION AND PLAY SET UP

From a traditional play therapy perspective, the issue of toy selection, or what toys to have on hand in the office, is fairly uncomplicated. What matters is that the child bring his or her unconscious to whatever play materials the office is supplied with, imaginatively superimposing onto them underlying needs, wishes, and conflicts. It is the supposed unique representational significance that the child accords the play object that assumes importance. If anything, toys, like Rorschach inkblots, should be ambiguous in form and use-value, the child's predetermined unconscious needs, wishes, and conflicts defining them and driving their use. Ideally, the toys themselves should embody no inherent potential to influence the child's play themes. Caution is exercised about having toys that might seduce the child to become ensconced in play, rather than talk. In this regard, board games are generally eschewed, although grudgingly permitted to loosen up an exceptionally guarded child by offering a benign distraction.

Contrastingly, toy selection is a fairly complicated affair for the therapist who underscores the play process (over symbolic play content) and the interactions and affects surrounding it. Insofar as emotions are viewed as psychic events that emerge, peak, and subside contingent upon varying degrees of interpersonal stimulation, careful consideration needs to be made to select a range of toys that pull for states of excitement as well as quietude. Likewise, the farther away we get from purist accounts of the unconscious, looking for the presumed predetermined unconscious meaning in the child's play, the less we become caught up in choosing "neutral" toys that are good receptors for children's projections. Indeed, the closer we get to a constructivist account of the unconscious in terms of diffuse experiences awaiting therapeutic interactions to give them substance and meaning, the more it becomes essential to have a wide array of toys that facilitate the manifestation and consolidation of a range of human emotions and relational events. We forget that the type of toys we make available tacitly communicates to the child what activity level will or will not be tolerated in the office, what emotions are acceptable, and how regressively or nonregressively they can be displayed.

Individual differences in the development of fine and gross-motor abilities across children requires that we deliberate over selecting office toys that reduce the potential for any child on our caseload recurringly being confronted with failure experiences—where he or she is unable to demonstrate manipulative mastery of any available toys. By the same token, toys that are too easily mastered and present little delay of gratification to utilize effectively can foreclose opportunities to build frustration tolerance.

At this point in the discussion it might be useful to identify a host of toys and play materials that offer promise with the participatory play therapy approach I am endorsing.

As for toys that children may gravitate toward for excitatory purposes, I have found the following useful: rubber swords and shields, dart guns, a magnetic dart board, a variety of Nerf balls, foam baseball bats and balls, ring toss games, Velcro mitts and accompanying balls, toy tanks, warplanes and soldiers, and plastic knights with transferable weapons. There are various board games and play materials that typically serve down-regulatory aims: Legos, Connect Four, Sorry, Don't Break the Ice, Barrel of Monkeys, chess, checkers, white eraser board with markers, and drawing paper and colored pencils. Predatory and cuddly stuffed animals, and cloth puppets resembling affectionate, as well as frightening animals and characters, can broaden the scope of communicative exchanges occurring in the play and the emotions their use evokes.

As we see in this chapter, what interests me are the interactions and emotions surrounding the playing of a game and the therapeutic potential they contain, more so than the symbolic content of the child's play, which is not to say that deep personal meaning cannot be divined from a child's play enactments. The issue is one of emphasis as active play scenarios unfold. Either way, there is benefit to considering the more obvious properties of a given toy before surmising its obscure referential features, as the following case illustrates.

After thirty minutes of continuous, animated mock sword fighting, in which ten-year-old Bianca repeatedly overpowered and cornered me, snarlingly pretending to cut off each of my limbs and stab me through the heart, despite me begging her to spare my life, I sat down on the couch announcing that I was exhausted and needed to rest. She kept with the high energy tempo exhibited in her sword play and began throwing a shield in the air, aggressively batting it with a sword. I expressed admiration for the force and accuracy of her hits in a voice tone that matched the shifting cadence of her actions as she moved from slowly raising her sword to rapidly and powerfully bringing it down on the shield. "The fierce Bianca brings down her sword with such might and fury that all in the land had better steer clear of her." The intensity mounted as Bianca became more and more aggressive in hitting the shield with her sword. Sensing that she was communicating something to me through aggressively hitting a shield, of all the play objects accessible in the room, with some anger in my voice I remarked, "Bianca, the way you are hitting that shield makes me think of you being angry at your mother for not protecting you, resulting in you being placed in foster care and adopted at such a young age. A shield is usually used for protection and you had a mother who did not protect you." Upon hearing this, Bianca lost all control and began wildly swinging her sword at the shield, yelling, "That bitch should have been a better mother. Why did that bitch not get her life together and take care of me. What a loser she was." Knowing how difficult it was for Bianca to recover from rage episodes, within time I suggested that we shoot darts at some targets in the office while continuing to talk about her memories of being placed in foster care. Bianca's rage turned to containable anger as she recollected hurtful experiences in foster care while shooting foam darts at targets I had placed at close range, with me gathering darts for her to reload into her gun.

EMOTION WORK

The case vignette on Bianca highlights sundry aspects of the emotion work that occurs during active play sequences. The type and intensity of emotion a child displays, as well as its duration, is contingent upon the degree of involvement by the therapist. By degree of involvement, I mean the rich interplay of speech content and prosody, physiognomic and tactile responses, and kinesthetic movements the therapist embodies in coordination with the child. Confident expectation in the therapist's sensitive involvement emboldens the child to manifest and more effectively handle a range of emotions of varying intensity.

Tracking, Matching, and Complementing

The affective communication processes of tracking, matching, and complementing occurring in the caregiver-infant dyad outlined by infant researchers (Stern, 1985; Trevarthen and Aitken, 2001) have applicability to clinical work with emotionally dysregulated children.

When we extend its use to the clinical situation, *tracking* simply refers to the therapist being emotionally present to the child's subtle and not-so-subtle shifting emotions in the play interaction.

Matching is when the therapist is emotionally moved by the child in ways that lead to the co-embodiment of a feeling. The therapist may spontaneously share in an emotion conveyed by the child, reproducing it in his or her own actions. A facial grimace might be matched with a facial grimace, a melodic voice tone with a melodic voice tone, a firm hug with a firm hug. These imitations are not prefabricated, contrived, or forced; rather, they flow naturally from the emotional resonance in the interaction. The therapist's matching of a child's feeling, imitating its vocal, linguistic, or postural features, reflects fluency at sharing in the child's feeling without modifying it. These experiences can be immensely valuable for the emotionally dysregulated child insofar as they allow him or her to more confidently dwell in a feeling or feeling state and acquire a primal familiarity with it. The sense of communion (Stern, 1985) between child and therapist resulting from these matching experiences can be vitalizing for children, leading them to playfully emit and experiment with a variety of verbalizations and nonverbal emotional gestures, bathed in the knowledge that what comes from the therapist on the "outside" coincides so reassuringly with what they are feeling on the "inside." A child's yearning to duplicate a game, with the same exchange of facial, vocal, and kinesthetic mimicry, can speak to a developmental need for such fundamental confirmatory emotional experiences.

Complementing pertains to the therapist joining with, yet modifying, a child's emotional expression. The therapist moves beyond mere matching and injects more complex verbal and nonverbal elements of an emotion into the interaction. The idea here is that the child can best assimilate and learn more elaborate forms of emotional communication from within the experience of sameness. For instance, a child may be enticed by the therapist producing a growl sound in reaction to his or her mimicked facial grimace. The child might respond by grimacing, growling, and making a fist. Taking the child's cue, the therapist might grimace, growl, make a fist, and initiate a verbal dialogue: "I am Dreg, the invincible warlord and I have come to gather troops to go to war." The child might reply: "I too am an invincible warlord. My name is Plug. I fight for myself, and myself only." Naturally, this can evolve into a rich play scenario where the child acquires a range of verbal and nonverbal communicative forms that are aggressively valenced.

The tracking, matching, and complementing processes that transpire in therapist-child interactions potentiate the child's ability to be emotionally responsive, as opposed to emotionally reactive, inasmuch as they anchor the child in his or her differentiated emotions and strengthen the child's emotional boundaries.

As the vignettes below illustrate, tracking, matching, and complementing should not be thought of as discreet events but as simultaneously occurring processes that acquire focal significance based on what the play interaction and the child's moment-to-moment affective capacities permit. Moreover, tracking, matching, and complementing can happen in the context of a pretend-play sequence, an actual emotionally charged interaction with the therapist, or a child's verbal disclosure about an upsetting or joyous past or present everyday life event, while engaged with the therapist in an ancillary play activity. By ancillary play activity, I mean some game or playful pursuit, usually involving physical movement, that occurs alongside a verbal disclosure, although having little ostensible symbolic connection to that verbal disclosure. Examples are dialoguing while tossing a Nerf football, or playing a game of Connect Four. For many children presenting with ADHD, opportunities to stay motorically busy can keep the tempo of a verbal disclosure going, its wordage more flexible, and its semantic content more coherent. In other words, the ancillary play activity, while having no apparent symbolic significance, still has organizational benefits.

While sitting on the floor directly in front of nine-year-old Francesca, I witnessed her pour out a tin of marbles on the carpet watching to see how I would react. I looked her in the eyes and smiled. Noticing that I did not experience her gesture as a provocation, Francesca began gathering the marbles and grouping them by color. In my therapy with Francesca she often tried to spoil close, affectionate moments transpiring between us, as if a mutual, positive feeling state was unsustainable for her. It was not out of the ordinary for her to abort a game she was enjoying midstream, skip around the office animatedly, all the while ignoring my requests for her to sit down, her threshold for emotional stimulation having been exceeded. This session was to be different. While she grouped the marbles by color she devised a game we could play together. She suggested that we both look each other in the eyes while picking out marbles. The one who selected the most red marbles would win. Whoever broke eye contact and looked down at the marbles would automatically lose. Francesca smiled shyly as we shared a warm gaze. I matched her expression, although less shyly. She was able to tolerate this intimate game, remaining seated and maintaining eye contact, while expressing her excitement with modulated verbalizations and voice tones: "Oh my God, I wonder who is going to get the most red ones!"

Ten-year-old Jamal picked up an unloaded dart gun and pretended to shoot at an imaginary enemy in the corner of the room. I picked up a similar dart gun and did likewise. Jamal began uttering, "The aliens are not going to know what hit them. . . ." I finished his sentence for him, " . . . when we use our advance technology weapons on them." Jamal lit up: "Yeah baby, watch out, ten months in the lab and we have the best technology around." He got on his knees behind an office chair and began making shooting sounds. I got on my knees beside him and made the same shooting noises, gradually rising the pitch and speed of my sounds. As he emitted faster and louder shooting noises Jamal began laughing loudly and rolling around on the floor. With some urgency in my voice I said, "Jamal, get yourself together, we have a tough fight ahead of us and the last thing I need is a comrade who is going to get us shot by acting all silly." Jamal immediately composed himself and went back to making the original shooting noises he had generated.

Eight-year-old Roberto asked if we could rearrange the office furniture to clear more space to play football on the office carpet. I obliged and assisted him in pushing back a heavy chair, uttering, "Roberto the Great, using his supreme strength to push, push, push." He seemed annoyed by my exuberance but denied it when I asked him. As we squared off to play football on the carpet he suddenly threw the Nerf football at me and yelled, "TOUCHDOWN!" Startled, I told Roberto that I was unhappy with him for throwing the football at me and that I needed to delay the game until I got over being unhappy with him. Roberto became sullen and sat on the couch staring blankly at the carpet. After a few minutes, picking up on Roberto's sadness, I inquired in a soft tone how he was feeling. He remained silent but lifted his head to show the frown he had on his face. I frowned back. Roberto spoke haltingly, "I thought you were making fun of me when we pushed the chair over to the wall." I replied with the same affective tone, "You thought I was making fun of you and it probably made you mad." Roberto continued, "Yeah, I was mad at you because I thought you were making fun of me." The discussion then led to how his older brother often teases him, with me prompting and drawing out Roberto's feelings, adding words and emboldening his gestures with those of my own.

Unable to contain his excitement any further, ten-year-old George burst into the office proudly announcing that he had been chosen for the all-star soccer team. His mood expansive and speech pressured, he paced around the office, telling me of his achievement in disjointed statements. My verbalizations were mostly a reiteration of his, with a different word or two added for emphasis. I found myself pacing with him, although my movements were less zippy. I interjected the pride I felt over his proud accomplishment with voice tones and facial expressions that were similar to his. George stopped pacing, picked up a rubber ball, and threw it to me. We threw the ball back and forth, with me more or less matching the force and direction of his tosses. George's speech became less pressured and his disclosures less disjointed.

These vignettes reflect how tracking, matching, and complementing usually involve rapid decision making at a conscious and preconscious level using intersubjectively communicated information, and incorporate a high degree of co-occurring emotional awareness and involvement with self and other in the clinical dyad. This is why I call it emotion work.

Optimal Arousal

A key, yet seemingly unrecognized, emotional dynamic that encapsulates various ADHD symptoms is unsuccessful internal management of intense emotional states that results in cognitive and behavioral disorganization. The child who is pre-consciously and consciously caught up in avoiding, handling, and recovering from potentially implosive and explosive emotional events is likely to be one whose cognitive processes inadequately support remembering well, following rules, listening to instructions and directions, reading subtle social cues, and generally being mentally focused. Upsurges in viscerally felt affects such as elation, shame, rage, and disgust, when routinely poorly self-regulated, can materialize in impulsive, haphazard, silly, overanimated, and aggressive behaviors. Hallmark ADHD phenomena such as difficulty in waiting one's turn, listening, following directions, and staying on task occur in social and interpersonal contexts imbued with varying levels of emotional stimulation. What we fail to recognize is how the child's ill handling of these varying levels of emotional stimulation might best account for the ADHD symptoms.

From this vantage point, it goes without saying that for play therapy to be efficacious with the ADHD child it has to create occasions for him or her to enter, tolerate, and recover from states of heightened emotionality more resolutely. Person-mediated, movement-oriented, sociodramatic play, in a play room where there is an ample supply of toys that pull for up-regulatory experiences, arguably creates the conditions necessary for the child to be appropriately aroused. This is where traditional play therapy fails ADHD children. The therapy is dead before it starts insofar as it holds fast to a nondirective, talk-tilted, sedentary ethos, thereby foreclosing occasions for suitable arousal.

When play therapy is working well with the emotionally dysregulated child, there is interactive and affective synchrony. Therapist and child cycle in and out of affecting and being affected by each other. Emotional push and pull dynamics percolate, with the therapist and child alternating between pushing for and being pulled into more amplified expressions of emotion. The play atmosphere becomes one in which the therapist responds to the child's moment-to-moment emotion-laden enactments with those of his or her own in ways that meet and enlarge the child's affective thresholds. Sometimes a spontaneous enactment of a more colorful expression of feelings on the part of the therapist covertly establishes a new parameter for what is acceptable in the interaction. At other times, a spontaneous enactment of a less colorful expression of feelings on the therapist's part covertly redraws a parameter for what is permissible. An example elucidates.

Without asking permission, twelve-year-old Miguel took it upon himself to take a half-filled plastic trash bag out of my office trash can and place the empty trash can in the corner of the room. I commented: "I guess you are feeling like pushing your weight around today Mr. Miguel." He availed himself with a rubber ball and began using it to "shoot baskets" into the trash can. I picked up another rubber ball and intermittently shot baskets into the same trash can, being careful to wait for opportunities Miguel left open for me. Intuiting that Miguel was pulling for a more vigorous interaction, before each of my shots I attempted to dribble around him before aiming my ball at the trash can, sarcastically making remarks like "Who says white men cannot dribble and shoot!" and "Does it take an adult to show a kid how to play a game properly?" Miguel, taking my cue, added some comments of his own, in a more edgy tone: "No, it takes a kid to show a shiny-headed, baldy adult how the game is played," and "You know I'm gonna win and you are gonna lose."

Before one of Miguel's tosses I positioned myself close to him and delivered a steady stream of noises and utterances: "Ba, ba, ba, ba, da, da, da . . . can the Great Miguel get the ball in the basket, or will he be so annoyed by me being soooooo annoying that he will lose his concentration and duff it . . . jo, jo, jo . . . will he get so frustrated that he will quit?" Under some duress, Miguel was still able to tune me out and make the basket. He came at me aggressively, growling and trying to get me in a bear hug. I matched his expression, grabbing him in a more subdued way, without growling. Miguel softened his hold and we went on with the game.

Optimal De-Arousal

In chapter 3, I disputed the orthodox psychodynamic idea that the liberation of emotion through nondirective play in and of itself leads to its modulation or neutralization. I also asserted my stance that self-regulation of emotion is not an emergent property of the child that unfolds when provided with the therapist's astute empathic mirroring or impartial interpretation of underlying feelings, mysteriously eventuating in self-calming tendencies. Rather, I proposed that the child's capacity to tone down emotional expressions and acquire a range of subdued facial, kinesthetic, tactile, vocal, and linguistic forms of affective communication is predicated on the therapist's vital subjective input. When I say vital subjective input, I mean the therapist's pointed use of his own down-regulatory emotional communications, in concert with those of the child, in ways that facilitate their assimilation.

Given the ADHD child's action-orientedness and susceptibility to becoming disorganized when energetic play infuses him or her with unmanageable levels of emotion, the therapist stewards the activity level in the room, gauging when the play threatens to become unproductively chaotic. The degree of directiveness or nondirectiveness assumed by the therapist to tone down the interaction and its emotional effects on the child depends upon the child's capacity to move out of regressive displays of emotion in due time and regain a capacity for mutuality in the interaction that seems to have been temporarily completely lost. This stewarding process can involve conscious deliberation on the part of the therapist and even be somewhat heavy handed.

On at least three separate occasions during a mock battle with light sabers, nine-year-old Danesha's aggression got the better of her and she seemed bent on hurting me. Such gentle reminders as, "Danesha, nobody can get hurt here" and "Danesha, it is okay to pretend hurt me with your light saber, but not okay to try to actually hurt me" were ineffective in curbing the intensity of her aggression. Eventually, I warned Danesha that if she tried to actually hurt me, instead of pretend hurt me, one more time, we would have to stop playing with light sabers and decide on a different game to play. Danesha promptly took a wild swipe at me. I firmly told her that she could either hand her light saber to me to place on top of the toy cupboard out of reach, or I could take it from her. The choice was hers. She threw it on the ground. I placed both light sabers out of reach on top of the toy cupboard. After helping her verbally process her feelings related to the abrupt discontinuance of the game, we mutually decided to play at ring toss. While taking turns tossing rings together, I linked up the incident that had just happened with common episodes of social friction Danesha faced in her daily life. "Danesha, what just happened makes me think of one of the reasons why your older sister refuses to play with you. You get so excited when she agrees to play with you that you lose control and hit, the game becomes less fun for her, and she refuses to play." Danesha appeared attentive and went on playing the ring toss game, although she evidenced little in the way of a verbal response.

On the other hand, down-regulatory maneuvers by the therapist need not be premeditated and governed by conscious choice. They can take the shape of rapid pre-conscious processing of intersubjective information eventuating in a series of offhand therapist enactments.

Using wooden blocks to build parapets for toy soldiers, nine-year-old Frank's tension mounted as the blocks he had haphazardly put together began crumbling. His breathing became more constricted as he stood up and appeared ready to kick down what remained of his battle scene. I quickly sat on the floor next to Frank, took a series of deep breaths, and began rebuilding the parapets using a trial and error approach to see whether the green ones or the red ones stayed in place better. Frank, who by this time was pacing around the office, stopped and seemed intrigued. He began breathing more fluidly, joined me sitting on the floor, and asked why I was using green blocks. I simply stated that they were bigger and heavier and would probably stay in place better. Frank, somewhat aggressively, pushed the red blocks off to the side and resumed building his parapets with green ones. I asked him if he wanted me to place my hand behind the parapets to keep them from falling over until he had finished constructing them. He responded in the affirmative, yet with some mild shame, perhaps because he had not thought of this himself.

My sympathetic response to Frank at a basic bodily/kinesthetic level can be seen as containing a host of subliminal solutions, if you will, for him to appropriate and thereby attain a state of de-arousal when in the throngs of frustration; namely, breathe more fluidly, use a trial and error approach to solve a problem, and agree to receiving help, even when your pride is injured. Conceivably, one component of enhanced self-regulation of high arousal occurs in the context of mutual enactment, at a basic bodily/kinesthetic level, where there is a sort of sympathetic acquisition process occurring. However, if gains in self-regulation of high arousal are to be made, the child has to have a clearer sense of where his or her emotional thresholds lie, and when he or she is on the verge of complete loss of control. This can be cultivated in therapy through verbal prompts that engender anticipatory thinking. In my experience, children are better able to attend to and integrate these verbal prompts when they are embedded in a positively valenced, mutually coordinated play activity that they want to prolong, but that their mounting excitement or tension imperils.

As ten-year-old Janice and I were playing with hand puppets, taking turns using them to dive off a pretend diving board that we kept imagining was positioned higher and higher in the air, her laughter became louder and her actions sillier. I drew my puppet closer to her puppet and had mine say to hers, "You are getting all loud on me, laughing like a great big hyena, and being sillier than a clown. I hope that your loud laughing does not become LOUD LAUGHING, and your silliness, SILLINESS, because this diving game is fun and I want to keep on playing it." Janice made her puppet talk to mine, "I promise I won't LAUGH TOO LOUD and act ALL SILLY. I guess I was getting too excited. It's my turn to dive, WHEEEEEE. Whoops, I mean wheeeeeee."

Overt and covert cues coming from the child can also signal a need for the therapist to bring his or her own activity level and emotionality into a range that is less bothersome for the child. These can be as subtle as the child averting his or her gaze, physically distancing him or herself from the therapist, issuing a disapproving glance, slowing down his or her rate of speech, or changing voice inflection. It is also not rare for the child to come right out and trumpet his or her objection to how the therapist is acting!

Eager to show me his new toy plane, seven-year-old Billy was thrilled by my suggestion that he show me how well it landed by using my arm as a landing strip. As he repeatedly pretended to land and take off his toy plane on and from my arm, I made sounds consonant with a plane landing and taking off. Billy irritatingly announced, "Will you stop being so hyper and just let me play alone with my plane." After several minutes of alone time, I helped tease out Billy's feelings. "I guess the noises I was making were annoying you and got in the way of us playing a fun game together?" Billy replied, "Dah, yeah, a B-52 bomber does not make those noises and when you were making them you were moving your arm around which made it hard for me to land my plane." I asked Billy to make accurate B-52 bomber noises for me to copy and agreed to try to keep my arm straight when he was landing his plane, although I added, "If you put too much pressure on my arm when you are landing the plane I cannot promise that I will be able to keep my arm straight the way you like it." Billy and I continued with the game without incident.

This example reveals how a mutually coordinated, positive mood state of the child's can suddenly be recast into a negative mood state due to interactive miscoordination, with the child explicitly indicating what is needed from the therapist to influence his or her emotional recovery in the moment. The miscoordination centered on me giving myself over to the play with too much abandon, losing my objectivity, and presumably being insensitive to any tacit signals Billy emitted, indicating that my emotionality was becoming unbearable. We are in the realm of countertransference here. My own subjectivity was too dominant in the interaction. However, insofar as I was able to regain a degree of objectivity and attend to Billy's feelings and wishes, incorporating them into the ensuing interaction, this asynchronous exchange had a productive outcome.

Suffice to say, the most severe forms of countertransference that impede effective work with ADHD children are those where the therapist is unaware of how his or her activity level is chronically out of step with the child's, or his or her level of emotional input does not shift with the child's, resulting in the child being enduringly underwhelmed, or overwhelmed.

Attention Seeking and Exhibitionism

As outlined in chapter 3, sometimes hyperactive behavior is best viewed through a developmental lens, in terms of childhood exhibitionistic needs gone awry. The child's perpetual "clowning" or "horseplaying" may simply be his or her desperate and unwieldy way to be seen and appreciated, or to pointedly draw recognition for a special talent. The special talent might be something indecorous, like spitting far, or making fart noises with one's armpit, that at first glance seem like nuisance behaviors. And they may very well be nuisance behaviors, but with a subtle interpersonal purpose—to communicate a basic need to be seen, heard, and appreciated.

I arrived at the waiting room door to greet eight-year-old Cameron before his session, only to discover that he was in the restroom. His mother, with whom I had good rapport, was there and we began joking about a picture on the cover of the magazine she was holding. When Cameron returned from the restroom, he detected his mother and me joking and his response to my greeting was a subdued one. His mother, who seemed to be caught up in the exchange with me, prolonged the discussion, and I respectfully followed along. While this was happening, Cameron, with his back to us, began using his hands to make drum noises on a nearby table. The noises he generated became unbearably loud, drowning out the discussion his mother and I were having. I walked over to Cameron, began gently rubbing his head with the palm of my hand, and inquired, "Is this your way of telling me that you are feeling ignored and want my attention? If this is how you are feeling, you can say so." Cameron kept making the drum sounds, although less vigorously and noisily. At the same time, he seemed receptive to my continued rubbing of his head. I took this shift in behavior as a gesture indicating that he was indeed feeling ignored and in need of attention. I added, in a voice with steadily increasing crescendo, "It can be a real struggle for kids to come right out and ask for attention, they often think it is babyish and are embarrassed to do so; however, if they do not, and act annoying instead, guess what, they often get an unkind adult, not a kind one." At this point, I brusquely tickled Cameron and we both laughed hysterically, with his mother watching on in amusement.

This is notwithstanding how demonstrations of indecorous special talents in and of themselves can contain efficacious and decisive body movements that, if they are to psychologically register for the child, need outside recognition. We forget how much of the child's ego, especially with boys, is wrapped up in what can be done with the body, no matter how inconsequential and obnoxious the behaviors seem to adults.

Cameron was restless and shifty as we sat on the office couch together talking about his week. He lifted up his shirt and began making rippling motions with his stomach. I was genuinely impressed and showed my amazement. "Cameron, did you learn that yourself, or did somebody teach you?" He proudly announced that it was his own creation and eagerly pleaded to show me other body movements. Clasping his hands together, he made his arms undulate. I attempted to copy him, but was unable to rival his dexterity and rhythm. My amazement was even more pronounced this time. "You've got that one down to a fine art. I bet that you could make some real cool dance moves using that." Cameron took my cue, stood up and began wiggling his bottom and undulating his arms vigorously. Throwing himself into the dance with abandon, his mild embarrassment was eclipsed by the sheer joy he seemed to derive from moving his body around so forcibly and capably. He stared hungrily into my eyes while dancing, and I beamed in delight with him.

If handled well, these exhibitionistic moments can be immensely valuable to both fortify a child's self-esteem and enable him or her to fully absorb and manage the attendant elation, without becoming uncontrollably giddy. It is not enough for the therapist to "mirror" the child, in an unnatural, stilted way. This runs the risk of mildly shaming the child in a moment of abandon and foreshortening the degree of joy in the interaction. If the experience is to be capitalized on, the therapist truly needs to join in the emotional tenor of the moment, injecting his or her own positivity into the interaction in ways that nudge the child into the further reaches of the joyous event. The therapist truly needs to enjoy the child's joy. In the above example, had I not egged Cameron on, both with my verbal invitations and conveyed gladness, his proud kinesthetic displays and the feelings they activated would arguably have remained somewhat constricted.

The state of emotional vulnerability that the child usually enters during exhibitionistic displays is explained by the simultaneously experienced hope that someone will be there to ardently confirm his or her proud accomplishments and the fear that he or she will be shamefully exposed for being so needy. It is to the latter that we now turn.

Shame, Rage, and Externalization of Blame

The role of shame-rage cycles in the aggressiveness shown by many hyperactive children may explain the social friction they are often embroiled in. In the throngs of shame, the child has the crippling feeling that he or she is "all bad," defective as a person, or unlovable. Actually, experientially, it would be more accurate to say the crippling feeling has the child, for shame has flooding effects that are not so easily warded off. A common interpersonal strategy to undo the agony and defenselessness shame induces is to convert shame into rage, lashing out at the perceived perpetrator or instigating event. There is nothing like a vendetta to sharpen one's consciousness, instate a feeling of dominance, and have the other acting as if helpless, intimidated, and exposed, rather than the self.

One of the main contexts in which shame-rage cycles typically erupt in play therapy pertains to complications surrounding the child's prideful displays of kinesthetic mastery. For children in particular, shame is about the body, how it looks, and what it can and cannot do. Active, dramatic play therapy that pulls for the child to display physical prowess and gamesmanship can be a fertile crucible to test what the child can and cannot do with his or her body and face the feelings that arise when confronted with personal limitations. When encountering personal limitations, shame is always a possibility, along with its darker counterpart, rage. This is especially the case when lapses in sensitivity and clinical judgment on the therapist's part aggravate the child's painful feelings of exposure.

Ten-year-old Roberto arrived for his session more agitated than usual, although upbeat. He elected to play a game of baseball with me, using foam bats and balls. Somewhat bossily, he assigned me the role of pitcher and I began throwing balls to him, varying the speed and height. His batting was exceptionally good and I told him so. He smiled, and in a cocky voice remarked, "I know. I'm hot today."

Sensing he wanted a more animated exchange with me, I notched up the pace of my throws and began simulating the gum-chewing and baseball-cap adjusting antics of a professional ball player. Roberto became perturbed when for the third time in a row, I struck him out. Being unaware of the shame that was operating and the degree of countervailing anger, I sarcastically commented to the effect, "Can you bring on a batter that can handle me." Roberto lashed out at me, threw the foam bat in my direction, and accused me of being " a sucky pitcher with a stupid throw and a big fat ass."

Realizing I had offended him I plaintively stated, "Roberto, Roberto, cool it. No name calling and no hurting of me. I think I just did something that upset you. When I made the sarcastic comment about bringing on a different pitcher after you had struck out, I guess I was rubbing salt in the wound. It probably led to you feeling worse than you already were, having struck out."

Roberto, who by now had regained some self-control, muttered under his breath, "You were giving me sucky pitches, that's why I struck out." In a moment of lightness I replied, "Sucky pitches, or strucky pitches." Roberto stifled a laugh. I added, "So my sucky pitches led to you striking out and that sucked." More outspokenly, he added, "yes, that sucked." Roberto was able to acknowledge that sometimes when he misses a pitch he feels like he sucks as a batter. I reminded him that just because I made bad pitches it did not make me a bad pitcher, just like making some bad hits did not make him a bad batter.

Not willing to let his name calling and aggressiveness go unheeded, I told him that I was bothered by these. "Roberto, I know my sarcastic comment stung you. But, your name calling stung me. And you almost struck me with the bat when you threw it. Talk about strike out!" Even though he was amused by my comment he insisted that I deserved it because I teased him. I persisted, "I did tease you and it was wrong of me. But, in my mind it was also wrong of you to try to hurt me." Roberto was silently receptive to my comments. I continued, "Is there something you can say that lets me know that you were out of line? Once we get that out of the way we can return to the game if you want." Roberto, seeming to feel pressure but not averse to providing an apology, stated, "Okay. Fine. I was feeling all ugly inside and I acted ugly. Sorry."

This sequence of events captures the central ingredients Scheff and Retzinger (1991) identify as formidable precipitants of violent outbursts.

These authors maintain that shame is likely to be converted into destructive rage when it is unacknowledged by the aggrieved party, leads to alienation from a needed attachment figure, and is "communicated disrespectfully" (i.e., an individual's total character is felt to be maligned, rather than some isolated misdeed). Roberto was unable or unwilling to articulate the shame he felt at the point at which he struck out. My sarcastic remark rapidly resulted in me being transposed in his mind from a helping person to a hurting person. My sarcastic remark also implied his deficiency as a batter.

Creating the conditions for shame to be acknowledged and interpersonal ties restored with the therapist is no easy feat. Awareness and verbal processing of shame reactions can be very difficult for well-adjusted adults, let alone hyperactive children. The fear may exist that to admit to vulnerability is to deliver up ammunition that might be used by the therapist at a future date. This fear is not so unfounded, since many a well-meaning therapist feels justified in referring back, out of context, to a painful self-disclosure made by a child, without the emotional supports to make it as appropriate to the here-and-now situation as it was when it was first disclosed. For the hyperactive child who is raised in a family where shaming is used as a means to eliminate undesirable behavior ("What's wrong with you. You are so active all the time. Why can't you calm down and be normal"), acknowledgment and verbalization of shame reactions can result in further humiliation.

The recovery process with Roberto described above reflects how active the therapist needs to be in edging the child away from destructive rage and into and beyond the underlying shame. The recovery process is essentially an interactive achievement, with the therapist using his or her more advanced emotive and cognitive abilities to shepherd the process along: Acknowledging transgressive behavior, offering the child face-saving ways of owning personal limitations, and proffering understandings that concretize the difference between poor actions and impoverished ability.

Undoubtedly, shame was also operating when Roberto externalized blame for his objectionable behavior. It was as if to confess his misdeed was tantamount to admitting he was a bad person. Shame-prone children often embody this dynamic, where they deflect negative attention away from themselves when reprimanded and frame their egregiousness as justified based on other people's perceived distasteful actions. As evidenced in the recovery phase with Roberto, if attempts to bolster responsibility-taking are to be effective, the child's ego needs to be mollified in advance. Put more metaphorically, in holding the child's feet to the fire he or she has to be soothingly warmed, and things can get hot, but the child is not to be burned. Humor, candor, and promises to resume a pleasurable activity also help!

INTERPRETIVE PROCESS

When engaged in fast-paced, active play with ADHD children, knowing when, how, and what to interpret about the child's behavior to promote self-coherence and self-understanding can be daunting. Interpretations are commonly experienced as unwanted intrusions into the play. They are often no substitute for direct counter-action when the child is behaving provocatively. One can never know for sure whether the child agrees with an interpretation because it helps make sense out of a bewildering experience or if he or she agrees just to fob off the therapist and prompt faster return to the play. There is always the specter that the child agrees with an interpretation simply to be done with the act of concentration that working over an interpretation requires. And yet, the interpretive process with ADHD children is an immensely important dimension of therapy for a variety of reasons. It can help with rudimentary crystallization and symbolization of diffuse emotional experience, engender interpersonally useful causal thinking, and indirectly provide the child with modular verbal expressions that can enhance his or her own communicative competency.

Organizing Function

Some children are susceptible to experiencing a range of feelings states as amorphous, quasi-physiologic forces that, once aroused, have flooding and disorganizing effects. This is especially true in the handling of primary emotions such as shame, rage, joy, and disgust. As discussed earlier in the book, ADHD symptoms can be a by-product of the disorganizing effects of poorly regulated intense emotion. Take the child who when in a joyous, expansive mood state becomes unpreventably giggly, clownish, overanimated, and given to repeatedly make nonsensical sounds. These behaviors may be defaulted to even when the child is in an upbeat mood, or when interactions with peers are mildly exciting. This same child may anger easily and protractedly, thwarting capacities to share, cooperate, wait his or her turn, listen to, comply, and follow through with directions, and stay sedentary when needed. Suffice to say, the organizational effects of the interpretative process at the level of containing and confirming affective experience can be one inroad to the treatment of ADHD symptoms.

The therapist's moment-to-moment tracking, verbalized differentiation and labeling of client feelings, as well as offerings linking up the client's outward actions with his or her underlying feelings, assist the child with defining and refining emotional experiences heretofore poorly formulated and communicable. Relatively consistent sensitivity and engagement of this sort can activate and sustain the child's willingness to unveil and more complexly work over diffuse emotional states. A child's desire to repeat a play scenario over and over may reflect its value to him or her in defining and refining expression of an emotion, or set of emotions, that have historically been foreshortened due to less than optimal containing and confirmatory input from the caregiving surround.

I have found two techniques particularly useful in eliciting children's receptivity to an interpretative process while keeping the play flowing. One is a "running commentary" approach where I assume the role of a pretend announcer, tracking and confirming a client's emotional reactions as the play unfolds.

During a game of Sorry at which eight-year-old Lilly was losing, she became glum, mute, then agitated to the point where aggressive stomping off was a distinct possibility. I gently assumed the role of a pretend announcer, holding an imaginary microphone to my mouth, and began whispering into it as to what Lilly might be feeling and why. "Ladies and gentlemen, I can tell from Lilly's face that she might be unhappy, worried, and mad about losing. Even though she is a very good Sorry player, she was having a hard time concentrating and made some unwise choices. Now she is at risk of losing. What will happen? Will she be so unhappy, worried, and mad that she will spoil the game? Or will she put her thinking cap back on, force herself to concentrate better, and keep playing the game? Coming to you live from Sorry Game Stadium we are wondering what Lilly is feeling and what she will do." Lilly took the pretend microphone from me and began talking. "I hate losing at Sorry. I should have picked the yellow pieces to play with. Yellow is my favorite color. Now I have green pieces and I have bad luck. I hate losing. This game sucks." I motioned to have the microphone back and replied, "Yes, ladies and gentlemen, it appears that Lilly is very unhappy about being behind in this game. Losing can hurt and Lilly is hurting right now."

Another is an "imaginary audience" approach where I pretend there is an outside person or nearby crowd to appeal to regarding what a client might be feeling and why. I may also speculate as to how a client's style of displaying emotion has problematic interpersonal effects.

While in a heated game of Nerf football using my office rug as a field, nine-year-old Jonathan celebrated a touchdown by wiggling his rear end at me, calling me names, and wildly running around the office making flatulence sounds. This type of disinhibited behavior frequently resulted in Jonathan getting in trouble at home and at school. I walked off to the side of the office and initiated a discussion with an imaginary referee about Jonathan's behavior. "Mr. Referee, take a good look at Jonathan. Clearly he is happy and feels great about his touchdown. He showed so much effort and strength when he knocked me over and ran the ball in. I admire that. But, does he need to make me feel bad in order for him to feel good? I know his older brother is a bad sport and often mocks him after defeating him at games. Does Jonathan need to do the same thing as his brother does? Surely Jonathan knows that I feel bad right now, just like he feels bad when his brother celebrates in mean ways?" Jonathan listened intently and toned down his celebrating.

Causal Thinking

In plain terms, for the interpretive process in play therapy to be productive, it has to inspire interpersonally useful causal thinking on the ADHD child's part. The mere act of proposing reasons for behaviors implicitly communicates to the child that feelings and motives can be separated out from actions and talked about. Embedded in the ADHD child's enactive communication style is an underacquisition of the capacity to verbally identify and articulate feelings and motives that govern actions. This vulnerability can have unpleasant interpersonal effects, as when the child seems oblivious to any need to explain his or her behavior at the very moment at which such behavior comes across as impulsive and haphazard. Insofar as the behavior is strictly seen by others as impulsive and haphazard, with no intelligible link to the interpersonal events that gave rise to it, the child runs the risk of being perceived as odd, if not dangerous. The child's ability to source reasons for his or her behavior that have some meaningful connection to events that transpired, might still result in social disapproval, but is unlikely to leave him or her being perceived as odd and dangerous.

This is not to say that there is arbitrariness to the interpretations that the therapist offers and that the child cognitively entertains. As covered in the chapter above, when it comes to interpretation, plausibility rather than veracity is the standard, with the therapist suggesting reasons for the child's feelings and actions based on experiential data derived from the immediate therapist-client play interaction and a grounded awareness of the child's family, school, and peer situation. A suggestive approach, where the therapist "wonders out loud" as to what underlying feelings, wishes, or intentions might explain the child's actions, respects the child's autonomy, injects a degree of patience and perseverance into the process, and stretches the child's active concentration and self-reflective capacities. An example illuminates.

For several weeks in a row, eight-year-old Cassandra ended her therapy sessions by stepping up her activity level and "accidentally" making messes, ignoring my pleas to help with cleanup. I held her by the shoulders, tried to secure eye contact, and in a soft voice began speculating aloud what might explain Cassandra's behavior. "I wonder if this is your way of telling me that you are unhappy when we have to end and that you wish we could have more time together?" (no response). "Maybe it's something else . . . is it that you want our session to last longer because you now have to go home and do your homework and you want to hold that off for as long as possible?" (no response). "Maybe it makes you mad when I rush you at the end of the session? I know that your parents can be very busy and you often get told to move faster and you get mad about that. Are you mad because I'm rushing you like your parents do?" (silence). "So, is it choice number one: 'Cassandra hates ending and wants more time with me?' Choice number two: 'Cassandra wishes she could hold off doing her homework for as long as possible?' Or, choice number three: 'Cassandra hates being rushed?'" (In a singing voice) "What is making Cassandra make messes and act silly, juicy choice one, two, or three? Juicy choice one, two, or three?" Cassandra smiled and said, "I'll take choice number one, crazy doctor. I wish we could play together for a whole day." I replied, "So you wish we could have much more time together and you are mad that we have to stop, and instead of telling me this you act like a Silly Billy and make a mess of my office? You know, it's better that you tell me with words rather than actions what you are feeling, Queen Cassandra, dear girl."

Interpretations as Relational Events

We forget how the therapist's delivery of an interpretation is a relational event with the imparted message being irreducible to words alone. The therapist's speech prosody; strength or weakness of voice tone; prolongation or discontinuance of eye contact; distal or proximal positioning to the child; and use or nonuse of physical touch, all influence how receptive a child will be to an interpretation, let alone construe its meaning. The therapist, knowing the child, may consciously choose some words over others for the desired effect. A decision may need to be made as regards how much physical distance from the child the therapist deems tactful during interpretative moments, or how strong a voice tone is needed, or whether eye contact should be forced, to command the child's attention. This is notwithstanding how alterations in the therapist's speech prosody, voice tone, gaze, and the like often occur spontaneously and nondeliberately, yet effectively, as a product of rapid pre-reflective processing of intersubjective information.

With ADHD children, the performative aspects of interpretations may be what essentially render them informative. Given their distractibility, difficulties with short-term auditory memory, and recoiling from acts of concentration, how an interpretation is executed may determine not only the ADHD child's receptivity to it, but also whether its content can be retained in short-term memory long enough to be mentally worked over. Depending on the emotional tenor of the moment, the child may be most favorably disposed to listen to an interpretation that is slowly whispered once directly into his or her ear, or repeatedly, loudly, and playfully sung in staccato style from across the room. Gently moving the child's chin to secure eye contact might prompt the child to pay attention and listen to an interpretation in constructive ways, or guarantee that it is immediately ignored. Much conscious and preconscious gauging of the interaction and liberal use of playfulness are needed to enliven the possibility that the child listen to and heed the content of interpretations. The vignette that follows captures how interpretations are assimilated by the child contingent on how they are borne.

At my invitation, Jamal's mother joined us during a session to discuss steps that could be taken to increase the likelihood that he finish his homework, store it in his binder, and hand it in to his teacher. While his mother and I talked, Jamal picked up a Nerf football and asked to toss it back and forth with me. I agreed as long as I could keep talking with his mother. As the tossing game unfolded Jamal's throws became increasingly aggressive, and on two occasions he "accidentally" hit me on the head with the ball. I quietly got up, sat next to him, smiled, and looked him directly in the eyes saying: "Mr. Quarterback, I think you are angry because your mother and I are taking time from your play session to discuss a problem that embarrasses you—getting your homework completed and handed in. Are your rough tosses a way of telling me this?" After a pause, Jamal sheepishly acknowledged that he was indeed angry because he felt I had "sprung" this meeting on him and was depriving him of expected play time alone with me. I, in a quasi-sarcastic way, added, "Hello . . . knock . . . knock . . . does Jamal not know that he can assert himself and ask his mother to leave, or propose that we have a separate family meeting to discuss homework issues, this time knowing in advance what will happen?" Jamal smiled, took a deep breath, and stated: "Mum, can you leave soon so Dr. G and I can have our session alone?" His mother agreed to leave in five minutes, if he shared his ideas as to what could help him finish his homework and hand it in. Jamal's initial hesitancy to agree with this arrangement dissipated when I let him use my watch to time five minutes. I pulled out a white eraser board and quickly wrote down the following remark, showing it to Jamal's mother, while Jamal squinted to see it. "Jamal thinks you do not keep your word." We all laughed, and Jamal's mother acknowledged that she was "a talker" and needed to honor her word and leave after five minutes.

Interpretations as Modular Verbal Expressions

At a tacit level, therapist interpretations embody linguistic expressions after which clients can pattern their own conveyed self-understanding. Bits and pieces of therapist interpretations, certain words or phrases, may show up in the client's interpersonal communications. It would be mistaken to think of this simply in "monkey hear, monkey say" terms, where the child passively adopts the therapist's language, undercutting his or her own distinctive expressivity. If the therapist is sufficiently attuned to the client, spontaneously hitting on words and phrases that emerge from the intersubjective field, it is erroneous to think of the content of an interpretation as unique to the therapist and its adoption by the client as a form of passive surrender. Rather, the therapist will be given to use words and phrases that have resonance for the client, that ultimately are jointly theirs.

If we assume that therapist interpretations covertly represent linguistic templates for the child to utilize to convey his or her own self-understanding, we want to avoid arcane language and clinical jargon in formulating interpretations, since these do not generalize well to everyday social situations for possible linguistic use by the child. Along these lines, depth psychological interpretations contain few profitable word choices that the child can use in normal interpersonal circumstances. The insight, "I am restless in my body because I wanted to suck my mother's breast dry over and over as an infant, and was denied this" would more than turn heads if even part of it was used as a verbal explanation for troublesome behavior by the child. Interpretations and the personal insights they impart need to be rich in child-friendly language and frame motives and explanations that have thematic relevance for children in everyday contexts.

In the middle of a foosball game in which nine-year-old Frank was behind five goals, he started snatching the ball from my striker and positioned it next to his, each time preventing me from scoring and setting himself up to score instead. I interpreted, "Frank, I wonder if you feel so crummy inside when you lose that you will do everything you can not to feel this way, even if it means cheating."

After her third attempt to unsuccessfully force two incompatible Lego constructions together to make a house, ten-year-old Carmen crumbled them apart with her hands in frustration. Moving close to her, I rubbed her back and stated, "Carmen, I think what happens is you wish you could magically be good at building, as if planning, being patient, and trying something again and again until it works doesn't matter. As if asking for help means you are a dummy."

Interpretive Enactments

Some of the most potent experiential learning in therapy with ADHD children occurs at the level of mutual enactment in dramatic, action-oriented play. This entails the therapist busying him or herself in the play and engaging in spontaneous gestures that wind up being interpersonally instructive for the client, even though there is no conscious attempt on the therapist's part to instill insight. The objectification of experience required by working over an abstract verbal interpretation is often beyond the ADHD child. Rather, enactment is the typical ADHD child's preferred language, if you will, and the therapist's willingness to and skill at partaking in behavioral dialogues ensures that the child is related to in a familiar medium.

Eight-year-old George began lining up toy knights on the shelf and shooting them down using foam darts from a Nerf gun. I pretended to make several knights talk as George was shooting at them. "You're too close, you chicken. I bet if you step further back and try to shoot us you'll miss." George embraced the challenge and stepped back before shooting, yelling, "Stupid knights, I'm still going to shoot you down and make you suffer." I had the knights reply, "Us suffer! Fat chance! You'll be the one suffering when you feel so bad because you keep missing us with your stupid darts." George kept missing the knights with his shots and upon looking like he was about to give up in frustration I had the knights utter, "I guess we got George all riled up when we challenged him. Now it is hard for him to concentrate hard and shoot accurately. We are really done for if he starts breathing deeply, becomes calm and starts to shoot accurately." George smiled devilishly, started breathing deeply, and held his gun with both hands to improve his shooting. In time, he hit one knight after another. I had the last knight standing pretend cry and fearfully say, "I am sorry. Please spare my life. The truth is that I was very scared when you started firing at me and I tried to hide it by being sassy and insulting. Please spare my life. I am so scared." George remarked, "Fine. This time I'll let you live. But don't ever get smart with me again."

A variety of implicit messages are embedded in this enactive play sequence. Acknowledging fear can make others show mercy; trouble can ensue when one masks fear with bravado; and, self-calming steps while angry can promote task accomplishment. It is arguable that one or more of these implicit messages could have been more consciously personalized and cognitively realized had I pulled back from the play and offered George some interpretations at key junctures: "George, you were so kind to show the last knight standing some mercy when he cried and admitted he was scared. I think you wish your brother would let up in hurting you when you cry and plead with him to stop. Instead, your crying seems to just make him want to ridicule you and hurt you more"; or, "George, I wonder if the knights are insulting you because deep down inside they are scared? Boys often try to hide scary feelings with angry ones, just like last week when you tore up your homework in anger because you were worried you could not complete it"; or, "George, you look like you are about to give up in frustration. You know that you have to calm down and concentrate more to do well at things, but it is hard for you to actually do what you know is good." However, this presupposes that the ADHD child is capable of abstracting him or herself from the flow of enactive play, can suddenly change cognitive sets and switch between "the pretend" and "the real," and concentrate and reflect on textured emotional experiences to cultivate self-understanding. Granted, with ADHD children these high-order mental processes need to be fostered, but inasmuch as they are underdeveloped, the point of contact for interpersonal learning is often enactive communications.

It is worth adding that enactive play sequences like the one depicted above tacitly beget a great deal of social know-how of the sort that ADHD children frequently lack. To reiterate, such children often know about the detrimental effects of impulsive actions, poor planning, compulsive skipping in line, failing to listen and follow through, and so forth. It is at the level of procedural demonstration of this knowledge, or showing what they know, that problems arise. Arguably, free-flowing enactive play sequences of the sort illustrated above provide the ADHD child a leg up as regards actually showing what he or she knows. For instance, in the vignette above George is getting practice displaying a measure of self-restraint in the face of provocation, respecting other's fear and reeling in his aggression, being dominant without acting ruthlessly, and redoubling his efforts to succeed when given a helpful suggestion.

IMPLICIT AND EXPLICIT SOCIALIZATION

Psychoanalytically oriented therapists are usually hesitant to consider therapy a form of socialization—the appropriate unit of exploration being the individual psyche, the stuff to be worked with the client's inner wishes, fantasies, and motives, and the goal self-understanding through insight. However, as relational ideas permeate the psychoanalytic paradigm, it becomes increasingly less tenable to deny outright that therapy is a form of socialization. I suppose this pivots on what we mean by socialization. If what we mean by socialization approximates something like: a greater awareness of a range of felt emotions and competence at communicating them tapping an array of face to face, kinesthetic, vocal, tactile, and verbal expressions that increases our ability to form and keep secure relationships, if not coexist with others, we are hard pressed to deny that therapy is a form of socialization!

It may seem like I am belaboring this point. However, when working with children one cannot sidestep the topic of socialization. In our consulting rooms we increasingly see children whose presenting symptoms center on underdeveloped social skills such as: sharing and cooperating, waiting one's turn, respecting other's belongings and personal space, empathizing with others when they are distressed or excited, initiating and maintaining conversations in a give-and-take fashion. I could go on. One has to wonder if the advent of computer games in our society leading to more sedentary, isolative, indoor play among children, in addition to smaller family sizes, the shrinking number of safe play spaces in the inner cities, reduction in recess time during school hours, less playful roughhousing with fathers due to divorce and father absence, and a variety of other cultural and technological changes all explain the rise in socialization difficulties being a front-burner mental health issue when children are brought in for therapy.

The socialization question is particularly relevant to ADHD. As mentioned previously, some experts have gone so far as to label ADHD a "social disability" (Greene, Biederman, Faraone, and Ouellette, 1996) or a "social learning disability" (Henker and Whalen, 1999) due to the average ADHD child's difficulties with sociability. In particular, it is sociability at the level of "procedural knowledge" more than "declarative knowledge" that the ADHD child struggles with. That is, knowing how to act across social contexts with a measure of emotional self-control and interpersonal versatility. This is in contradistinction to knowing what is appropriate to do or say at an informational level. The distinction is not a subtle one, nor is it unimportant. If the ADHD child is to improve, the therapy needs to be rich in occasions for the acquisition of more sophisticated and effective forms of socioemotional communication that can be lived out.

Therapist Self-Disclosure

Therapist self-disclosure, whether indirectly, in the context of pretend role playing, or directly, in the context of an emotionally charged actual therapist-child interaction, can be one vehicle for the child to learn about other's "inner" wishes, motives, fears, desires, and how they line up with their "outer" behaviors. Indirect and direct therapist disclosures can also be poignant experiential lessons helping the child to realize the subtle and ostensible real-life consequences to actions.

During pretend role play the therapist can talk through a persona that is being adopted, or a puppet that is being used. The pretend nature of the play and the use of an object or role through which to represent his thoughts and feelings can give the therapist creative license to embellish, which can expose the child to a richer source of socioemotional information. The socioemotional information may be rendered more usable by the child insofar as it is embedded in a nonthreatening, relatively enjoyable interaction.

Upon discovering that I happened to have a Lamb Chops puppet in my collection, one of her favorites, seven-year-old Pam impulsively rammed her hand up in it and began making it shout: "BAH . . . BAH . . . BAH . . . BAH . . . BAH . . . BLACKSHEEP HAVE YOU ANY WOOL." I reached for a small chicken puppet and spoke through it, reflecting my being startled and annoyed by Pam's impulsive and vociferous behavior. "You startled me, Ms. Lamb Chops. At first I did not want to say anything. I was frightened. But, my fear quickly turned to irritation and I knew if I did not say something I would go numb inside. So, I just had to tell you about my feelings. I am trying real hard to use words and hang on to what I am feeling without getting real mad, or going all numb inside. I knew if I either got too mad at you, or went all numb inside, I would not be able to play well with you." Pam listened very attentively.

The child's receptivity to direct, authentic feedback regarding his or her here-and-now problematic behavior is largely dependent not only on what the therapist says, but how it is said, its timing, and the degree of congruence between the feelings conveyed surrounding it and the emotional tenor of the interaction. At a global level, the child's receptivity to direct feedback is also a function of the value the child attaches to the relationship with the therapist. The therapist who is perceived as a valued figure due to making him or herself recurringly available for play consonant with the child's activity level and characteristic emotion regulation abilities can be someone whose self-disclosures carry weight. Of course, genuineness, using child-friendly words that highlight transitory behaviors and feelings, rather than perceived global personality attributes, and speaking with a degree of intensity that captures the child's attention, without blanketing it, all apply.

Eleven-year-old Salvador began rifling through my desk drawers looking to see if I had any gum. This crossing of personal boundaries was typical of Salvador, who over the three months I had been working with him had on separate occasions "mistakenly" placed one of my toy soldiers in his pocket, tried to turn on the laptop computer on my desk without asking, had left the office abruptly to go to the bathroom without any clear indication of what he was about to do, and passed gas at will. My interpretations to the effect that the frustration he felt when he did not get his needs met immediately seemed too much to bear had fallen on deaf ears. Also, his short attention span precluded me from speculating as to psychogenic reasons for him needing immediate gratification of his needs. Playfully enacted communications sometimes worked, as when I chose to reach for my air freshener when he passed gas and indicate, "What is this, chemical warfare?" while I sprayed a wall of air freshener between me and him to concretize that a personal boundary had been transgressed and needed to be reasserted.

On this occasion I did not feel like being playful. Waiting until his mild distress over discovering that I had no gum dissipated, I took Salvador by the hands, placed myself at his eye level, and put my concern to Salvador directly and sincerely. "You know by now that I am a pretty friendly and agreeable guy, Salvador, and all you have to do is ask, and most of the time I will oblige. I really don't like it when you go through my belongings without asking. Can we have an agreement in here where you ask when you want to go through my stuff?" Salvador, appearing mildly, but not overly shaken, replied, "I guess so." I smiled and added, "You guess so, or you mean so?" Smiling he added, "Okay, I mean so . . . now can we get the foosball table out? I thanked him for asking and suggested that we both put it down on the floor together since it was so heavy.

Of course, therapist self-disclosure is not always a verbal affair, nor elective, in the ordinary sense of the word. What I have in mind here are the myriad ways in which the therapist, naturally and subliminally, communicates to the child by way of posture, facial expression, voice tone, and automatic choice of words. Communications do not have to be made conscious to be socially meaningful or useful.

The notion that pretend play gives the child license to exhibit him or herself more free-flowingly because what ensues is "just pretend" does not solely apply to the child. When dramatic role play unfolds between the therapist and child, the therapist also is freed up. It is important that the therapist not just adopt a role, but *inhabit* it. In this way the therapist can make reflexive use of a host of affectively suffused nonverbal and verbal expressions that spontaneously occur to him or her that the child might tacitly identify with. The therapist's more evolved socioemotional development and sophisticated use of cross-modal expression of emotion make him or her a fertile source of implicit relational learning.

Often it takes the therapist inhabiting a role, and not just adopting it, for the child to do likewise. This is important since the liveliness and intensity surrounding mutual role inhabiting, where therapist and child enactively play off each other, fosters a more complex exchange of implicit, as well as explicit, communicative stimuli. The positive feelings and expansive mood that the tempo of the play generates can prime pre-conscious and conscious social learning.

For several weeks in succession, nine-year-old Robert and I gravitated toward repeating a game in which we both hid behind separate chairs in the office and fired darts back and forth at each other. We would vie to see who would be first to run up to the other and commandingly announce, "Drop the gun. DROP THE GUN, NOW." Whoever was first to act got to take charge and it was expected that the other look sincerely startled and be speechless, jump back with a constricted body posture, breath held in and eyes wide open.

Across sessions, when I assumed the persona of the captive person, I expanded the verbal and nonverbal expressions I used to communicate all I was feeling in that role. "Back off, you are scaring me . . . I SAID BACK OFF BUDDY YOU ARE SCARING ME" (in a tone that started out sheepish, but ended up stern); "What would my friends say if they saw me now, being so pathetic as to let my guard down and be captured" (with sad expressions); and, "I have no way of escaping, the best thing I can do is be friendly with you and maybe you will have mercy on me" (with plaintiff expressions).

Over time, I projected myself more thoroughgoingly into the role of captor, generating a host of nonverbal and verbal emotional responses suitable to that stance. "You probably think I will show you mercy, don't you . . . I SAID DON'T YOU? (with thinly disguised sadism); "I was just lucky to run up on you first, is that a reason for me to treat you badly" (with a mixture of confusion and muffled compassion); and, "Oh what the heck, let's just arm wrestle and get this over with . . . JUST KIDDING . . . hands above your head, I said HANDS ABOVE YOUR HEAD . . . THAT MEANS NOW."

Robert delighted in this game. When he was in the alternating roles of captor and captive, feeding off my reactions, he experimented with a variety of gestures and remarks, spanning from the sadistic to the merciful, the terrified to the empowered.

Had I stepped back from the play with Robert and speculated as to the psychogenic reasons for him needing to startle and be startled, catch and be caught, undoubtedly my behavior would have become subdued. This surely would have deprived him of the chance to be exposed to and add his personal imprint on an array of socioemotional expressions happening before him—expressions with socialization ramifications: How to convey shock and fear to an aggressor, assert one's need for personal space, display a feeling of empowerment, show mercy, accept that luck and chance enter into achievements, use humor to instill lightness into an interaction, and display sadness evoked by a defeat, to name but a few.

Relational Insights

A participatory style of clinically treating ADHD children requires a redefinition of insight work. The emphasis is less on what the child's actions reveal about him or herself as an individual, and more on what they reveal about how he or she relates to others and expects to be related to by others. Even when contemporaneous play interactions are viewed as symbolic reenactments of past unsettling events in the child's life, requiring the therapeutic focus to be on the child processing feelings about what happened "then and there," insight work is tilted in the direction of how past interactions with important others have created present relational expectations.

Upon arriving for her session, ten-year-old Bianca had an edge to her. Her sweatshirt hood was up over her head and there was a glower on her face. I caught the tail end of a conversation between Bianca and her foster mother, witnessing her openly berate Bianca for appearing like a gang member by having her sweatshirt hood on. Bianca denied being bothered by her foster mother's derisive comments, basically ignored me, and started throwing metal darts at a magnetic dart board located on the inside of my office door. On her first try, all three of her darts missed the board, instead hitting the door with a thud. She had made no effort to aim them. When it was my turn I took ample time to aim and shoot, and each one hit the dart board.

On her second try, Bianca's throws were even more unruly. I inquired whether she was trying to tell me through her actions that she was angry at her foster mother. At that point Bianca's vexation surfaced and she turned on me. "Would you just take your turn and quit with the questions." I indicated that I was not going to continue the game until I had some assurance from her that she was not going to throw darts erratically at my door. Her anger became even more pronounced: "YOU AND YOUR ASS-WIPE RULES."

I interpreted, "Bianca, I think that it is your foster mother and not me you are really angry at. For that matter, maybe you're mad at the fact that you are in foster care at all. I bet some of your foster parents in the past had ass-wipe rules."

Bianca replied, "You got that right. The second foster mother I had used to lock me in my room all day if I did not eat my whole breakfast." I looked aghast and said that I could not imagine how that must have felt for her. She added, "I can. Like crap. That's how it made me feel, like crap." Bianca went on to exceed the characteristic two to three minutes of talk that was her maximum when exploring her painful past.

The play segued into her wanting to draw pictures. She began drawing a nondescript face, as did I, taking her lead. I returned to the issue of her second foster mother and asked Bianca what she looked like. Bianca stepped in and finished my drawing, trying to capture a resemblance of her second foster mother. When she completed it, I snarled, "We just got us a new dartboard!"

Bianca, still half angry, but somewhat amused, picked up on my cue and started throwing darts at the picture, which I had taped to my leather chair, knowing that it could easily withstand darts being tossed at it. All of Bianca's darts hit the target this time. While she threw her darts, she emitted a steady stream of angry profanity, identifying each of her foster parents from the past.

Later in the session, while we were having a snack break, I rather nonchalantly remarked, "Bianca, when rules are unreasonable you have every right to be angry. But, I don't think that my rule earlier was that unreasonable. I think because you have had so many unreasonable rules in the past that all rules seem unreasonable to you now. When you act nasty when confronted with reasonable rules, some adults are going to see this as due cause to come down even harder on you." Smiling, I injected, "Am I right, or am I right?" Bianca reflected for a moment, smiled, and replied, "I guess you're right."

Unpacking this clinical narrative will allow us to delineate some key ingredients of the insight-imparting process with externalizing children. Such children are often used to being lectured and chastised for acting heedlessly and develop an emotion-regulation style of affective numbing, rapidly flashing to affective eruption, in the face of other's objections, reprimands, and criticisms. We can see this when Bianca goes from ignoring me to attacking me during the dart game. The here-and-now relational pull can easily become a negatively valenced one with externalizing children like Bianca, where the therapist is drawn into actions commensurate with other, seemingly punitive figures in the child's life. In the example above, I am inducted into correcting Bianca's behavior due to its provocativeness. My subjective reactions center on curbing Bianca's disruptive behavior. "Past" and "present" bleed together for Bianca and she elevates my reprimand to the level of the punitive actions of her foster mother. However, since I am not essentially constituting myself as a punitive figure, it is easier for Bianca to realize that my rules are not unreasonable, that I am not the living embodiment of her foster mothers, and to more cognitively grasp that not all rules are unreasonable.

In more conceptual terms, by responding to Bianca from my own subjectivity and asking for reassurance that she would not throw darts wildly, I risked becoming an "old-bad object" for her—a reprimanding, criticizing, authority figure. However, I do not let my annoyance ripen into derisiveness. I am personally affected by her provocativeness but do not personalize it. As such, I become a "new good object" for Bianca. She can have the experience of there being rules set down in response to her unruliness without this being a derisive enterprise, as expected.

In the end, Bianca appears to have acquired several relational insights; namely, she is predisposed to react provocatively to all rules and when she does so, adults might actually tighten their grip on her; and, she anticipates being treated derisively by adults even when they are trying to reasonably execute authority. Their assimilation is made possible by their interpretative grounding in the here-and-now interactions transpiring between Bianca and me. Additionally, arguably, her receptivity to my interpretation of her relationship expectancies was primed by my use of words that were in keeping with her vernacular. I also "struck while the iron was cold," or waited for a nonthreatening moment to deliver my insights, and interjected a mixture of sincerity, humor, and lightness into the interaction. Last, but not

least, the insights and the here-and-now interactions supporting them, occurred in the context of active play between Bianca and me. Occasions to
stay motorically busy and have physical outlets for her anger allowed Bianca
to move in and out of using speech as a communicative tool, because it was
not expected to be her sole communicative tool.

Tempering Omnipotence and Engendering Mutuality

For a certain percentage of children presenting with ADHD-like
socialization deficits, the more overriding concern can be one of narcissistic vulnerability. These are children whose sense of entitlement is age-
inappropriate and entrenched, impeding their capacity to take turns, share
and cooperate, follow rules, empathize with others who are euphoric or in
a state of distress, or generally allow for mutuality and reciprocity in relationships. Granted, we expect strong needs for interpersonal control and
fantasies of omnipotence to be present to varying degrees throughout early
childhood. But a true narcissistic vulnerability begins to coalesce when the
school-aged child's dominance needs exact a social price and the child recurringly finds him or herself relegated to the margins of his or her peer
group, overrelying on an omnipotently tinged, isolative fantasy life to bolster self-images of invulnerability and super specialness. Ultimately, if play
therapy experiences are to have an impact with such children, they have to
incorporate tolerable challenges to their grandiosity and help them realize,
and want to counteract, the loneliness that trenchant needs for interpersonal
control exact.

Nine-year-old Margaret came to her session sporting a flashlight. She
haughtily announced that whichever toy knight on the bookshelf she
flashed her beam at would immediately be melted and destroyed. I franti-
cally gathered up the knights, speaking through them. "Oh, no. We have to
move fast. Great Queen Margaret wants to destroy us all." I opened up my
cupboard door, stuffed all the knights inside, and had them say behind the
protection of the cupboard door, "Great Queen Margaret may be our
leader, she may have a great deal of power, but it is not right for her to think
that she has all the control, like control over whether we live or die. We
need to keep ourselves safe from her because she wants too much power."

Margaret looked perturbed over the fact that I had unilaterally decided
to lock the cupboard door with a key, which I had hidden in a planter when
she was not looking. She asked me where the key was. I replied in a falsetto
voice, "We never give away the Secret of the Key." Margaret became angrily fixated on finding the key, which she eventually did. As she moved to

unlock the cupboard door, I grabbed some puppets, used them to block her path, and had them utter, "Great Queen Margaret. Why do you want to destroy the very knights who serve you well? Will you not be lonely without them?" Margaret aggressively pushed the puppets out of the way, opened the cupboard door, extracted the knights, and shone the flashlight on them one by one, declaring, "Stupid, stupid knights. You should know better than this. I have complete control. It is time for you to die."

From across the room I had the puppets say, "Great Queen Margaret is really losing it. For now she may be enjoying showing so much power and killing off the knights. But, what she does not know is that she is going to be so lonely later on without the knights around and with everybody in the land avoiding her because she needs too much power."

Margaret stopped herself from killing off the last knight and said, "Okay. You get to live because you have been my most loyal knight." I picked this knight up and had it say, "Great Queen Margaret, thank you for showing me mercy. You know that I will always respect you as my queen. But, if you go around needing to have all the power in the land I will be scared of you and want to hide." Margaret grudgingly replied, "Fine. I'll give you some power. You can be my prince."

This example illustrates how the child's need for omnipotence can be confronted indirectly and metaphorically through sticking with enactive play. This is often the most advisable way to work with such children, since their brittle self-structure preempts direct reference to their proclivity for entitlement and the social alienation it causes. Accommodating to the needs of others, admitting defeat, settling for competence over omnipotence, showing mercy, asking for help, acknowledging that he or she is not above the rules, are all tendencies that the child might manifest in pretend play, because it is "just pretend."

The interpersonal exchanges that transpire surrounding the play can be another mechanism to attenuate the child's dominance needs and foster mutuality. Questions posed to the child with candor during games and activities can prompt a perspective-taking stance on his or her part: How do you think I feel losing all the time? What would make this game more fun for me? Do you think I'm more excited about having won than guilty over beating you? These types of questions as they organically arise in the play can activate the client's openness to experience the therapist as an objective subject, more than a subjective object—someone who is mostly there to provide attunement, confirmation, and gratification of important needs. The child's willingness to answer questions put to him or her pertaining to perceptions of the therapist's inner world potentiates an emergent aptitude for realizing that others have needs and wants independent of the self, that somehow need to be contended with.

The therapist can also position him or herself as more of an objective subject and self-disclose a genuine desire for more mutuality in the play. The increased likelihood that this type of self-disclosure is acceded to resides in it being couched in a way that still honor's the child's narcissistic needs.

During a game of checkers, eight-year-old MaryAnn arbitrarily changed the rules to her advantage, jumping her pieces over multiple squares at a time, leading to her winning game after game. I gently placed my arm around her shoulder and addressed her as follows. "MaryAnn, I know that you love to win and like to feel that you are unbeatable at checkers. But, this game is getting boring for me because I keep losing and am having trouble following the good rules you are making up. Is there a way that we can make this game more fun for me? Better yet, more fun for the both of us?" MaryAnn suggested that I get to jump my pieces over three squares each time, not just one. She wanted to jump her pieces over four squares each time. I agreed and returned to the game with renewed enthusiasm.

Mutuality fostering can also be built into the office rules the therapist establishes. Special attention to office rules is imperative with children whose sense of entitlement is aggravated by being raised in a permissive household where codes of behavior are not laid out and consistently enforced. For instance, the therapist might agree to do his or her utmost to start sessions on time and not keep the child waiting, as long as the child leaves the office on time at the end of the session and does not keep the therapist waiting. There may be a requirement that "whoever makes the mess, cleans it" at the end of sessions. The snack policy might be one where if the child gets a snack, the therapist is allowed one too. With such children, the process of setting down office rules, and their enforcement when tested, encapsulates an important treatment dynamic in and of itself.

Coaxing Sublimated Expressions

ADHD children often need active assistance not just with tempering the intensity of their emotionality in interpersonal situations, but with finessing their outward expression of a range of specific emotions in socially adaptive ways. Their characteristic modes of expressing anger can be off-putting, steeped in totalistic and offensive wordage (e.g., "You're stupid and a lousy friend"), and embody overly constricted or effusive nonverbal behaviors. Similarly, happy feelings frequently are conveyed either too faintly or too boomingly for them to elicit wished-for recognition.

Delicate and socially fluent ways of verbally and nonverbally communicating emotions are best picked up by the child when they are embedded in active play. This is the case because they are acquired in a spirit of playfulness, experimentation, initiative-taking, and mutuality, rather than in one of obligation, indoctrination, and duress, which often color the everyday contexts in which ADHD children are prompted to improve their behavior.

Coaxing more sublimated expression of emotions in the play can take the form of the therapist enactively matching, yet efficaciously altering, a child's delivery.

In the midst of a mafia-type game, where ten-year-old Jonathan was Guido, the Big Boss, and I was Franky, his underling, Jonathan took umbrage at me for not following his orders fast enough. He got in my face and directed a stream of profanity at me. I matched his anger, omitting the profanity, and kept a respectful distance from him, commenting, "Guido, you are talking to me like I am on the side of the Gambino family, the enemy, instead of a loyal friend. I listen and follow orders better when somebody does not get all up in my face and cuss me out." Jonathan, in role, stepped back from me and chose his words more carefully, while still being angry. "Franky, I just want you to move faster. Get a move on. The Gambino family will be here any minute and we need to get our guns loaded."

Alternatively, the therapist can request different words and behavior to render a feeling more acceptable, putting the onus more squarely on the child.

Jonathan and I pretended to sneak up on imaginary Gambino family members and fire our dart guns at them. He exhibited his joy over "taking out" the leader of the Gambino family with uncontrollable exuberance, running around the room and screaming, "WE TOOK OUT THAT SON-OF-A-BITCH, WHOOOYAHH." I ran alongside him, less energetically, although still excited, and stated, "Boss, I know you are happy, and I am too. But, we did not take out the whole Gambino family. Is there a different way you can show your happiness since you are being too loud and what you are saying might piss off those Gambino family members that survived? There are Gambino family members close by and they will know our location if you are HAPPY (loud voice and more animated gestures), instead of happy (soft voice and less animated gestures)." Jonathan thought about what I said and modulated his excitement. "Good point Franky. I am so stoked that we took out the leader of the Gambino family" (in a quieter voice, no longer running around the room, motioning to give me a "high five").

At a more basic level, interventions aimed at curbing more primal expression of feeling and imposing thought before reflexive aggressive actions can center on reminding a child that it is acceptable to "pretend hurt" during a play interaction but not "actually hurt."

Michael stockpiled all the biggest rubber swords he could find in my office in preparation for our mock battle. Taking two of them, one in each hand, he ran at me swinging wildly. I positioned my shield to block his hits and Michael took delight in fiercely stabbing my shield. One of Michael's stabs reached my stomach and I pretended to be gravely injured, groaned, and flailed around on the floor. Michael stood over me, loudly proclaiming his victory, "You will have your head cut off and all your body parts fed to my dogs." He aggressively took hold of my neck and roughly positioned his sword next to it. I reminded him that it was okay to pretend kill me and chop me up, but that I did not want him to actually hurt me.

A request with a therapeutic outcome can even be one that exhorts the disinhibited child to keep certain thoughts to him or herself! Not all vulgar or aggressive thoughts need to be spoken aloud. Sometimes in therapy the child needs to be told directly that a rude or disrespectful thought is acceptable to think, but not speak. This may seem counterintuitive since therapy is supposed to be free-associative in nature, liberating the client from the prohibitions of everyday discourse. However, Western society has changed considerably since the time of Freud and children are exposed to all manner of permissiveness, rudeness, shameful behavior, and unfettered expression of aggression through the mass media and video games. Given this state of affairs, interventions that playfully instill tact, diplomacy, and social sensitivity at times have merit with impulsive children.

SUPPORTING PERSEVERANCE AND ENGROSSMENT

A classic ADHD trait is premature discontinuance of tasks that are experienced as onerous. Diagnostically speaking, tasks that are mental in nature and that entail active concentration, such as math problems or spelling skills, are the ones usually targeted.

However, when working with ADHD children one also notices task avoidance and abortion across a variety of kinesthetic and socioemotional domains. The child who recoils instantly at the sight of homework, rushes through it or leaves it incomplete, may be the same child who refuses to get back up on the monkey bars after falling off, and the same child who flips a chessboard in frustration when losing to a perceived inferior player. Phenomenologically, it seems impossible to differentiate between failures in perseverance and engrossment due to "neurological deficit" versus "self-deficit." The former zeros in on brain abnormalities that undercut executive functions. The latter highlights the child's regressed personality style: a preparedness to avoid tasks that cannot be instantly mastered, to perceive a trial and error or stepwise approach to most things as an insult to his or her grandiosity, to view asking for even a reasonable degree of help to complete a task as an act of impotence, or to adopt a "deus ex machina" mentality, silently expecting that someone or something will swoop down and impose solutions to problems. Regardless of whether we account for failures in perseverance and engrossment in terms of neurological deficit or self-deficit, the desired treatment goal is still the same: To help the child experientially link up outcome to planning, perseverance, engrossment, and outside help that brings a task within his or her reach with moderate effort. Interactive regulation of the frustration aroused during the completion of challenging socioemotional, kinesthetic, and mental activities is also a key component of the work.

There are myriad occasions to stimulate the child's task persistence during a typical play therapy session. The context can be the setting up or breaking down of games, finishing one play activity before moving on to another, completing drawings and construction projects, adhering to agreed-upon rules to games, or any number of seemingly innocuous events. (I have an old cupboard in my office with an antiquated key that requires dexterity to use. Many a child has had to endure my intervention aimed at mastering use of this key to open the lock that leads to the cupboard in which lie the shelves where enticing toys are kept!) In these contexts, the stance of the therapist deviates from the nondirectional one usually endorsed by traditional play therapists: Sensitively counteracting the child's impulse to abort a task that cannot be immediately mastered, nonimposingly channeling the child's attention back to the task, promoting engrossment in the task by making it alluring, and reconfiguring the task to render it accomplishable with moderate effort. Holding and gentle physical corralling of the child are sometimes necessary to prevent him or her from ruining a game, activity, or construction project before it can be redone, as well as optimize his or her ability to stay in the appropriate area. Obviously, there needs to be dutiful attunement to and interactive regulation of the child's mounting frustration all the while. The sense of satisfaction and positive emotion imbuing accomplishment of segments of a project, reinforced by the therapist's praise, can embolden the child's motivation to persist and see the project through to completion. The extended clinical example that follows should bring these dynamics to light.

Seven-year-old MaryAnn pulled out a container of Legos and dumped its contents on the carpet, announcing that she was going to build a dollhouse. I sat down in close proximity to her on the carpet and began spreading Legos out with both hands, saying, "Let's get them all spread out for you to see. If the house is going to be a strong one we will need to find you pieces that fit well together. Do you need my help?" MaryAnn grunted a preference for me to not help her and merely nodded in agreement, not looking up, to my suggestion that I build my own dollhouse alongside her on the carpet. I began talking out loud to myself. "Okay, let's see, I will need a plan. I want my house to be made up of red and green pieces so I'm going to collect those only. Next, I just want pieces that have four sets of dots or more on them since those will make strong walls for me." I busied myself making my house according to my plan.

MaryAnn, who seemed oblivious to my presence, started randomly forcing pieces together that were ill-suited, did not squeeze them sufficiently to make even the compatible ones connect well, and growled in frustration when her feeble construction began to crumble. She threw what was left of her house on the ground, stood up, and began riffling through a basket in my office looking for toys. I walked over to her and, putting my arm around her, steered her back in the direction of the Legos, commenting, "Oh gosh, MaryAnn, I can see that you are so frustrated over not being able to build your dollhouse. You started out with so much excitement and now you are down in the dumps. It would be a mistake for me to let you give up so easily. I was getting into the whole idea of us building dollhouses together. Can you try again? I will search through my cupboard for toy figures that might fit in your dollhouse if you try again."

MaryAnn's mild resistance to me physically steering her in the direction of the Legos lessened and she ambled over there of her own accord, although still looking glum. I sat down next to her and pleaded with her to let me provide assistance. "MaryAnn, I know you think it is weak to ask for help, but I think this is one of those times when you really need help. What if I help you with a plan?" She angrily insisted that she did not want to restrict herself to pieces of a certain color or size, as I had. However, she did go along with my suggestion that we remove from her pile all the pieces with three sets of dots or less since they were not good for building big houses. While she launched into her building project I sat next to her, adlibbing a song in a soothing voice: "Houses, houses, are what we build. One piece after another, squeezing them tight. Houses, houses, are what we build. One piece after another, squeezing them tight."

On one occasion I abruptly seized the entire structure and made some minor alterations to ensure the whole thing did not collapse, stating, "Woopsadaisy, Houston we have a problem. The BIG GUY needs to step in to make sure that we don't have a BIG PROBLEM." MaryAnn smiled at this and continued building with added focus when I returned the structure to her. On another occasion I expressed my concern that if she kept doing what she was doing the roof might fall in. She was receptive to my cue and stopped what she was doing, although she did not appear to have a solution at her disposal. I pressed my fingers up against a Lego beam holding up the roof and motioned with my eyes for her to press down on the roof, which she did.

Once the roof was firmly in place I urged her to take a snack break. MaryAnn heartily agreed. I praised her for making such a realistic roof, using flat pieces that would make the rain run off easily. While we sat eating our snacks we talked about how hard building projects can be, but how good it feels when you see the finished project.

When the house was eventually completed MaryAnn could barely contain her excitement, to which I responded, "I am so glad that you decided to continue working on your dollhouse. Look at it, with its multicolored walls and strong roof. All the effort and focus you put into it paid off. It is beautiful." I asked her if she still wanted me to select toy figures to insert in it, as I had promised. She let me know that she thought this was a silly idea because none of the toy figures I possessed would fit.

I was dutiful to preserve the dollhouse for the duration of my treatment with MaryAnn and showcased it for her, off and on, reminding her of the effort and determination she exerted to ensure its robustness and beauty.

5

WORKING WITH PARENTS

The amount of parent involvement deemed proper in child psychotherapy has been a bone of contention since the field was founded. Anna Freud (1946) viewed positive rapport with parents as a prerequisite for successful child treatment and was not above conducting home visits and doling out advice to parents. Melanie Klein, on the other hand, was notorious for keeping her distance from parents and perceived such a stance as necessary to activate the child's primal fantasies, unfettered (Smirnoff, 1971). Yet, ultimately, both these founding mothers, to a greater or lesser degree, subscribed to a model of child therapy in which symptoms formed and were transformed as a product of the child's "interior world," which they believed somehow could be separated out from the child's "external world" of everyday life interactions with parents. The main agenda of traditional play therapy continues to center on individual contact with the child to realign psychic structure or alter self and other representations, as if the parent's characteristic ways of relating to the child can be suspended as essential contributors to these phenomena (Chethik, 2000). It is a dubious enterprise to extract the child from his or her primary relationships and treat these relationships and their effects, largely, as mental representations, modifiable through symbolic play.

From a relational perspective, the rationale for parent involvement—or, for that matter, sibling and extended-family member involvement—in child therapy is rooted in the notion that symptom coalescence, maintenance, and amelioration are inextricably linked to past, present, and anticipated mutual regulation processes existing in a given parent-child dyad and expanded family system. For example, a father may chronically feel intimidated by his son's susceptibility to angry outbursts and frequently vacillate between fearfully capitulating to his demands and vociferously denying them, both of which perpetuate tendencies within the child to be entitled, easily frustrated, and shame-prone. The mother, for her own defensive reasons, may be selectively attentive to the father's moments of intolerance and resentment, furiously warding him off and leaping in to console the son, leaving the father feeling undermined and phobic about disciplining his son. The son may, in turn, seem outwardly brash that he has won through intimidation, although inwardly petrified that his father's future potential for rage has been stoked. To complicate matters, the son's younger sister, who has witnessed this emotional interplay over and over again, may be given to secretly provoking her brother to get him in trouble with the father, as a means to building a father-daughter alliance, thereby satisfying a need that she shares with the father to have a close, conflict-free relationship with someone in the family. This cluster of emotionally charged family interactions, if frequently manifested, can support or aggravate an ADHD symptom picture in the son of low frustration tolerance, motor restlessness, externalization of blame, and entitlement-driven task avoidance and discontinuance. Needless to say, with this scenario in mind, if child therapy is to be productive and effective, parent work cannot be seen as merely preparatory, ancillary, and sporadically implemented, but as integral, intensive, and ongoingly necessary.

It is the rare case where parents seek therapy for their child due mainly to life-enhancement or self-fulfillment reasons. By the same token, even in our psychology-savvy culture, children tend not to ask for therapy. More often than not, the initial context of therapy is one where the child's protracted behavior problems have resulted in the school issuing some sort of treatment mandate and where parents pursue professional help with a mixture of desperation and reluctance. This is especially true when the child's condition embodies classic externalizing symptoms—impulsivity, aggression, and shunning of responsibility. Parents, siblings, grandparents, and teachers are likely to be more in conflict and distressed by the child's actions than the child him or herself. We can assume that the child's behavior has led to his or her parents being dealt with unsympathetically and subjected to moral judgment by outside parties charged with caring for the child. In short, whether acknowledged or not, during their first encounters with the therapist, parents often feel a blend of helplessness, shame, and anguish that sets them up either to take too much responsibility, or too little, for their child's condition. This situation is worsened by countervailing cultural beliefs seeming to offer parents a forced choice of either blaming their child's brain, or blaming themselves, for the problems that exist.

The former short-circuits any meaningful understanding of parental contribution to and remediation of children's problems. The latter unfairly magnifies parental guilt and feeds a naïve optimism that parents can completely override the effects of biology and complex social processes in altering children's behavior.

Ironically, by the very adoption of a bio-psycho-social model of human development, by knowing in one's bones that the etiology of all child problems involves a bewilderingly complex intermingling of biological, psychological, and social forces, the clinician embodies the quiet confidence and nonjudgmental stance necessary to disabuse parents of the belief that they are all to blame. At a covert level, the line of questioning employed by the therapist begins to parcel out the myriad interlocking causes for the child's difficulties: Were there any birthing complications? Looking back, how has Mary taken to sleeping and eating routines? Has Frances been afflicted with any illnesses or medical problems over the years? What were separations and reunions with George like in the early years? Did your family have access to an affordable, high-quality preschool or nursery? What have Tamara's relationships with teachers been like? What do each of you stress in your parenting role? Does Miguel have any natural talents? Does Jamal's activity level vary depending on how tired he is, whether he is at home or at school, or how calm or stressed you are as parents? Under what circumstances, and engaged in what activities, have you found Helen's attention span to be longer? Does Jimmy have any friends with whom he is better able to share, cooperate, turn take, and suffer defeat gracefully? What is Cosmo's best friend like and how do they relate to one another?

Indeed, an overarching positive relationship with parents is foundational to render the overall therapy auspicious. There is little to be gained from sitting back, detachedly listening, with eyes and ears trained on detecting parental dysfunction or pathology. The parent needs to know that the therapist thinks of him or her as essentially a good, well-meaning person, who gets tripped up by habitual ways of overreacting or underreacting to his or her child. Put differently, we start from the premise that the parent is a good person who acts badly. Or, more comprehensively, we start from the premise that the parent is a good person who acts badly in reaction to his or her child acting badly for good reasons. It takes conscientiousness and verbal versatility to capture this bidirectional and gracious way of framing child problems: "You dislike it when you get so mad at Juan when he smarts off at you, especially when in your calmer moments you realize that he is angry because you have to work so hard as a single mother and are gone from his life a great deal"; "The more you lean into

Maria and force her to take ownership for her objectionable behavior, the more she tries to shift the blame over to you to get away from feeling ashamed in the moment. When she makes it look like you are the bad one, it burns you up inside and you rip into her. You become the sort of parent that you swore you would never be, and most of the time are not"; and, "Billy seems to use all the wrong ways of getting the attention he craves from you. Understandably, you are put off by his frenetic demands for you to witness his demonstrations, whether he is drawing, swimming, running, or even brushing his teeth. But maybe your being half there during these moments of prideful display contributes to his relentless pursuit of attention?"

These interpretative formulations contain subtle confrontations and injunctions to change. Maintaining an overall positive stance and a spirit of collaboration increases the parent's openness to the subtle confrontations and injunctions to change nested in bidirectional interpretive formulations. It also helps the parent buy into the idea that even though a child's upset is both the cause and the effect of parental reactivity, the parent is the one who assumes the greater impetus to change.

Another reason for establishing and cultivating positive rapport with parents stems from the need to gradually address their stylistic ways of expressing emotion and how these influence the child's symptoms. In my experience, children's symptoms are less apt to be associated with distinct repressed memories, isolatable parent-child conflicts, or circumscribed life traumas. Rather, more often than not, symptoms represent, in part, failed attempts to contend with or adapt to the characteristic modes of expressed emotion exhibited by key caregivers—as when a child habitually tunes a parent out who is too soft in communicating expectations, or a child acquires an overexuberant style of social engagement culled out of relentless efforts to enliven a depressed father. Whenever we discuss an emotional style we are dealing with entrenched aspects of the personality, which leave even the most sanguine of persons sensitive to criticism. Automatic ways of showing feelings can be so imperceptible to parents, yet so perceptible to the therapist, making parents liable to feeling painfully exposed when such tendencies are highlighted. Productive self-reflection is aided by the awareness that the therapist views the parent in an overall positive light and has the best interests of the parent, the child, and the parent-child relationship at heart.

It is easier to be benevolent and merciful with parents when we stay appraised of the sociocultural pressures circulating that undercut their effectiveness.

PARENTHOOD OVERBURDENED

Compassion for parents is readily mustered when we realize how Herculean a task it is to raise children well in contemporary American society. More is being asked of parents concurrent with them being caught in a "time crunch." The explosion of electronic games, computer technology, and multi-media devices has thrust a burdensome oversight role upon parents to ensure that children are not exposed to inappropriate adult material. Every new gadget seems to have its risks and benefits. The same fancy cell phone that can be used to call a parent to check in after school—even provide pictorial proof that the child is at karate and not carousing the streets—can be used to access lewd photographs on the Internet. Our capitalist culture and free speech ethos are not friendly to political lobbying for tighter control of the content and distribution of Internet resources, electronic games, television programming, and the like, that might safeguard children. This oversight role falls squarely into the laps of parents. Moreover, steady increases in homework requirements and competition for slots in respectable schools and universities have resulted in parents functioning more as would-be tutors and academic coaches. Orchestrating and supervising play dates, extracurricular activities, and "enrichment" programs, once again, requires parents to step up.

As parents scramble to accommodate these new roles, socioeconomic forces have squeezed the actual time parents have to perform them. Compared with the previous generation, parents now have less vacation time, work longer hours, and have to complete more education and training to achieve and maintain the same professional status (Ciulla, 2000). To boot, waves of corporate downsizing and outsourcing of jobs, erosion of traditional pension plans, rising health insurance costs, and expectations of geographical mobility to stay professionally competitive, all have made for a more anxious workforce (Ross, 2003).

In the past several decades, the face of children's play has changed dramatically. It has gone from being primarily kinesthetic/social, and taking place outdoors, to sedate/nonsocial, and occurring indoors (Elkind, 1994). Children, especially boys, are more apt to be cloistered at home alone, or in the company of siblings and friends, mutely playing electronic games, than to be outdoors in the neighborhood, energetically pursuing a game of cowboys and Indians. To circumvent our trumped-up fears of lawsuits and random violence, and to provide our children with a "competitive edge," we feel compelled to enroll them in an ever-expanding array of organized sports, music programs, and extracurricular activities. As mentioned, precious little parental time then has to be spent organizing and watching over children's play activities. The amount of time children have for any kind of play, let alone free play, is shrinking due to cutbacks in recess time during school hours and increased homework demands after school. The upshot of these transformations is that our children are deprived of countless occasions for socioemotional learning once embedded in the very nature of common play. Arguably, electronic games and adult-structured activities lead to more scripted and constricted social interactions than spontaneously occurring, peer-mediated, free play. Indoor, sedentary play is no match for the kinesthetic and outdoor brand as regards eliciting a range of emotions and communicative opportunities within and between children.

More alarmingly, DeGrandpre (1999) makes the compelling argument that as children become saturated with television viewing, electronic gaming, and computer use, they crave more speed, stimulation, and instant results while resisting "conditions of slowness" conducive to mindfulness, perseverance, and deep mental processing. Boys may be particularly vulnerable here. They may gravitate toward asocial, visually loaded technology which, in turn, curtails in-the-flesh social engagement and verbal sharing. The more hooked on new technologies children become, the more restless, cantankerous, and impulsive they are when their immediate social milieu demands that they be motorically still, attentive, and reflective. Such social milieus cut across the average classroom environment and place of religious worship, as well as being out in nature. As for the former, school officials and religious clerics are rushing to incorporate new technologies to educate children and administer to the faithful; the noble aim being one of staying current with the awesome informational and representational potential inherent in new technologies; the less noble aim more like a caving in to social forces to entertain and stimulate, or suffer obsolescence. As for the latter, the upcoming generation of children and families appears to be turning away from nature, preferring a virtual relationship with the outdoors to that of actually being among the flora and fauna (Louv, 2006). This despite the fact that one antidote to ADHD symptomatology appears to be playing in open areas that are lush with greenery (Taylor, Kuo, and Sullivan, 2001).

The social pressure to conform to existing play formats and avail children with trendy technology is tremendous. Parents almost have to become trenchantly countercultural to prohibit or limit children's exposure to electronic games and television, as well as balance their involvement in organized sports and extracurricular activities against opportunities for athleticism and unstructured play time that transpires organically, outside of adult supervision. Shouldering the medical and legal risks associated with improvised, spirited, peer-mediated play, sadly, has become a social reality for parents. Having a neighbor child break an arm while swinging from a tree in your backyard, with your daughter watching on, and you listening to Bach in the home office, is no longer simply an unfortunate event, or even an expectable part of childhood, but proof of the need for an "umbrella liability insurance policy." Also, it is regrettable that public institutions have scaled back on the number and type of open-play spaces and structures made available to children, for economic and legal reasons. Yet, if more enhanced socioemotional learning is to transpire, children need ample doses of outdoor, peer-mediated, kinesthetic, spontaneously occurring, imaginative, socially rich play. Diplomacy, social tact, turn taking, cooperation, knowing when to back down, aggressively asserting oneself, celebrating the superior ability of a group member, challenging the false claims of a group member bent on dominance, silencing someone who is using emotionally regressive ways of seeking attention, consoling a friend with a true need and a painful affliction—these are all socioemotional skills that are honed in the optimal peer group, outside of, or even complimentary to, parent involvement.

SYMPTOMS AS SIGNS

One of the great calamities of viewing ADHD narrowly, as a neurological disorder, is that symptoms are not seen as meaningful communications that can inform child and family change processes. Even terms like *impulsivity* and *hyperactivity* are mechanistic and genericized, connoting random, meaningless bodily movement. When we phenomenologically define terms like *impulsivity* and *hyperactivity* we start to see the human face of ADHD: "Hits brother when overexcited"; "Unable to complete homework when left alone at the dinner table"; "Can play videogames for hours, but has a short attention span in algebra and science classes"; and "Gets distracted and fidgety in noisy classroom."

Not uncommonly, the hyperactive-distracted child is a veritable canary in the coal mine, signaling parents that family life is out of balance and that aspects of the larger culture that foment disquietude have encroached too much into family life. The dominant belief is that maturation largely accounts for children developing frustration tolerance, impulse control, self-direction, and optimal emotional regulation. Children's brains are thought to be hardwired to automatically equip them to progressively order and organize experience. In short, all that the child needs for self-regulation is considered to be internal to him or her. When children persistently act silly, whine, are restless and fidgety, leave tasks unfinished, are forgetful, and emotionally implode and explode, we are instructed to think that something is awry that is purely internal to the child. However, it is more accurate to think of young children, in varying degrees, as naturally impulsive, distractible, and disorganized and in need of well-regulated family and school systems that interact favorably with their maturational predispositions in ways that promote self-restraint and cognitive engrossment. The symptomatic child is perhaps signaling a need for a different kind of socialization, in the broad sense, than he or she is currently receiving. It is socialization of emotional communication that I emphasize in this book and pick up on below. However, the requisite socialization I have in mind also extends to salutatory routines and structure in the home.

Treatment bodes well when parents are inclined to examine their lifestyles, outside work and professional commitments, obligations to extended family members, and everyday routines, to determine to what degree these keep the child symptomatic. Fixed bedtimes, nighttime rituals that induce states of restfulness, good sleep, scheduled mealtimes, ready access to parents in times of distress, ample opportunities for vigorous free play and exercise, limited television viewing and electronic game use, plain old family "down time," and planned leisurely vacations, are some run-of-the-mill inducements of self-regulation. The self-examination engaged in by parents, spawned by the child's symptoms, may eventuate in the realization that parenthood cannot be tacked on to a harried career and that over-scheduling the child, ironically, leads to an underscheduling of time for family togetherness. In no uncertain terms, the symptomatic child may be the gateway to the parents seriously questioning undesirable intergenerational parenting trends, zeroing in on the values and legacies they really want to hand down, and creating salubrious changes that raise the emotional quality of life for all family members.

From time to time, the mismatch, or serial mismatch, between a child's learning style, or cognitive stage, and the pedagogical approach adopted by his or her teachers is the overriding explanation for an ADHD profile. We are seeing more of this in our offices with the national push toward "teaching to the test" and the expectation that kindergartners be edged more rapidly into reading, writing, and formal academics. This is the child who overregulates his or her emotions at school, straining to sit still, steeling him or herself, minute by minute, in the face of cognitive and academic competency requirements that are out of step with his or her emergent learning style or developmental timetable, who at home emotionally backslides and is distractible, impulsive, labile, easily frustrated, and generally disruptive. When therapists advance the possibility that these symptoms are indications that the child might not be ready for kindergarten, or needs a more progressive educational school placement in line with his or her learning preferences, they may be doing the family a great service.

In general, conjoint exploration with the parent as to the meanings, purposes, and functions symptoms serve is indispensable for guiding what remedial action to take. Along these lines, sometimes hyperactive-disruptive behavior is the child's desperate and belated way of satisfying archaic narcissistic needs to be seen, heard, and recognized. A fuller understanding of this dynamic can sensitize the parent to tuning in more wholeheartedly during the child's exhibitionistic moments. Then again, hyperactive-disruptive behavior can signify the child's permeable emotional boundaries, whereby he or she perpetually becomes silly and behaviorally dysregulated in affectively charged everyday contexts. An awareness of this can help parents and teachers orchestrate the child's life more to reduce the frequency and intensity of such episodes, such as avoiding play dates and classroom seating assignments with overly rambunctious children, and closely monitoring the child in social situations to raise his or her awareness of when emotional thresholds have been crossed and down-regulatory steps need to be taken.

INFORMED CONSENT

There are risks inherent in a more active play approach, where states of emotional arousal and de-arousal are cycled in and out of, that parents need to be alerted to before therapy with the child commences. Touch and physical contact are not only unavoidable, but at times clinically imperative. Mock wrestling, rubber-sword fighting, or a energetic game of tag might create the stimulus conditions necessary for the child to tap and negotiate high arousal; however, they also introduce physical and verbal aggression into the equation, albeit jestingly, and harm can occur. There is always the chance that the therapist's best effort to prevent harm will be unsuccessful, whether of the physical sort, as when a child gets bumped and bruised, or the emotional sort, where a child misconstrues a therapist's playful actions as a purposeful attempt to injure. And yet, even these unfortunate events can represent potent occasions for socioemotional learning. For instance, the therapist's soft words and gentle massage of the wounded area might prompt an emotionally constricted boy to cry upon accidentally bumping his head on the corner of the couch; or, a meaningful discussion might ensue about what made a child think that a line had been crossed where the therapist went from playfully displaying aggression to actually trying to inflict real pain.

Before I engage in any vigorous play with a child I insist that furniture be moved around in ways that preserve safety. This step is not only practical but therapeutic insofar as the child has to somehow hold back his or her excitement until a safe space is constructed. It helps to stock one's office with furniture that can withstand rough treatment and whose design is friendly to the body upon contact!

Parents need to know that different forms of touch are emotional communications that can strengthen the child's attachment to the therapist, enliven and deepen the treatment, and expand the child's socioemotional repertoire. I consider rubbing a child's back, patting him or her on the head, or poking and tickling him or her to be legitimate ways of engaging children— *when they are supported by the emotional tenor of the interaction, when due regard is given to the child's age and gender, and when the gestures appear clinically useful.* Often these gestures are mutually engendered and enacted, with a child tickling back, kicking the therapist coltishly on the rear end, or sitting adjacent to the therapist while swinging his or her legs in the therapist's direction for gentle contact. It is children who lose out when we as professionals succumb to a staunch view denying any physical touch with children. However, this way of working requires that we have ironclad boundaries around acting out any latent inappropriate urges with children and develop bedrock trust with parents whereby they acknowledge, and even welcome, touch for benign and clinical reasons.

Parents also need to know that in extreme situations, the therapist might make use of physical restraint to down-regulate an agitated, out-of-control child. In fact, when the child's presenting problems encompass an amalgamation of entitlement, ruthlessness, and a susceptibility to dangerous and jarring displays of agitation or aggression, all ineffectively contained by a permissively valenced parenting system, profound therapeutic benefits can be yielded from the clinician backing up his or her warnings of physical restraint with its actual implementation when the child is behaving dangerously.

Eleven-year-old George's father, Hank, was in the habit of requesting father-son meetings when there was bad news to deliver to George that might roil and agitate him. George's mother had long since abandoned the family, leaving no traces of her whereabouts. Hank was traumatized by her departure and even after years of his own therapy and medication use was so demoralized by his life prospects that he had little energy to actively parent George. Midway during a session early on in treatment, Hank suddenly announced to George that he had changed his mind and would not buy him a new Gameboy, as earlier promised. Stepping up his angry demands in reaction to his father's refusal to purchase the Gameboy, George leaned over and slapped his father in the face. Hank recoiled in fear. I told Hank that he needed to forcibly communicate to George that his behavior was unacceptable. Hank beseeched George to stop, unconvincingly. I told George that there was a rule that nobody could get hurt in my office and that I would physically hold him to help him get control of himself if he did not stop. George ignored me and kept slapping his father. I took hold of George's wrists and physically moved him onto the office carpet, face down, arms splayed wide, with me sitting on his legs. My head was positioned far back to protect me from George's attempts to head-butt me. In time, I enlisted Hank's help to hold George firmly, and coached him to spell out the conditions for George being released: "If you keep your left leg still for a count of thirty seconds, I will let go. The same applies for me to let go of all your other limbs." I whispered in George's ear that perhaps he was more hurt than angry when he has no control over his needs being met, especially his need to see his mother who decided to disappear from his life. George began weeping uncontrollably and Hank and I went from holding him down firmly to rubbing his back.

The availability of toys dialing into aggression, such as swords, dart guns, soldiers, and army paraphernalia, may not square with a parent's value system. This might have to be discussed. An enlightening dialogue could ensue regarding the difference between combative fantasy play and actual demonstrations of violence, underscoring how opportunities for dramatic, physically enlivening, aggressive fantasy play are a valuable inroad for the average child to access and give gestural and verbal form to normal human urges. The dialogue might segue into how acting out in a quasi-aggressive way might be boys' normative way to signal underlying hurt, and how hindered boys are by their overuse of electronic games where themes are scripted, the body is relatively passive, and the violent imagery increasingly hyperrealistic.

The confidentiality question is an interesting one when the clinician chooses to work concurrently, although mostly separately, with child and parents. The justification for having sturdy treatment boundaries, structuring therapy mostly around individual contact with the child, augmented by periodic parenting sessions, is derived from the adult model of care. The idea here is that the child has a need to play out and talk through conflicts and issues pertaining to noxious events suffered at the hands of parents, and that if he or she is to be freed up to do this, parents cannot be in the know. It is presumed that the child's dependence on the parents makes him or her vulnerable to deleterious reactions should the parents become privy to honest disclosures. However, we are living in an age when a sizable population

of parents welcomes honest disclosure by their children over acting out behavior that has mystifying effects. We are also living in an age when treatment dynamics are more likely to revolve around the child's nonconflicted,
open demonstration of disfavor with a parent or parents, than the child's
conflicted, inhibited conveyance of such disfavor. This state of affairs has
ramifications for the flow of information between children and parents ob-
tained from separate sessions. To work effectively with children and parents,
the issue sometimes is not whether information will be shared, but how.
Frequently, what children need is not staid promises of privacy, but indications that their concerns will be raised with parents, with the child's ap-
proval, in ways that the parent can digest and make productive use of. Likewise, the parents can use the therapist as an emissary, so to speak, with their
endorsement, to bring up weighty issues in a way that the child is responsive to.

This is notwithstanding the fact that a play therapy approach that underscores process over content, and emphasizes here-and-now challenges to
the child's reflexive emotion regulation strategies, more so than uncovering
repressed memories and childhood traumas, minimizes the risk of deleterious disclosures of sensitive family information. In addition, information ob-
tained from parent sessions regarding the parent's crystallized ways of expressing emotion, whether rooted in the therapist's in vivo subjective
reactions to the parent, the parent's admittances, or both, when generically
and benignly shared with the child, can have therapeutic effects. Children
can find it immensely validating to have dim, although conflicted, perceptions of a parent confirmed. The wording of comments made by the therapist regarding the parent's affectivity is all important to preserve privacy.
The therapist countenances the child with his or her own general perceptions of the issues rather than resorting to a "he-said, he-did," or "she-said,
she-did" lexicon: "*I think* that your mother sometimes gets pretty worked
up when people do not agree with her. What do you think?" and "What if
your dad is someone who gets anxious easily and his worries keep him from
letting you play aggressively for fear someone will get hurt?" Speaking in
the third person, in a way that makes personally relevant insights seem like
generic feedback, can also work in favor of preserving privacy: "Fathers are
a peculiar breed, they aspire to professional success and busy themselves
greatly to provide for the family, feel guilty that they are neglecting their
children, then deal with their guilt by being too lax with discipline." Of
course, all these information-sharing principles work in the other direction
when therapeutic communications garnered from individual sessions with
the child are brought up with parents: "I wonder if your daughter is one of

those children who needs extra encouragement to persist during moments when she is about to give up?" and "The way your son plays with me makes me convinced that he needs more predictable contact with you."

When setting down the rubric for therapy, I also like to press for both parents to be present, if it is a nuclear family, as well as in divorce cases where there is a dual parenting situation and a low degree of acrimony. The ADHD child's self-regulatory needs require a high level of joint parenting. Also, parents are encouraged to hold me accountable for the quality, productivity, and effectiveness of the interventions I provide. This step can add a spirit of earnestness to the overall treatment and prompt helpful discussions about responsibility-taking.

WEARING DIFFERENT HATS

Working effectively with parents of ADHD children requires shifting in and out of different roles. The therapist needs to be prepared to flit between an explorative/supportive stance and a parenting consultant/coach stance as circumstances demand. The dynamic tension between these two stances is often great during initial visits with parents. Parents solicit answers and solutions simultaneous with there being a thin understanding of the child's life situation and little emotional capital amassed in the therapist-parent relationship to pave the way for the delivery of sensitive feedback. Insofar as the therapist is able to show genuine care, contain his or her own anxiety, resist the temptation to leap in and intervene, actively listen, acknowledge underlying feelings, remain level-headed, and so forth, the parents get an implicit lesson in self-restraint. The therapist is unwittingly modeling how to stay composed under pressure and how not to be overwhelmed or underwhelmed by the emotionality of others—the procedural knowledge constitutive of an emotionally responsive, as distinct from an emotionally reactive, way of relating that will serve the parents well. It goes without saying that during ongoing, intensive parent work the steady drumbeat of the therapist's measured, caring, reflective involvement becomes an implicit relational template upon which the parents may model their own capacities for emotional responsiveness, and which may in turn, largely prereflectively, be transmitted to the parent-child relationship, and ultimately to the child him or herself.

And yet, it is not enough to just mirror, contain, and reflect. Nor is it constructive to romantically assume that parents possess a latent parenting knowledge base that can be teased out of them with nondirective listening and sensitive prompting. Furthermore, when the parent looks to the therapist as a parenting mentor, or coach, it is misguided to see this simply as the parent abdicating his or her authority or sidestepping his or her individuality. At the same time, it is ill-advised for the therapist to become overzealous and kingly or queenly in his or her consultative role. The process in which desired changes in parenting practices are generated is a collaborative one. Sometimes it is the parent who is in the driver seat describing a problematic parent-child interaction, retrospectively examining "what went wrong," self-identifying improvements, and mustering determination to "do it right" next time. Sometimes it is the therapist who takes the reins, surmising out loud "what went wrong," as well as "what went right," offering concrete suggestions of future courses of action, nuanced phraseology, limits and consequences, and alterations in everyday routines and parenting practices. When the therapist assumes more of a foreground role in advancing solutions, the task is one of communicating whatever knowledge he or she has to offer in ways that render it personally convincing and procedurally useful to parents.

Other roles also have to be judiciously accommodated. From time to time it is fitting for the therapist to act as a child-advocate with the school, recommending classroom accommodations to enable the child to function optimally and musing aloud with teachers over preferred ways of engaging the child that heed his or her emotional thresholds and susceptibilities. There is even a place for the therapist to step in as "child development expert," to use his or her authority with certain family members or key caregivers who are culturally and characterologically suited to this, to hasten the execution of needed concrete changes in the child's life. An example of this is contained in one of the case studies at the end of the book, where a formal meeting was scheduled with an "old-fashioned" grandmother to educate her on the pitfalls of infantilizing her grandson and offer guidelines for her to build his frustration tolerance and self-directed task mastery.

STABILIZING THE ATTACHMENT SYSTEM

The overlap between ADHD symptoms and problematic parent-child attachment patterns is frequently so pronounced that assessment and modification of the latter can be important for treatment of the former. Negative acting-out behaviors that are emblematic of ADHD, such as failures to listen and follow through with adult requests, disruptiveness, and untoward attention seeking, can typify a long-standing parent-child attachment pattern in which the child has learned to amp up his or her behavior to elicit proximity and continued involvement on the part of a parent who is experienced to be inconsistently available. Even chronic clownish, overly rambunctious, reckless behavior that is disruptive, but not aggressive, can serve this same function. The vicious cycle seen by therapists of the child behaving negatively leading to parental withdrawal, causing the child to rev up his or her noxious behavior, precipitating immediate, although embittered, parental involvement is an all too common interpersonal dance. It is a dance that has primordial significance insofar as children would rather have an angry or overwrought parent in their immediate presence, than no parent, for biogenetic-evolutionary-survival reasons.

There are other types of parent-child attachment dances with effects that interface with ADHD characteristics. Inattention, forgetfulness, distractibility, and disorganized work habits can reflect overdependence in the parent-child attachment system. The child has tacitly learned that a parent's interest is piqued when the child presents as ineffectual in remembering information, staying focused, and self-completing tasks, and if he or she holds out long enough, the parent will out of expediency, convenience, or a dubious need to rescue the child provide copious amounts of assistance and direction. A dynamic where parents are continually too emotionally available at the wrong times and not available enough at the right times, from the standpoint of the child's need states, can foment general agitation, impulsivity, and high frustration in the child. Then again, a dynamic where parents are continually flat or disengaged in the face of the child's expressed needs for comfort or shared joy can lead to the child restricting and blunting his or her own affectivity to preserve a tie with the parents. This can manifest itself in the child overcontrolling his or her feelings with deleterious cognitive and socioemotional effects, ranging from problems vicariously identifying with and handling others' emotions and limited empathy skills, to difficulties attending and concentrating due to the prereflective mental labor involved in keeping his or her emotion system in shut-down mode.

In our work with parents how are these dances altered, from the parent's end? Obviously, any enduring, seemingly ossified parental ways of responding to the child have deep psychological roots in the parent's own family-of-origin attachment history and are not easily transformed. If a beginning collaborative therapist-parent working relationship evolves into an ongoing, intensive one, patterns of emotional closeness and distance, and reactions to pivotal separations and losses across generations can be explored and addressed, the cardinal focus being how these affect the unconscious relationship expectations that parents act out with their own children.

At a more surface level, there are usually habits, life commitments, and reflexive child-rearing practices that parents are amenable to changing that aggravate an already vulnerable parent-child attachment, tipping it into crisis. For instance, a preoccupied, inconsistently available single mother may take a job with unpredictable hours, shift the bulk of transporting her daughter to school over to a neighbor, skip set mealtimes, and exhaustedly fall asleep in her daughter's bed in a seemingly random pattern through the week. The child, ordinarily restive due to having little leverage over when, for how long, and in what way her mother is physically and emotionally present, now becomes behaviorally unmanageable. The mother, resentful that she is having to parent all alone, with a daughter who does not appreciate her efforts to keep the family afloat financially, finds solace in endless telephone conversations with a string of friends, which further alienates and inflames the daughter. Interventions in this situation might be having the mother question the pros and cons of a job with unpredictable hours, designate (with input from the daughter) and keep to set days when the mother drives the daughter to school and is available for mealtimes, base any co-sleeping arrangement on the daughter's needs and age, and talk on the phone when the daughter is asleep or away from home.

In my experience, the average parent is intrigued by and receptive to child-rearing advice culled from attachment theory. There is something primal to the simple idea that in times of troubles we all, especially children, need someone to stand by us. Parents tend to buy into this basic idea. The more complicated endeavor is getting parents to see how their child's impulsive and unruly behavior signals neediness within the child and is a desperate ploy to have the parents be near him or her. It may seem counterintuitive to the parent that a child's rejecting, hostile actions actually signal a misguided desire for parent-child closeness. Reflecting on and accommodating to the particular ways in which the child might need the parent to "stand by" him or her in moments of distress is also an area of challenge for parents. For instance, many mothers hurtfully recoil when their sons are nonresponsive to their attempts to have an emotional discussion about sources of distress in their sons' lives. The preferred mode of solace for these sons might be some predictable time alone with their mothers, where the focus of the discussions are games and toys that pique the boys' interests. These "shoulder-to-shoulder" intimate moments may be the backdrop for pointed emotional disclosures.

Generally speaking, throughout childhood, children are attachment sensitive and need some measure of control over when they have contact with parents, the degree of emotional closeness or distance that contact entails, and how long it lasts. This attachment sensitivity becomes magnified when family transitions and crises raise the child's anxiety concurrent with parents being more emotionally and physically absent. As therapists, we need to be mindful of this state of affairs in our therapeutic probing and advice giving: Does a mother's or father's career demands and work hours introduce an unintentional degree of randomness into when they are able to be with the child and for how long? Can realistic changes to this be made that do not compromise the family's economic well-being? Is there a way for parents to have firmer boundaries between their work and parental roles, such that when they are with the child they are more emotionally present and better able to give him or her doses of undivided attention, and when they are at work they put to rest any worries about the child? What parent-child interactions and activities typically bring the child joy? Can more of these be predictably built into family life? How are everyday separations and reunions handled? Are school dropoffs and pickups rushed? Do they leave enough time to touch on and momentarily process fleeting feelings of anxiety the child might be experiencing or to thoughtfully respond to any oppositional pushing-away behavior? If there are to be prolonged separations by a parent, is the child given advanced notice and concrete ways of staying in touch with the parent, and allowed to participate actively in the reunion, if wished? When should the parent's bed turn into the family bed, a "safe base" for the child to retreat to during anxious times, or when should it remain the parent's bed, lest co-sleeping infantilize and overstimulate the child?

As outlined above in this book, the father-child bond can be strengthened with ready access to vigorous play experiences. Fathers are apt to push their children, especially their sons, to the outer reaches of physicality and into heightened states of arousal, whether it be excitement or aggression, during play. The child's emotional development can profit from these experiences due to the multiple occasions they offer for tapping and managing emotional highs and lows in concert with the father's up-regulatory and down-regulatory play gestures. It need not be the biological father who is the valued playmate, but someone who assumes a paternal role in the child's life with constancy and predictability. We are not fishing in barren waters when we accord a modicum of causality for boys' restlessness and agitation to deprivation of vigorous paternal play. Fortunately, many men tend to be primed to want concrete solutions and are open-minded when the therapist prescribes more active paternal play, especially when given a rational explanation for its benefits!

DISCIPLINE

The etymology of the word *discipline* is similar to that of *disciple* and touches on notions of instructing, mentoring, and emulating. As such, discipline is more than a course of action that is meted out when a child misbehaves. It encompasses the totality of the parent's way of being with the child to preserve his or her safety and assist with building frustration tolerance, recovery from implosive and explosive emotional episodes, navigation of conflict, and general regulation of his or her emotional life. In our encounters with parents it is useful to think of discipline in this way since it dramatizes the need for them to think of themselves as the preeminent socializing agents in the child's life whose actions are inextricably linked to the child's acquisition of self-discipline. This is particularly true when working with parents of ADHD children, where the rudiments of self-discipline—perseverance, engrossment, openness to instruction, and emotional versatility and self-restraint—are underdeveloped.

Parental Emotional Responsiveness

Parents' incremental improvement in reducing their reactivity in heated emotional exchanges with their children is a centerpiece for the child acquiring emotional versatility and self-restraint. Even under the best of circumstances, young children's egocentricity and diffuse emotional boundaries result in them zeroing in and fixating on parent's anger and frustration during conflicts, showing a remarkable obliviousness to how their own behavior has ignited the parent. The ungracious comment, "Why are you being so mean to me?" made to the irate parent by the child who has been stingingly disrespectful is well-worn. The permeable emotional boundaries and ego vulnerabilities of ADHD children can set them up to be flooded, more so than just infused, by the negative mood states of parents during conflicts. This can result in emotional blunting, use of physical or verbal aggression to impel the parent to back off, or a variety of other self-protective reactive steps. Any opening to have the child listen to or self-reflect on his or her part in the imbroglio is lost.

This negative cycle can be avoided or broken the more the parent is able to embody and exemplify emotional responsiveness, rather than reactivity, during tense parent-child interactions. As with attachment patterns, stylistic ways of handling strong emotion have deep psychological roots and are not so easily mutable. However, there are communication skills and tactics the therapist can offer the parent to utilize when under duress to embolden the parent's capacities for differentiated emotional responsiveness. One is "empathy coaching" or being "an amateur therapist." The parent is advised to step back during conflicts, actively listen, and make reflective comments as to what the parent thinks the child might be feeling. This may seem alien to the parent and he or she might have to "fake it until you make it." Parents often fall into the trap of assuming that when they are acknowledging a child's feelings they are ipso facto agreeing with or acquiescing to the child. The parent needs to be brought to the realization that he or she can acknowledge a child's underlying feelings, while still disagreeing with the child's point of view and refusing to accede to the child's demands: "Marjorie, I know how much you like watching the Simpsons on TV and discussing the episode with your friends the next day. I can see you are so upset that I am asking you to turn the TV off and get ready for bed. It hurts me too to think that you might not be able to share in the discussion with your friends tomorrow. However, it is your bed time and I need you to head upstairs."

It is also useful to hone the parent's awareness that he or she can acknowledge a child's feelings while challenging their objectionable outward expression: "Marjorie, I understand that you are angry at me. I had to switch off the TV for you because you were stalling. It might feel to you that I am being bossy. But, I don't like it when you storm off and slam doors when you are angry. I would rather that you tell me how angry you are with words. If you want to be alone for now and have your door closed you need to open it and close it more quietly for me. How many minutes do you need to calm yourself before I come upstairs to talk with you about what just happened between us?"

Lessons learned by the child on how the outward expression of feelings, the emotion words used, voice tone, and overall comportment all have wished for or unwished for interpersonal effects are best learned situationally and experientially, during and after poignant parent-child interactions; not in a lecturing, didactic manner, rather, such that the parent sensitively provides subjective feedback to the child with due regard to aspects of the interaction that indicate whether the child is tuned in or out. Modulation of speech prosody, short phrases, "I" statements, whether to maintain eye contact or use touch, position oneself close or distant to the child, all become relevant in parental communications. This is the best means for the child to assimilate the natural socioemotional consequences of his or her actions. The parent can also hint at alternative verbal and nonverbal expressions the child might use, or might have used, to improve his or her chances of being listen to, heard, understood, and responded to. The therapist can pepper these ideas and thoughts into discussions with the parents. The therapist can also coax the parent to self-reflect on and playfully rehearse with the therapist optimal modes of delivering subjective feedback to the child; not "in the abstract," but salient to everyday scenarios the parent commonly finds him or herself in with the child.

As parent work unfolds, the therapist can listen in for possible ways in which the parent's emotional reactivity is governed by projection and projective identification. Aspects and tendencies of the child the parent finds so unpleasant may be personified by the parent him or herself, although disavowed. Opportunities for drawing these comparisons during parent work—replete with sensitivity, candor, humor, and goodwill—can have humbling effects and bolster the parent's compassion for the child. Then again, projective identification may be operating whereby the parent is unconsciously and overzealously locked into needing a child to be a good student, a fine athlete, an obedient person, or all of these, incessantly reacting with disfavor when the child shows any frailties in these areas. It is as if the parent needs to keep these qualities and life pursuits alive in the child in order for them to have any viability for the parent him or herself. The child's imperfections are not countenanced with ordinary disappointment but received by the parent as a massive personal failure. The loss of self-other boundaries here can be delicately addressed with cognitively oriented interventions: "You were once a great student and athlete, and naturally you want your son to be the same. But, maybe his strengths lie in other areas?" and "You were the sort of kid who obeyed and respected his father and this seemed to work out for you. Or did it, all of the time? Were there times that you felt your being obedient compromised your ability to be true and honest to yourself, or make you too passive? I wonder if your son's talking back is his awkward way of being honest with his feelings and making sure that he will not be too passive of a person?"

In cases where parents' ill-acquired self-other differentiation, characterological issues, or mood instability severely foreshortens their ability to refrain from "fighting fire with fire," finding them perpetually striking back emotionally at the child when he or she is intractable, a central part of parent work becomes establishing enough credibility to float recommendations that the parent undergo a medication evaluation, seek personal therapy, or both. Periodically, the therapist simply has to "lay in wait" until a major parent-child conflict causes the parent so much anguish that he or she feels there is no option but to seek a more rigorous level of intervention.

Aiding Emotional Recovery

Parents are often at their most stymied when faced with a child who is susceptible to implode in shame, explode in rage, or be in the throngs of a state of clownish excitement. It would not be completely off the mark to view these episodes metaphorically as types of emotional seizures and to consider them no more able to be willed away or commanded to stop than an actual seizure is. Reestablishment of emotional equilibrium requires much down-regulatory input from the caregiving surround. Letting the child ride out a negative mood state alone often leads to a more protracted situation, where the child is unduly subjected to painful emotional over-stimulation. Refraining from priming mutual opportunities for pardon and reparation can deprive the child of valuable lessons in relational upkeep. When these tendencies occur excessively, they run the risk of convincing the child that his feelings are beyond the pale of human relationships to handle. Despair, despondency, social friction, and cognitive and emotional disorganization, regrettably, all become possibilities.

Parents are encouraged to keep a log of, or be otherwise prepared to come to sessions with rich descriptions of incidences when the intensity and duration of a child's emotional reactions seemed conspicuously out of proportion to the precipitating event. A retrospective analysis of these events is conducted to unpack elements that might have been narcissistically injurious for the child that were or were not recognized, and what the parent did or did not do to attenuate the child's mood state and help him or her transition out of it. The therapist switches back and forth between prompting a then-and-there recounting and analysis of the event under investigation and facilitating a here-and-now processing of the parent's feelings as they recall the event. Helping the parents contain and make sense of feelings that arise during these disclosures is fundamental to sharpen and texture their memory of events, acknowledge any contribution they may have made to the child's emotional episode, and stay cognitively flexible in entertaining ideas about possible future ameliorative actions in similar situations with the child.

The therapist might even use countertransferential responses gleaned from his or her individual play therapy sessions with the child to confirm the parents' perceptions of the child and offer possible down-regulatory actions for the parents to take when the child is emotionally overstimulated: "I, too, have noticed that Helen has a short fuse when I disallow her to engage in an activity that I think is risky. What I finds helps is to stand far away, rather than close to her, say something softly that recognizes her sense of outrage, wait for her to make one of her usual sarcastic comments, meeting it with one of my own, and eventually direct her to other activities I know she likes."

Parental level of affectivity, voice tone, speech prosody, choice of words, distal versus proximal position to the child when he or she was upset, and efficacy at ushering the child out of a heightened positive or negative mood state are all dimensions of the retrospective analysis and advice-offering process.

The task is often to move the parent in the direction of first showing empathy for the child's injured pride embedded in emotional outbursts. It is also getting the parent to realize that his or her gestures and verbal communications in helping the child transition out of heightened emotional states influence the self-talk and down-regulatory behavioral options available to the child to self-recover over time.

Full retrospective analysis of a mutually hurtful incident in the parent-child relationship requires a focus on any attempts at reparation and restoration of affiliation that were made by the parent, or the child. Was the parent able to take the lead and acknowledge the part he or she played in the hurt caused, thereby modeling good responsibility-taking behavior? Were any apologies made based on mutual readiness and genuineness, or were they made to gloss over smoldering conflict? Did the parent fall prey to using any totalistic and accusatory statements (i.e., "You never want to own up to the hurt you cause"), thereby closing off opportunities for the child to take ownership for his or her behavior? Were there any indications of the child wishing to make amends embedded in his or her postconflict conduct, no matter how awkward or obscure? How might the child have responded if coaxed to take ownership for his or her "part"?

Emotionally compromised children will often descend into shameful self-loathing once their rage has passed, which can put the parent in conflict regarding holding the child responsible for his or her original actions. It is a virtuous skill to know how to caringly talk the child around, and gauge when the time is right and what degree of emotion is needed to face the child with his or her unacceptable actions. Laboring with parents to define possible word choices for use in these torturous moments can be invaluable: "You are not a bad person, and certainly not an evil person. You are a good kid and I love you very much. That said, you are a good kid who made some bad choices, and when you are feeling better we need to look at those."

Another area worthy of therapeutic discussion with parents pertains to how positively valenced redirective gestures are important to help children transition out of negative mood states. This is a delicate endeavor, since the parent's attempts to inject levity into an interaction, conversationally redirect the child, or steer him or her toward a soothing activity, if mistimed or employed in asynchronous ways, can have emotionally invalidating effects.

In reasonably well-organized households, where parents have been indefatigable in their efforts to be judicious, calm, actively restorative, and positively redirective in dealing with the child's frequent emotional outbursts, yet they persist unabated or even worsen, the diagnostic gaze of the therapist and parent may need to be trained on the possibility of a mood disorder or other serious psychiatric condition in need of pharmacological intervention. Having said this, we always have to counterbalance the suspicion of more serious mood disturbance against the realization that collapsing and becoming emotionally undone can be a healthy form of regression for every child. Controlling his or her emotions at school to keep a still body, and be a good pupil and likable classmate, can be enough to ripen the child's need to emotionally unravel at home. Paradoxically, the child's tendency to fall apart at home can speak to how secure and safe he feels with his or her family. The magnitude and the frequency of the child's outbursts at home may be explained, in part, by the degree of emotional self-restraint and kinesthetic inhibition, as well as unbidden cognitive tasks, his or her school experience compels, relative to the child's chronological and maturational age. Of course, when the child presents radically differently across home and school environments, we as therapists always need to contain any anxiety we, or the parents, may feel about the child fitting the criteria for a more serious psychiatric disturbance. Needless to say, we also always have to rule out the more commonplace reasons for the child's labile mood states (i.e., transitory fatigue, chronic fatigue, over and understimulating households and schools, caregiver reactivity) before we reach for our psychiatric manuals.

Task Scaffolding

The need to scaffold tasks to bring them within the efficacy domain of the child, measured against his or her transitory mood state, age, and ability level cannot be emphasized enough with parents of ADHD children. The types of tasks I have in mind here are the stuff of everyday life and range from self-dressing, proper personal hygiene, chores and bed making, to board game playing, drawing/construction projects, and homework assignments. Nonintrusively disallowing the child to quit, or leave off finishing a task, rechanneling his or her attention back to it, making it alluring, reconfiguring it to make it achievable with moderate effort, being emotionally responsive to the child's mounting frustration while still pressing for task continuance, praising the child's efforts and final achievement—are all indispensable parental actions. Obviously, the parent has to pick his or her battles, and the child's level of fatigue and agitation should always be considered to circumvent an insurmountable situation.

A seemingly perpetual risk for parents of ADHD children is to either leap in and unilaterally complete tasks for them, or be complicitous with their incompletion or abandonment of tasks by storming off in anger. While these are understandable pitfalls, given the ADHD child's distractibility and task resistance, neither of them help the child build requisite frustration tolerance and incrementally acquire greater self-efficacy.

Limit Testing

Parents often fail to grasp that there is a lived-experiential dimension to the setting and enforcement of limits whereby the child needs to test a limit and the parent actually has to enforce it, for it to be a real limit. The ubiquitous parental anthem, "I've told him a thousand times to stop hitting his brother and he keeps at it," is testament to the common parental belief that issuing a directive should be sufficient to beget compliance from children. It also reflects the common parental belief that warnings and the mere saying of "or else" ought to be enough to keep the child in check. It is the enforcement of the "or else" part that legitimizes the warning for the child. Helping the parent realize that the child's limit testing is inevitable and, in fact, sets the occasion for a more thoroughgoing internalization of rules and expectations, can lessen the parent's penchant for reactivity in situations where the child opposes and transgresses.

Time-outs

The harm-reduction potential of using time-outs can be spelled out for parents. Firmly instructing the child to go to an appointed quiet place or space in the house (i.e., a "calming chair") can separate parent and child before a tense situation becomes an inflammatory one, allowing the parent to regain sufficient composure and objectivity to reflect on reasons for the child's upset and set in motion a level-headed course of action. Parents can even self-impose a time-out, all the while articulating what they are feeling in the moment and specifying a desire to back off to prevent the conflict from worsening. This both models self-restraint for the child and associates time-outs less with punishment and more with self-control. From the child's end, time-outs sometimes offer the emotional space necessary to feel guilt over his or her behavior and imagine reparative gestures that might, in turn, mollify the parent. However, this requires that the parent be attuned and receptive to any reparative intentions imbuing the child's post-time-out maladroit behavior: "Mommy, do you know where my flower tee-shirt is?"; "Daddy, the dog just went poop"; "Daddy, Mary (sister) just came into my room when I was on time-out and stole some of my Legos."

THE MEDICATION QUESTION

Parents are often in a quandary whether to pursue a medication option with their ADHD child. So much confusing and contradictory information pervades the social discourse on the benefits and safety of ADHD medications. I concentrate on psychostimulants (Ritalin [methylphenidate], Dexedrine [dextroamphetamine], and Adderall [dextroamphetamine plus levoamphetamine]) in my discussion because this class of medications remain the most widely prescribed for ADHD (Gallardo, 2005)

On the one hand, there is the medicalized perspective, in which ADHD is framed strictly as a "brain disorder," treatable first and foremost, if not exclusively, with medication. To paraphrase the oft-quoted idea, one should no more deny an ADHD child a psychostimulant than a diabetic child insulin. Parents are advised to weather medication side effects, usage risks are downplayed, and benefits are underscored. Since psychostimulants tend to have rather immediate global effects in reducing impulsivity and enhancing cognitive vigilance, they may have special appeal to harried parents desperate for speedy resolution.

However, this medicalized approach obscures the fact that there is no medical test for ADHD that categorically differentiates ADHD and non-ADHD children. It is now commonly accepted that psychostimulants boost the attention and concentration of ADHD and non-ADHD children alike and that a positive response to medications is no proof of a preexisting disorder. Also, a casual approach to prescribing psychostimulants belies how noxious the side effects can be and, arguably, hinders parents' willingness to enter into a cost-benefit type discussion with their physician regarding the pros and cons of using a given medication with their child, based on its "side-effect profile." Typical side effects to psychostimulants documented in the literature are: appetite loss, insomnia, mood changes, weight loss, irritability, stomach aches, and headaches (Fitzpatrick, Klorman, Brumaghim, and Borgstedt, 1992; Swanson, McBurnett, Christian, and Wigal, 1995). Tics and compulsive behaviors have been observed in subpopulations of ADHD children placed on higher doses of psychostimulants (NIH Consensus Statement, 1998). Moreover, certain ADHD medications are now required to carry a "black box" warning label alerting users to the increased risks for hypertension, cardiac arrest, and stroke (Walraich, 2006).

Indeed, the justifiability of using medication as a sole treatment option for ADHD has come under empirical scrutiny in recent years. Several significant studies have demonstrated how a combination of medication and psychosocial interventions has superior therapeutic advantages for ADHD children over medication alone (Connors, Epstein, and Marsh, 2001; Pelham et al., 2005). Perhaps of greater concern is the dearth of research on the long-term effects of psychostimulant use, as well as the trend to not include a placebo group and to fail to publish unfavorable findings in studies of ADHD medications (Schachter et al., 2001).

It is also important to remember that medication does not somehow download social learning into the child. The medicated ADHD child may be more attentive and less impulsive and aggressive in global ways, but no more able to start and sustain a mutually satisfying conversation with peers, laugh at a joke in a socially acceptable manner, emotionally process failure experiences without alienating others, access a range of verbal and gestural ways of expressing anger, or implicitly judge what degree of excitement will cue a friend to join in a game. Not surprisingly, a variety of researchers point to the questionable effectiveness of medications for remedying the socialization difficulties of ADHD children (Murphy, 2005; Whalen and Henker, 1991).

These ideas and findings would seem to dispel any belief in medications being a panacea, or risk-free treatment agent, for most ADHD children. This said, it would be wrong-headed to dismiss the mountain of evidence substantiating the beneficial effects of psychostimulants in alleviating core symptoms of ADHD, such as hyperactivity, impulsivity, distractibility, and reduced attention/concentration, at least over the short term (Charach, Ickowicz, and Schachar, 2004; Gorman, Klorman, Thatcher, and Borgstedt, 2006; Klimkeit et al., 2005).

All things considered, what can be gleaned from the literature to advise parents should they have general questions regarding if and when a medication consultation with a physician might be a worthwhile step to take to assist their child? Before I answer this question, perhaps I should share some thoughts on the very notion of the therapist placing him or herself in a position to comment to parents on medication issues with ADHD children. Obviously, no nonphysician therapist has any legal and professional authority to make direct recommendations regarding specific medications and their effects for any individual child. However, nonphysician therapists might have a clinical and ethical responsibility to avail parents with opportunities to discuss fears and concerns regarding their child being placed on medication and exchange information regarding general research-based medication findings. As for the latter, given their educational background conducting and analyzing empirical research, psychologists may be uniquely qualified to play a consultative role with parents about overall patterns in the literature regarding medication effects. It is the rare physician who has the time and training to address parents' depth psychological attitudes toward their children being on medications, as well as comment on complex trends in the literature regarding pharmacological and nonpharmacological treatments of ADHD. For that matter, it is the rare physician whose educational background prepares him or her to formally and intricately assess children's psychosocial, cognitive, and academic development, and distinguish between normative and nonnormative variations. Consequently, it is not enough for the nonphysician therapist to always fall back on the old safety maneuver of directing all questions and concerns about medication use to the child's medical doctor.

Some useful guidelines are available to facilitate therapist-parent discussions regarding when a medication referral might be indicated. These guidelines are based on a survey of over one hundred psychologists and physicians designated as ADHD experts (Connors, et al., 2001). These experts recommend that medications not be a first-order treatment for preschool-age children, or those whose ADHD is mild and characterized more by everyday socialization difficulties and a tendency to internalize, rather than externalize, emotional pain—presumably, a susceptibility to shyness, anxiety, dysphoria, emotional implosion, or shame. Psychosocial interventions are underscored in such cases. A medication referral arises as a more distinct possibility when the child's ADHD is severe, and when the child externalizes emotional pain, such that explosiveness, aggression, oppositionality, and chronic social friction dominate the clinical picture. In such cases medication may afford advantages, over and above psychosocial interventions, to more swiftly bring about changes in the child's overt behavior necessary to preserve his or her school placement and reduce crisis-level discord within the family.

6

CLINICAL CASE PRESENTATIONS

C ontained in these pages are two extensive case studies that show the human face of ADHD and its remediation through participatory play therapy. To preserve the confidentiality of the children and families involved I have changed names, factual information and, at times, details about the child's actual life situation. However, as much as possible I try to recount circumstances and occurrences as validly as possible to enable the reader to appreciate the complex interplay of affect-dysregulation dynamics, narcissistic vulnerabilities, attachment-related concerns, student-pedagogy mismatches, and other factors raised earlier in this book, that often emerge in therapy with ADHD children. I refrain from any deep analysis of the play therapy interventions covered, instead inserting some surface analysis here and there to punctuate my narratives, preferring to leave it up to the reader to reflect on the meanings nested in my descriptions; meanings, I hope, that derive from how I conceptualize the etiology and treatment of ADHD throughout the book. In both cases I detail how closely I worked with parents and assumed an advocacy role vis-à-vis ensuring the child's optimal school situation. This may be somewhat surprising to the psychodynamically oriented clinician who is more accustomed to working individually with the child, with outside parenting sessions and school contacts being ancillary and less frequent. However, I trust that the reader will grasp how neither depth nor effectiveness in the child's individual play therapy need be compromised by ongoing close contact with parents and involvement with teachers and school officials.

SAM

Sam, the product of an African American mother and Asian American father, was brought in to see me a few months before his seventh birthday. His mother, Frances, was concerned about Sam's frequent references to feeling sad and being picked on by peers at school. Sam's teachers had noted a proclivity to abort tasks if he was unable to show immediate mastery of them and a habit of positioning himself as a victim with peers, lamenting over their unfairness and meanness with him. He was also minimally able to switch out of states of exuberance transitioning from the playground to the classroom, rendering it almost impossible for him to sit quietly and complete academic work after recess and lunch. Also worrisome was Sam's quickness to resort to physical aggression during conflicts—hitting, biting, and kicking—although this occurred almost exclusively in his after-school program where there was less structure and adult supervision, and where Sam was grouped with younger as well as older children evincing varying levels of impulse control.

In a consultation with Sam's teacher she informed me that he was prone to rising out of his seat at will and strolling around the classroom. On more than one occasion, on impulse, he had sped out of the classroom to catch up with an older friend whom he had seen sauntering past the window. His perceived short attention span made it difficult for him to remember and follow directions, and his disruptive behavior necessitated frequent visits to the principal's office. Sam was often observed by his teacher rifling through his pockets and playing with small toys that he had sneaked to school when he was supposed to be participating in group activities with other second graders. He attended a religious school with a strict behavior code and in my phone calls with his teacher I got the distinct impression that she saw it as her personal mission to reform him. She disclosed to me during a phone consultation that her youngest son was diagnosed with ADHD and she had "whipped him into shape."

A family background inquiry revealed that Sam's father was an international businessman who kept mistresses around the world. Frances had become increasingly disenchanted with the direction her life was taking around the time of her pregnancy with Sam. She was growing tired of the relentless traveling with her husband, of his drug use and infidelity. She had hoped against hope that her marriage to him would stabilize and cement their life together. Instead, the marriage was short-lived and within weeks of Sam's second birthday, Frances moved with him across country to break away from her husband and start life anew. From then on Sam's visits with his father were seldom and occurred strictly on his father's terms. A typical scenario had his father calling from a local airport announcing that he had a stopover en route to a business meeting. He would insist on seeing Sam, showering him with presents that were purchased without much forethought at the airport, and leaving as abruptly as he had arrived. Sam only ever spoke of his father in glowing terms and adamantly opposed any negative characterizations of him made by Sam's mother.

Frances was one of six children born to middle-class African American parents who worked long hours to ensure the economic survival of the family. She was raised essentially by a variety of extended-family members. She excelled at music in school, eventually becoming a successful musician in the entertainment industry. She was perpetually guilty over being unavailable to Sam and repeating her parents' mistake of allowing their careers to eclipse their parental roles. It was not uncommon for Sam to endure long school days, going from regular school to an after-school program, being picked up by a nanny and not seeing his mother until the late evening. Frances confessed that she routinely opted not to tell Sam in advance when she had career trips planned, preferring to depart before he had arisen on those mornings, rather than endure the "huge scene" that would erupt anytime she told Sam of travel plans in advance. Frances was convinced that everyone benefited by her calling from the airport to say goodbye once Sam was awake. Guilt over her unavailability due to career obligations led to Frances being overly permissive in tolerating Sam's rages and unrepentant bossiness. Frances was also given to feed off Sam's negative mood states, becoming sad when he was sad, and angry when he was angry, only to capitulate to Sam's demands out of fear of emotionally damaging him or adding to his already beleaguered life situation. Her childrearing approach, honed in dialogues with her countercultural-leaning friends, reinforced her belief that what children needed was love and nurturance, and their obedience and respect would naturally follow.

In our parenting work together, I expressed concern over Sam being on the young end for second grade, and about the mismatches between the school's pedagogical approach and Sam's current socioemotional proclivities. Frances disclosed that the decision to place Sam in his current school had been rushed into, chiefly governed by the fact that Sam's best friend attended it. He was the one who had begged to attend it and she had acquiesced. As it turned out, Sam had been enrolled in and withdrawn from three preschools and two elementary schools based on Sam's fickle requests and her many career-related relocations. I offered to do a formal assessment with Sam to determine his current level of cognitive, academic, and psychosocial functioning so that Frances and I could have a comprehensive discussion regarding an optimal school placement for Sam, all things considered. Since Frances had the economic resources to place Sam in any school that would accept him, she was amenable to this. Her endorsement of this plan also spoke to her guilt around being professionally preoccupied at the expense of Sam having a better quality of life. These dynamics were fueled by the death of her teenage nephew in a gang shooting. This event had thrown her into a sort of existential parenting crisis.

My assessment concluded that, although Sam had a high-average IQ and was above grade level in most academic areas, his socioemotional functioning ill-suited him for the second grade, especially in a school that had a strict behavior code, overemphasized rote, sedentary learning and "teaching to the test," and underemphasized the more kinesthetic, hands-on, individualized approach that Sam seemed to need. Frances and I researched local schools that posed to be a better fit for Sam and I agreed to write letters of recommendation when the application period arose substantiating Sam's academic/cognitive adeptness. In the meantime, I consulted with the school principal to advocate on Sam's behalf, imploring her to place him in a second grade class with a male teacher whom Frances had heard through the parenting grapevine was both nurturing and "ran a tight ship." The principal agreed to this and the switchover proved to be auspicious inasmuch as Sam complained less about going to school and paid attention in class more. His antics were more apt to be ignored or viewed as expectable behaviors to be worked with, rather than detestable behaviors to be eliminated, because in the words of Frances, "his teacher gets what boys are all about."

In the early weeks of therapy, Sam insisted upon having his mother escort him to my office from the waiting room. He presented as shy, fearful, noncommunicative, and emotionally constricted, although intrigued by my playful attempts to draw him away from his mother, whom he mostly shadowed. We repeatedly played the squiggle game (Winnicott, 1971) on a white eraser board and Sam's emerging attachment to me was reflected in his overt joy seeing my squiggles steadily match or amplify the wildness of his, with me repeatedly turning his wild squiggles into something recognizable. This interchange found me playfully and conspicuously expressing my mounting excitement with flashy/swishy lines in response to his mounting excitement and use of flashy/swishy lines. I saw this as him testing to see if I could manage his interpersonally engendered emotional intensity and accept him at his most excitable. The surging wildness of Sam's squiggles appeared to be contingent on my complementarity, me synchronistically feeding off of his affectivity with due regard to his potential for being overwhelmed and need for containment.

Within time, Sam showed a preference to have sessions alone with me. This was facilitated by me suggesting that if he wanted to "say hello" to his mother he could knock once on the wall separating my office from the waiting room, twice if he was missing her, and three times if he needed his mother to run to the office immediately. Frances knew of this plan and agreed to match Sam's single knock with one of her own, broadcasting a "hi" back, or two knocks if she was also missing Sam. At the same time it was made evident to Sam and his mother that she might want to enjoy reading a magazine in the waiting room and not want to return knocks. I wanted to sow the seed for Sam being able to respect his mother as a separate person with her own needs, simultaneous with giving Frances permission to be her own person and not worry about his safety outside of her care. Everyone agreed that if Sam knocked three times it meant that he desperately needed his mother to deliver herself speedily to the office door. Just knowing he could exercise this emergency operation if needed seemed to be enough for Sam, since he never ever used it during therapy. He did, however, make liberal use of the single knock system, which his mother consistently responded to on cue.

There was a quasi-didactic dimension to the weekly parenting sessions I had with Frances in the beginning months of treatment. She was genuinely fascinated by the knocking system we devised and what it revealed about Sam. In layman's terms, as best I could, I sketched out relevant separation-individuation concepts and attachment theory ideas that would shed light on matters. I suggested that since Sam's father was essentially absent from his life he had nobody to identify with in ways that might embolden his pulling away from her. I proffered that my sessions with him appeared to be a safe context to rework his anxiety around separations and reunions. He already confidently expected that I would be there to join with him at the beginning of sessions and she to reunite with him at the end of sessions. This basic interchange had anxiety-reducing effects for him.

We discussed how his father's sudden appearances and disappearances as well as Frances' erratic travel schedule might elevate Sam's overall level of separation anxiety, as well as aggression. I explained how young children with a history of abandonment and prolonged separations can carry inside much anxiety and agitation that is aggravated if they continue to have limited control over key caregivers' coming and going. Frances became tearful when I mentioned that Sam probably felt that she was all he had, his veritable lifeline, and each time there was a separation, he might feel in some small way the terrible fear that she was never going to return. She remembered feeling similarly as a child when her mother would leave for work before sunrise and return well after sunset. I gently proposed: "I suppose you awoke many times with her not there. Perhaps because that happened so many times and you made the adjustment, you feel that Sam should make the adjustment when you travel and leave without telling him before he is awake." I stressed that I was not saying this to instill guilt, but to help us rethink parenting practices for the better. Frances was galvanized to change day-to-day parenting habits that our explorations together deemed less than optimal. On her short list were pledges to no longer leave on trips unannounced; reduce travel to what was absolutely necessary to sustain her career; start each week off by sitting Sam down and sketching out when and at what time she would pick him up from school; purchase a child-friendly cell phone that he could call her directly on at designated times; and generally keep Sam informed as to her commitments and whereabouts.

Not surprisingly, in time Sam's marked excitability stood out in treatment. His idealization of me was thinly veiled and his elation and expansive mood state during visits with me would spill over, resulting in him becoming disorganized in his verbalizations and outward behavior. I would comment on how happy he seemed spending time playing and talking with me, and how hard it must be to wait all week for the happy times we had together. Or, how thrilling it seemed to be for him to spend time alone with me and have my full attention, since there were times when he did not have his mother's full attention, and certainly not his father's, when he needed it most. Or, that he was so happy to be spending time with me that his happy feelings bubbled out all over the place. Once, I playfully gestured that perhaps we should walk around my office gathering up his bubbly, happy feelings so that there was room for us to play. This would find us both skipping around my office, me slightly less ebullient than he, imagining we were collecting up bubbles.

Sam's idealization of me, and the affects surrounding it, had to be handled with exquisite sensitivity since the potential for his feeling exposed for being so needy was always just below the surface.

This said, the dissolution of self-control that Sam experienced in relation to intense positive feelings was not restricted to his idealization of me and the expansive mood state surrounding it. It was more emblematic of his affect-regulation style. On those occasions when his initial excitement and disorganized behavior flourished into unbridled silliness and goofiness, with my confirmatory recognition of his feelings simply serving to rev him up, my stance became more directive. Typically, I would narrow his selection of games to those that were more low-key yet still allowed for a modicum of active play (ring tossing, building with Legos), assert that I desired to play together but was worried that he was so full of energy that it might be difficult for him to effectively play any game, or self-disclose how much all the excitement was wearing me down, and ask him to join me in a snack break. I posed interpretations to him, springboarding off my here-and-now reactions, aimed at bolstering his overall social awareness: "Sam, I wonder if your friends feel what I'm feeling right now. This boy is sure fun to play with, but when will he slow down so we can have a break!" and "Sam, I'm tired and want to play a different game, one where I can sit down and be calm in my body. I wonder if your friends are able to let you know when they would rather play quieter, calmer games, when they get tired of playing energetic games with you?"

Sam was also prone to upsurges of intense negative affect. Early on in treatment during a session in which his mother and I sat adjacent to each other on the floor watching on, Sam attempted to assemble an anatomical puzzle made out of sponge body parts, his frustration mounting all the while. He got up and started to kick me in jest. Playfulness turned to agitation, as his kicks became attempts to actually harm me. I started by wondering out loud why he was becoming angry all of a sudden: maybe he was angry because he was unable to put the puzzle together right away (challenge to his omnipotence needs), or because he was used to having his mother all to himself and did not like sharing her attention with me (oedipal theme), interpretations that he seemed to experience as indirect invitations to continue aggressing. I told him that it was fine for him to be angry but that kicking was not allowed and that he would do better to use words. He persisted kicking me at which point I informed him that if he continued I would need to hold him to calm him down.

My final warning went unheeded and I eventually moved in to physically restrain him as nonaggressively as I could. For the ensuing twenty minutes he screamed, wriggled, and flailed. I lightened and tightened my grip contingent on the degree of resistance he manifested, and whether I sensed his sudden movements to be deliberate attempts to hurt me, or just awkward ways of repositioning his body. I repeated variations of the following statement, with voice tones that shifted in relation to Sam's conveyed distress: "Sam, I know you are so very, very angry with me. But I don't like to be kicked and I will hold you until you feel calm inside your body. I have a watch on my wrist and when you are able to stop yelling and stop wriggling your body I will start a two-minute countdown. Let me know when you are ready to start the countdown." Throughout the duration of the hold, Sam raged at me, calling me names and vociferously accusing me of hurting him, even as I lightened my grip to ensure that I was not applying too much pressure.

Sam's mother looked on tearfully and became quite alarmed when at one point he began screaming: "Mom, mom, make him stop. He is hurting me. Help me. Help me. Please don't let him hurt me." I reassuringly told Frances that I knew this was all upsetting but that I was trying to help Sam get himself under control and was confident that when he was ready, he could calm himself. Sam did eventually collect himself for the specified two minutes and left the session red eyed and full of righteous indignation over my having hurt him and his mother's refusal to protect him.

The parent session scheduled with Sam's mother later in the week was timely. She reported that Sam had been surprisingly more manageable and less unruly in the days subsequent to our eventful session. Part of Frances was grateful to have witnessed firsthand a firm response to Sam's uncontrollable aggression without him seeming to be "damaged." Frances always feared that she could permanently emotionally damage Sam, even with a single episode of egregious loss of control. I inquired as to the possible childhood roots of this belief and she wept bitterly, remembering a time when her mother had brutally beaten her, and how her relationship with her mother had never really recovered from this. The beating incident was a dramatic and vivid example of how she more generally experienced her mother: harsh, loud, and unnurturing. Together, we mused over how Frances seemed to have swung in the other direction and was overly affectionate with Sam, at the expense of imposing limits and expectations. I impressed upon her the need to curb Sam's behavior when he acted dismissively and ragefully, suggesting that Sam might even be desirous of some firm discipline, the evidence for this being his more composed presentation in the days after I physically restrained him. Frances and I took several sessions to map out the conditions under which she herself might physically restrain Sam at home, and how to implement this effectively and nonaggressively. She accentuated her need to administer a nonaggressive hold, since she did not want to aspire to deliberately harm Sam, in contradistinction to her own mother whom she felt derived satisfaction from inflicting pain. We also mapped out a set of consequences that Frances felt she could effectively and realistically utilize with Sam. The idea of the "punishment fitting the crime" appealed to her, where the type of consequence imposed varied in relation to the severity of the infraction.

To swallow the whole idea of discipline being an indispensable aspect of parenting, I had to provide Frances with a rationale that squared with her more libertine, love-at-all-costs worldview: "The child who is unable or unwilling to follow rules, give as well as take, adapt to routines and structure, is a child who will fast become unliked by peers and adults. Rejection, compounded on rejection, obviously will leave the child feeling unlovable." My rather heavy-handed comment seemed necessary to break through to her.

In the early phase of my individual work with Sam, he was inclined to discontinue games that he could not immediately master. A favorite activity of his was piecing together an anatomical puzzle made of spongelike human organs. Conceivably, this reflected the emotional chaos he felt inside, how emotional states left him in a state of disarray because of their felt-diffuseness, and of his need to articulate, assemble, and organize them. Periodically, Sam was oblivious to the benefits of a trial and error approach and insisted on forcing incompatible pieces together, resisting any help from me, all of this eventuating in him prematurely giving up and furiously catapulting the puzzle across the room. Sometimes I empathized with him over how maddening it was not to be able to put all the pieces together instantly. At other times I would take a more active approach: "Hold your horses, Sam. Hard puzzles cannot be done right away. Why don't I get involved here." I would give him two or three pieces to select from to insert in an area, or provide him with the correct puzzle piece and challenge him to rotate so that it would fit. My structuring the puzzle task to align it with his skill set, with due regard for his current level of frustration, enabled Sam to have success experiences that seemed to fuel his task persistence on the same puzzle during subsequent occasions.

Off and on during the course of therapy Sam took delight in running ahead of me from the waiting room and slamming shut the door of my office before I arrived. The length of time I would be kept waiting varied and Sam did not hold back from announcing his plan to let me in when he was "good and ready." Sometimes I would proclaim from the other side of the door: "I am looking forward to playing with you and it is so hard to wait and keep all the excitement inside. I wish I knew when you were going to open the door because it's really tough on me not knowing and keeping my excitement inside." At other times, on gaining entry to my office I would interpret: "You got here early today and had to wait for me to come and get you to play. I wonder if you closing the door on me is your way of having me feel what you were feeling, that's it's no fun being kept waiting, especially for something you're looking forward to." Or, "I can see that you enjoy me being the one who is shut out and kept waiting for once, when you are the one who usually has to wait for your mother or be shut out by your father."

Session endings also prompted enactments of Sam's need to master the powerlessness he felt in response to his father's sudden appearances and disappearances, as well as his mother's unpredictable schedule. Sam would either suddenly exit my office when told how many minutes were left, or prolong contact with me by making a mess that would take time to clean up, insist on starting a new game, or lie lifeless and noncommunicative on the floor.

On one of his visits, approximately a year into therapy, Sam ran ahead of me from the waiting room to my office, slamming the door shut before I arrived. I waited quietly. After a few minutes he swung the door open and invited me in. He had dumped out most of the toys in my hamper to get at the rubber swords and shields, selecting the most sturdy sword and shield for himself and tossing me the shabby ones, announcing: "Only start when I say the word *superhero*." I responded by saying "Understood. You're the boss." Sam began professing his invulnerability, noting that if I injured him with my sword he could simply touch his sword against his imaginary toy box and he would be healed. He informed me that I could be healed also by touching his toy box, but that if I touched it with my sword in the wrong place I would explode. Naturally, I asked him if he could point me to the right places and the wrong places on his "toy box," or for that matter where I might even find his toy box, because I did not like the idea of me exploding. He replied: "Too bad. I know but you don't get to know." Moreover, he pointed out that if he swiped me on the legs with his sword I no longer had use of them and had to kneel. The same applied if he wounded me on either arm. In a deep, haughty voice I replied: "Good luck. I am Ivanhoe, the Great Warrior Knight and due to my years of fighting I do not get sword swiped easily. When I battle it's the other person who needs to watch out." Sam beamed, and thrust himself into the play with added resolve to "wipe me out." Each time I injured Sam he touched his sword against his imaginary toy box and zestfully ran at me.

In time, I conveyed to Sam that it was futile to try to locate his imaginary toy box and that I wanted to take my chances and just stab him, maybe even twice in quick succession, before he could reach for his regenerative toy box. He was perturbed by this and ran at me successfully sword swiping my legs. I fell to my knees and kept fending him off, swinging both my sword and shield around. His maneuvers to skirt my swipes were impressive and I said so, keeping with the dramatic play enactment: "The Great Ivanhoe has never met such a match. Sam may be quicker on his feet than even me. His fancy footwork is amazing." At times Sam got carried away and began ferociously swinging his sword in my direction. I interrupted the play and firmly reminded him that he could pretend hurt me, but not actually do so, and that it was not permissible to sword swipe above the shoulders. Sam adhered to these rules without testing them.

I managed to poke my sword around Sam's shield and wound him in the heart. Sam reacted by stating that he was now a ghost and that I had no way of knowing where he was located in the room at any given time. I went along with this and swung my sword in the air aimlessly, showing my exasperation over the fact that I was essentially vulnerable and he invulnerable: "The Great Ivanhoe cannot see where Sam is. All is lost. I have no power and he has all the power. I am as good as dead."

Sam took delight in pretending to kill me off, systematically cutting off my arms, then my legs, stabbing me in the genitals and lobbing off my head with his sword. He then piled cushions on my body, jumping off the couch on top of me to celebrate his victory. At no time during this sequence of events did his behavior really spiral out of control or did he deliberately attempt to hurt me. Indeed, after several minutes of landing on the cushions covering my dismembered body he expressed a wish to play chess, allowing me to adopt his rule of jumping as many players as one wanted in a single move.

This session captured Sam's emerging self-regulatory emotive capacities, where he was increasingly able to maintain a level of organization and rule following in the face of intense emotion. Additionally, the session captured the full flowering of oedipal and phallic themes in the play and his underlying yearnings to be invulnerable and all-powerful. These dynamics manifested themselves in many sessions over the unfolding months, as I steadily challenged his needs for omnipotence.

In the later stages of therapy, Sam arrived at his session one day seeming rather plucky, picked up two Star Wars light sabers from my toy collection, and nonchalantly referred to them as two "jumbo penises." He proudly wagged them around next to his crotch. I immediately switched into enactive play mode and with a fake French accent stated: "That's too much power for one boy to have. One jumbo penis is enough." I picked up a Nerf dart gun and began shooting at the light sabers, commenting when I eventually hit one, "Ping. I hit it. Sam is now down to one jumbo penis." Sam, seeming to anticipate his dilemma, remarked in a mock German accent, "Not so fast. Don't you know about Hydra. These penises grow two more when killed, so now I have three jumbo penises." I recoiled, scratched my chin, and remarked, still with a fake French accent: "This boy is clever. Hydra will keep having too much power if I do not do something fast about it. I shall have to retire to my laboratory to invent something to make this boy realize that more than one jumbo penis will weigh his body down and leave him too heavy to defend himself." Sam was taken in by my appraisal. When I returned to the play and threw a pretend "smoke bomb" at him that had been designed to make extra jumbo penises regenerate only if Sam felt his life was in danger, Sam seemed only too willing to go along with this.

In the final months of therapy, Sam chose to play a baseball game with me using foam bats and balls. For many sessions in a row, he darted to my office and orchestrated a more or less identical game. He designated five bases at different locations in my office. He was to be first up to bat. The rule was three catches and a batter was out. I supplied a running commentary: "Ladies and gentlemen, we are at the ball field. Sam is up. I wonder if he wants a high pitch or a low pitch." At other times I abruptly and unilaterally made the decision for him: "Sam had better watch out because he is getting a high pitch (or a low pitch)." Sam would strain to contain his excitement, keeping his bat elevated and staying focused on the pitch. At times I delayed my pitch or faked one, causing him to become even more excited and strain even harder to maintain his poise. He delighted in hitting the ball into dark crevices of my office where its retrieval on my part took so much time that he could get one home run after another.

During one of these baseball games I caught all three of his hits and gleefully announced that it was my turn. He insisted that the three catches were not cumulative and that each time he managed to run to a new base he had a clean slate. I earnestly replied: "Sam, I know you enjoy winning, and your batting skills have really come along. In fact, I had to really work hard to get those three catches. I feel I really deserve to have a chance to bat since I caught three balls from a good batter." I went on to tell him that in all honesty I was starting to get a little bored because he was getting to win so many bases and I was left chasing balls around the office. My expressed admiration for Sam's batting, combined with his seeming concern to make the game mutually enjoyable, resulted in him backing down from his demands. Indeed, when it was his turn to pitch he threw me balls that were easy to bat, and he seemed to hesitate tagging me when he had an opportunity to. When I probed, "Sam, are you feeling bad for wanting to win so much of the time and trying to make this game more fun for me?" he smiled and unconvincingly denied it.

Sam's therapy was eventually cut short because his mother moved out of state. At the time we discontinued our work together Sam no longer met the criteria for ADHD, as he had at the onset of therapy. He was more secure in his attachment to his mother and had developed a close relationship with her new boyfriend. His omnipotence needs had abated, such that he did not become uncontrollably elated, explode in rage, or implode in shame around winning and losing, or when demonstrating mastery or failed mastery. Nevertheless, when he was in conflict with peers it usually was around his need to orchestrate the game or bend the rules to enhance the chances of a victory. Sam's task persistence and containment of frustration vis-à-vis challenging socioemotional, kinesthetic, and academic challenges were greater. In general Sam was less restless, anxious, aggressive, and overly excitable.

WILLIAM

William was eight years old when his parents sought treatment for him to avert his being removed from yet another school due to disruptive and aggressive behavior. William had been expelled from a preschool for poking a child in the face with a pencil while in a fit of rage and in kindergarten the persistence of his tendency to hit, kick, or spit when angry had eventuated in a similar fate. The incident that precipitated the need for therapeutic intervention involved him threatening to kill a peer in his second-grade classroom who had teased him about his weight. School officials, zealous to enforce their no tolerance policy vis-à-vis threats of violence, informed William's parents that his eligibility to remain enrolled was contingent upon him receiving professional help.

During the initial session held with both parents alone, William's mother broke down in tears, woefully revealing that perhaps she had given birth to a "demon child." She had lectured him endlessly about the need to "use his words" when angry and to refrain from acting aggressively, all to no avail. As an elementary-school administrator herself she was profoundly embarrassed at having to face fellow school officials regarding her son's errant behavior, which had resulted in added lectures, threats of punishment, and virulent expressions of disappointment being directed at William. She guiltily confessed that she was exasperated with William and was avoiding him more and more, maintaining longer work hours and insisting that he play alone in his room. His father, who was a foreman on a construction crew, was incensed over William "never listening," being in "his own world," and needing constant reminders to comply with requests. He rhetorically asked the therapist why it was that as a child he only needed to be asked once before obediently complying with parental demands, whereas William seemed to repeatedly ignore him, "drag his feet," become easily distracted, whine, complain, and leave tasks unfinished.

Both parents dreaded homework and mealtime situations. A typical homework scenario might find William complaining of boredom within minutes of starting an assignment, issuing relentless requests to go to the bathroom, wandering off when unattended to, fidgeting, frequently initiating conversation unrelated to the task at hand, and acting silly or staring off into the distance in response to stern warnings to complete work. It was not uncommon for homework assignments to be completed with parents supplying the answers out of desperation, or with William rushing through his work simply to be done with it.

Mealtimes often found William refusing to eat what was served, grousing about stomach aches and nausea, "accidentally" dropping cutlery on the floor, plaintively claiming to be too weak to fetch it, and generally acting restless. William's parents disclosed that twice a week or more, on account of their exhaustion from long commutes and work days, to "keep the peace," they allowed William's grandmother who lived with them to cook him a different dinner than the one served. Dinner times were generally hurried affairs with conversations centering on preparations for the coming day, and a parental eagerness for the meal to end fast so as to steal some rest and relaxation from the little time left available in the evening.

William had entered pre-school late, at age four, when his grandmother was no longer able to care for him during the day due to her moving out of state to care for an ailing sibling. William's grandmother, who was non–English speaking, had assumed the dominant role in his childrearing ever since his mother returned to work within three months of his birth. When William was five years old his grandmother returned to live in the household. At the initial session, William's parents referred to the grandmother as "Old World" in her parenting practices. They were appreciative of her being available to assist with childrearing but communicated misgivings about her tendency to "spoil" William. A detailed inquiry into the particular practices involved uncovered a history of infantilization and overprotection, whereby William was fed, dressed, and washed by the grandmother out of step with his emerging independent motoric capacities or need for assistance in an age-appropriate manner. As a matter of course his grandmother would anticipate and gratify his needs with limited verbal input from him, a process that was complicated by William's lack of fluency in his grandmother's native tongue. Indeed, at age six his grandmother had still routinely picked out his clothes, assisted him with getting dressed, tied his shoelaces, and cleaned up after him. Periodic bedwetting was handled by the grandmother dutifully washing the soiled bed linen and redressing William's bed without complaint.

Contact with his teachers and access to school-based reports provided additional information. William's speech articulation was delayed and his teacher had considerable difficulty communicating with him, especially in emotionally charged situations. During peer conflicts, which were many, when addressed by teachers, he was in the habit of either appearing mute and emotionally shut down, or disorganized in his behavior, laughing uncontrollably, sometimes even running and hiding under tables and chairs. Furthermore, the teacher often observed that William needed constant redirection to keep him focused on his work. He handed in work that was incomplete and sprinkled with careless errors, was off task frequently, hummed to himself, found extraneous stimuli irresistible, and attempted to talk with peers, when the expectation was that he work independently. William typically played by himself, with fleeting forages into peer play typically devolving into him being ostracized because of his inability to share, cooperate, tone down his excitability, or handle negative interactions without aggressive outbursts.

On the second visit William accompanied his parents. His gaze was downcast as his parents delivered a litany of grievances. I empathized with how frustrated they were with William's behavior, with how awful it was to live in fear of getting calls from school when he "acted badly," and I countered with how upsetting it must be for William to hear only what he was doing wrong, without any mention of what he was "doing right." I mentioned how sometimes it is easier for both children and grownups to listen to criticism if they have first been reminded of their positive attributes. Picking up on my tacit recognition of William's shame, his parents shifted the tone and content of their disclosures and began discussing how loving William could be with his dog, how protective he was of his younger cousin, and his beautiful smile. During the ensuing silence, William picked his head up and looked around the office. Acting on his outward signs of increased social comfort, I wondered aloud if he was curious about the toys in my office and invited him to examine them with me. William sat motionless and nonresponsive. I opened up my toy chest and uttered aloud, in a soft and jocular voice: "William is obviously too nervous to look right now, but if he was to look he would see that inside this remarkable toy chest there are toy dart guns, rubber swords, board games, and lots of pens and papers to draw with." I indicated that there were more toys in the room somewhere that he could discover for himself when he felt comfortable.

Persisting in my attempts to engage William, I inquired if any of the toys I possessed interested him. He pointed to the white eraser board and markers located behind the cupboard, remaining inert in his seat. I indicated that he was welcome to use them, humorously interjecting: "Since you have legs and the eraser board does not, you will have to walk over to it." William smiled but continued to present as mute and emotionally remote. Adjusting to the situation I replied: "Since this is our first time together and this is a new place I will make it easy for you. Swish, I wave my magic wand and give the eraser board legs for thirty seconds, just long enough for it to walk over to William." William laughed, quickly covered his mouth with his hand, and furtively looked up to receive the drawing materials I was delivering to him. He proceeded to scribble aimlessly on the white eraser board, with lines of varying colors and shapes jutting out in all directions. His productions, which he executed with flat affect and an empty gaze, embodied no recognizable form. Tops of markers were either left scattered on the floor beneath his feet, or replaced on wrong colored markers. I interpreted the following: "Looking at your drawing makes me think that you have so many big feelings inside that are so hard to control that you get confused, mad to the point of wanting to hurt somebody or break something, or go numb. Let's you and I meet together, and play and talk in ways that will help you get less confused, out-of-control angry, and numb in your body." Thus began a two-year course of psychotherapy with William, with supplementary weekly parent sessions that tapered off over time as his symptoms abated.

In the early phase of therapy, heavy emphasis was placed on meeting with William's mother and father to address parenting practices that offered promise as regards enhancing his frustration tolerance, independent functioning, and acquisition of nondestructive ways of communicating anger. It was sensitively and nonjudgmentally brought to their attention that sometimes William's disruptive behavior might signal an acute need for more involvement on their part. The parents were intrigued by information I provided them on attachment and its relation to problem behavior in children: "Sometimes children who have experienced difficult separations—like parents having to return to work shortly after the birth of a child on account of unavoidable professional demands or economic pressures—who have undergone multiple early school transitions, or suffered the sudden departure of a trusted caregiver during the preschool years, all of which are relevant to William, require more predictability concerning parents' coming and going in their life, and will take desperate measures to elicit physical closeness and involvement on the part of parents." Upon reflection, they acknowledged that William's outbursts at school appeared to be more frequent when the parents' jobs and extended-family commitments consumed more of their time and energy, as well as resulted in alterations in everyday routines and absences from the home. They began to reprioritize their work and extended-family commitments to free up more time to spend with William, which they were less apprehensive about doing since his behavior was gradually improving. William's father was responsive to suggestions that the father-son bond might be strengthened by an infusion of rough-and-tumble play and that William might be less inclined to ignore and treat his father with dismissiveness if he felt that to do so would be to jeopardize their increased closeness. The potential benefits to William of this rough-and-tumble play vis-à-vis unleashing, taming, and experimenting with angry feelings were discussed.

Another focus of parent sessions was the deleterious effects of the grandmother's childrearing habits, even though her intentions were to be nurturing and supportive, in ways that were culturally familiar to her. I speculated that William's task-avoidance and low frustration tolerance may, in part, be related to his lack of practice accomplishing skills of daily living independently or with age-appropriate assistance. The connection between the grandmother's infantilization of William and his problematic "magical" expectation that other people decipher and gratify his needs and wishes without him taking initiative was not lost on the parents. Enriched awareness of these interpersonal dynamics and their psychological effects was achieved as William's mother voiced concern that her husband suffered from the same passivity and overripe needs for assistance as her son, stemming partly from the grandmother's style of parenting. The father concurred and felt drawn to alter an intergenerational pattern but feared incurring his mother's wrath or provoking alienation in their relationship should he confront her directly with his concerns. It was agreed that I would have an "educational discussion" with the grandmother using my authority as a doctor to prescribe specific parenting practices that she should adhere to, thus enabling William to feel strong and capable. The parents could then remind the grandmother of the "doctor's orders," rather than risk inciting a more personalized dispute over childrearing and the possibility of irreconcilable conflict. The parents also decided that William's English-language skills and social and emotional competencies would undergo more rapid advancement if they enrolled him in an after-school program every other day at the YMCA rather than have him routinely picked up by the grandmother only to wile away the afternoon hours in sedentary television viewing.

At the parent's behest, I maintained regular contact with William's teacher and school counselor, monitoring his progress and advocating for empathy, commitment, and patience on their parts given William's psychological vulnerabilities. His teacher's entrenched readiness to perceive William's behavior as a sort of "moral failure," coupled with the fact that his classroom environment remained rather chaotic and disorganized, prompted the parents to request a classroom change. The parents and I marshaled forces and met with the principal to outline the reasons for a classroom change. It was agreed that I would complete a formal assessment with William, evaluate for co-morbid learning disorders, and make recommendations to the school. William tested in the average IQ range in both verbal and nonverbal domains, and his scores on achievement tests revealed grade-level status in reading, writing, and arithmetic. In short, there were no ostensible signs of learning disorders. It was recommended that William receive speech therapy and be placed in a more tightly run first-grade classroom with a teacher who was firm, but nurturing, who exhibited clear behavioral expectations, and who was inspired to bolster William's independent work habits and social and communication skills. Based on prior consultation with the parents, and in accordance with their wishes, it was recommended that if there was no significant improvement in William's behavior over a six-month period, a psychiatric consultation to assess for possible medication usage would be pursued.

In my early work with William, he recurringly gravitated toward play themes in which characters set themselves apart from the group and bullied others, thinking nothing of using physical force to preserve physical boundaries, wrest control of desired objects, or generally overexert dominance. Yet, the bully characters struggled with feeling alone and making themselves desirable friends, relinquishing aggressiveness in favor of sociability. These very issues permeated William's interpersonal world outside the office. The session I now describe was characteristic of numerous ones during the early phase of therapy. Mutually enacted dramatic play with puppets centered on giving coherent verbal and gestural expression to diffuse emotional experiences arising in mock social situations where aggression and assertiveness had a bearing on peer exclusion versus inclusion.

I introduced William to a new hawk puppet that I had just added to my collection. He inserted his hand in the opening and began making it fly across the room. I took all the other puppets out of the container and pretended to have them converse: "Wow, there's a hawk flying above us. I wonder where he came from. Mr. Horse, can you go talk with the hawk?" William flew the hawk over to where the dart guns were stored and began loading a gun. Each time a puppet approached the hawk "to get to know him" William made the hawk fire darts at it and laughed hysterically. I simulated moans and groans coming from each puppet that was hit, mentioning that they would nonetheless survive under a doctor's care. William pleaded with me to have the puppets approach the hawk after they had recovered from their wounds. He then ruthlessly shot them, jumping around and laughing devilishly.

At one point, I made the horse puppet savagely attack the hawk puppet before William had a chance to reload the dart gun. William reached for a foam bat and began striking the horse yelling, "time out Enrico, time out." I backed off, quietly had the puppets regroup, and made them say in unison: "We are through with that big bully eagle who attacks us when we just want to get to know him. We'll get him back. We will refuse to be his friend and he'll be all alone." At this point, William's mood became mildly deflated and he flew the hawk over to the other puppets moving its beak and saying: "You guys, I'll let you all hide from the snow under my wings." I had each of the puppets approach the hawk, albeit apprehensively, "to see if he could be trusted." Each one knocked on his beak and asked to be protected: "You are so big and strong and your wings are warm and cozy. Can you give me protection from the snow?" William had the hawk puppet expand its wings each time to make room, squawking: "Hurry up and come in, it's cold."

As therapy progressed, other important treatment dynamics and interventions included: prompting and supporting William's independent task mastery without undue implosive and explosive emotional effects; productive signaling as to when my affectivity during play interactions exceeded his tolerance level; therapist here-and-now self-disclosures aimed at building relational insight into the likely consequences of troublesome actions; and efficacious self-regulation of emotion during energetic game playing to facilitate the following of rules, strategies, and social decorum. All of these dynamics are contained in these next sessions that occurred about six months into therapy.

William elected to play a game of Sorry, gesturing for help to set up a variety of puppets around the game board. To tease out the specifics of the game he had in mind, I asserted, "Can you let me know what game you want to play, and with what puppets, using ideas coming out of your mouth, rather than just pointing and having me read your facial expressions." This prompted William to sigh and state: "I need you to help me get the puppets out so that they can play each other at Sorry." Faking as if to pry open his skull, I replied: "You sigh like you're frustrated because I can't just look into your head and know what you're thinking, as if that were possible."

As was his usual habit, he sat back and waited for me to take the puppets out of their container. I told him with a measure of frustration that it was not fair that I had to do all the work and that his help would be appreciated. He seemed concerned and proceeded to pull the heavy puppet box out of the toy chest with one hand, ill aware of the futility of this strategy, as if help would arrive magically without any ostensible request. I voiced my concern that all the puppets might fall out of the container and make a big mess if William continued thinking that he could move such a heavy container without giving it his full attention, or asking for some assistance, if absolutely necessary. Consequently, William grabbed hold of the container and used all his might to pull it out of the toy chest and across the room to the play area. I animatedly interjected, "Ladies and gentlemen, you just witnessed William do such a big boy thing. He used his superhuman strength to remove the puppet box out of the toy chest. His grandmother usually does things for him and he lets her. But now we are seeing William do even the most difficult things by himself. Ladies and gentleman, what an impressive show of strength by the young man."

William, beaming with pride, but appearing slightly put off by my theatrics, replied: "Enrico, can you stop being so hyper and help me set up the puppets to play Sorry." Toning down my reaction and switching from a jocular to a sincere mode of relating, I stated: "William, I guess I was getting a little carried away, it was just my playful way of letting you know how glad I was that you did not give up in frustration when carrying the toy chest across the room by yourself. You are so used to having things done for you and I think that you expect help without needing to ask for it, or feel weak because you cannot succeed at doing things on your own."

William seemed more focused on continuing with the play than listening to my utterances. He started to line up puppets around the Sorry game board, voicing his irritation that I was sitting back and not participating: "Enrico, can you hurry up and give me the hawk puppet and put Lamb Chops next to the blue Sorry pieces." William took control of the hawk puppet next to his station on the Sorry game, as I placed puppets next to each of the remaining game stations. The game was played in a low-key fashion, with each of us sticking to agreed upon assignments as to whose responsibility it was to roll the dice on behalf of a given puppet. Mutual turn taking, counting off dice numbers patiently and accurately, and moving game pieces along the board based on achieved dice scores were all accomplished without incident.

This organized, systematic, rule-adhering style of playing the game was exhibited by William in the face of potential distractions and disorganizing emotional upsets introduced by my playfulness. I picked up the Lamb Chop puppet and began to make it talk: "Hey, Mr. Hawk, do you really think that you can beat me at this game? I mean you are a big powerful hawk, I can see, but it might be my lucky day, and I might win. How are you gonna feel then?" William picked up his puppet and made it talk: "Hawks might not be kings of the jungle but they sure are powerful. I'm going to try my hardest to win." I abruptly positioned the Lamb Chops puppet close to the hawk's beak and in a somewhat shrill voice suddenly had Lamb Chops announce: "Well, you may be a big tough hawk, but I'm not scared of you." William had the hawk puppet wrest control of the Lamb Chops puppet and throw it across the room. I had the other two puppets talk to each other: "Wow, Mr. Hawk was so out of control with his anger. He's one scary dude. Why didn't he just tell Lamb Chops that he was getting too close, talking too loud, and needed to step back and speak in a quieter voice?" Running across the room, I picked up Lamb Chops and had him say, "Yeah, Mr. Hawk, I know I was being too loud and got too close to you body, why didn't you tell me that in an angry voice instead of tossing me across the room like a big bully?" William made the hawk say: "Ok, you're right. I was so mad that you got in my face. Can we keep playing? I should have asked you to not be so loud." I had the Lamb Chop and dog puppets say in unison: "Mr. Hawk is not such a scary guy after all. Let's keep playing."

When I announced that the session would be over in five minutes, William complained that time had passed too fast. He nodded his head when I suggested that he wished he could play with me for longer and was angry that sessions ended according to my schedule, not his. All the while, William ignored my requests for clean-up assistance and rolled around on the office floor. I empathized with him further regarding how sad and mad he must feel with our enjoyable time together coming to an end, but said that we had played with the toys together and were jointly responsible for putting them away. I reiterated the latter statement in a more forceful tone when William tuned me out and persisted in rolling around on the floor. Once again, William failed to comply. Rankled, I asserted: "I am starting to get annoyed because you are not helping me. I guess this is similar to how it is at home. You want more time with your parents, they have other things to do, and you respond by acting up to force them to pay attention. Like you would rather have angry attention than no attention." In response, William executed a half-hearted helping gesture, throwing one puppet into the container from across the room while still lying on the floor. Annoyance giving way to amusement, I brought the container closer to him and stated: "Well, if that's the way you want to help me clean up, I can live with it. Just make sure that Mr. William Michael Jordan himself lands as many puppets in the container as possible." William then alternated between playfully shooting puppets into the container and picking them up in earnest.

Another session found William demanding that I line the puppets up for a "surprise delivery." I told him that I would be glad to do this if he could ask me in a less bossy voice, which he did. He had the Barrel of Monkeys land on a plane and spill out on the floor, jumping around crazily and mumbling nonsensically. I had one of the puppets declare, "I can't wait to play with the monkeys. They are so funny and entertaining. Wait a minute, these guys are too hyper. I'm worried that they will not be able to control their excitement, or that they'll end up hurting someone because they are out of control." William began rolling around on the floor with the Barrel of Monkeys on his chest, grunting, mumbling, and making loud vocalizations. I had the puppets talk among themselves and designate the snake to talk to the monkeys: "Monkeys, we really, really like you guys. You are so entertaining and funny. On behalf of all the puppets, I want to inform you that we would really like to be your friends and play with you, if only you could be less hyper and rowdy." William's overenthusiastic play resulted in the monkeys being scattered all over the floor. I took hold of the hawk puppet and announced that there was an emergency and that the monkeys needed to be "rescued from their rowdiness." I used the hawk puppet to make multiple rescue missions, saying to each batch of monkeys: "You guys, I'm taking you to a calm room where you can get yourselves together and afterward play with the friendly puppets."

In time, William walked over to where I had the monkeys stashed, picked up several at a time, and had them ask to play with the puppets. Before the session ended William requested that I give him paper and a pencil to write a letter from the puppets thanking the monkeys for calming themselves down and asking to play.

At the six-month mark, during a regular biweekly parent meeting we reviewed William's progress and the appropriateness of a referral for a medication evaluation. His parents were pleased with the substantial reduction in William's aggressiveness, the noticeable difference in his behavior around mealtime and chores, and his improved verbal communication. In general, he seemed less bossy and more capable of give and take in both peer and adult-to-child interactions. Play dates and sleepovers were no longer nail-biting affairs for his parents waiting by the phone for the inevitable call.

Suggestions I had made at earlier parent meetings regarding reducing the randomness and one-sidedness in their separations and reunions with William had been implemented. William was told each day the exact time he would be picked up from his after-school program; his parents gave him time cues based on when they anticipated departing for work, rather than leaving suddenly without warning; and he had built-in playtime with his father two evenings a week, a commitment I had frequently badgered his father to "hold sacred." Both parents had striven to be less emotionally reactive with William, to step back, and enforce agreed-upon consequences in a matter-of-fact way, rather than succumb to mutually unpleasant haranguing lectures. Soothing bedtime rituals involving dim lights and mellifluous music were employed. To avert sudden devolutions in William's behavior during everyday transitions, extra preparation time was allotted. His parents no longer hastily tied his shoelaces and stuffed his backpack with homework and snacks, out of convenience, in a frenzied bid for all to be on time. They had been persuaded by my ardent speeches on mundane tasks being "teachable moments" where a host of social and emotional lessons could be learned surrounding the mere tying of shoelaces, cleaning off the table, putting on one's socks, stuffing one's own backpack, and the likes! TV viewing was limited to the weekends, eliminating the daily battle of getting it turned off, which ate up precious time in the morning better allocated to planning for the day ahead. On the rare occasion when William wet the bed, the expectation was that he participate in stripping it and washing the sheets.

Although his parents were hesitant, they did elect to pursue a medication consultation due to William's recurring difficulties focusing and staying on task at school. I recommended a child psychiatrist who would not be perturbed by their preference to take an experimental approach, or "try and see" attitude toward medication, and who would be receptive to their poignant questions (informed by their talk-show viewing) surrounding whether medication use might incline him to use drugs to alter his mood when he gets older, stunt his growth in puberty, or ruin his appetite and sleep. William was put on a therapeutic trial of psychostimulant medication with moderately successful results. The complaints from his teacher about distractibility, incomplete schoolwork, and keeping his hands to himself persisted, although they were less frequent. In consultation with his psychiatrist, William took "medication breaks" during school vacations, without untoward effects at home.

As we entered our second year of therapy, William's play demonstrated increased organization and fewer themes of destruction, his verbalizations were longer, and more coherent, and assertive, and he was less apt to vacillate between states of unbridled excitement and emotional flatness. Several play scenarios captured these qualities.

William requested that we resume playing with a Lego plane constructed the week before and placed in the special box assigned to him for his keepsakes. (The availability of a box to store creations and keepsakes can be immensely valuable in concretizing a feeling of specialness in the child, as well as reinforcing task persistence insofar as constructions are returned to, successfully completed, and made available to be showcased at the flip of a lid!) I pulled out a small plastic snake and spoke through it: "Hey, how about taking me for a ride in the sky?" This peaked William's interest and he emerged from an emotionally reserved state to one of subdued excitement as I placed the snake on top of the Lego airplane, cuing him to take the snake on a tour of the office.

During the ride, I intermittently pressed down on the airplane with the snake such that it narrowly avoided collisions with furniture and made sudden, abrupt descents. I also maintained a running commentary: "Wowee, yipeee, this ride is sooooooo fun. Oops, my stomach just dropped, now it is up in my head somewhere. I'm sooooo excited that I can't bear it." When my airplane ride was over, William insisted on taking a toy lizard for a ride by himself, insinuating his displeasure at my exuberance: "My lizard is going to be just happy, instead of excited like your snake." His flight descents were less abrupt than those demonstrated by me, although he came closer to making his airplane collide with furniture. William's airplane stunt differed from mine in one other important respect; he landed to refuel and took off afterward in a smooth fashion.

In an attempt to initiate conversation at the beginning of a different session later that month, William informed me that he had just seen the movie, *Finding Nemo*. I playfully mused that *Nemo* rhymed with *torpedo*. William wanted to know the name of "the other thing under the water that explodes." I told him that I could draw it and maybe he could guess. On a white eraser board I scribbled a picture of a mine under water and he excitedly recalled its name. He added a thick black chain to the mine, securing it to the ocean floor. I asked if I could draw barnacles on it and explained what these were when he asked. William drew crabs crawling up the chain to eat the barnacles. I mused out loud that I was worried that the crabs were getting so big from eating the barnacles that they might set off the mine. William instead drew a "matchbox torpedo" heading in the direction of the mine in a bid to be the one who had control over any explosion that was to materialize. Seeking his permission, I gathered together red and orange markers for us to color in an explosion once his torpedo hit the mine.

At the moment of impact, we wildly scribbled all over the white eraser board using red and orange markers simulating an explosion, complete with sound effects. William seemed uncomfortable with the messiness of the drawings and the level of arousal in the room, taking it upon himself to wipe the board clean, stating: "You are getting too crazy, Enrico. Next time can we just have a little explosion since a single mine doesn't blow up the whole ocean?" I sincerely apologized for letting my "fun feelings get all blown out of proportion." William resumed playing the same drawing game, this time instructing me to draw my own mine and color in my own explosion, while he drew his exactly as before on the side of the white eraser board he had designated as his own. We each had explosions caused by different events, his via impact with a "torpedo matchbox," my rendition being due to crabs expanding from eating too many barnacles and setting off the mine. I summed up: "I am glad that you can let me know when my excitement is so out there that you are annoyed and that you can play in your way, and me in my way, and we can still enjoy the activity."

A drawing produced by William toward the end of treatment epitomizes how far he had advanced. During an uncharacteristically low-key session, William chose to draw a volcano on a white eraser board. In the middle of the volcano, running from top to bottom, enclosed by a thick black line, he depicted a chamber with an opening, letting me know that this was where the lava was stored and flowed out. He added box-shaped rooms adjacent to the lava chamber, mentioning that these were places for people to be alone to "chill out." One of the larger box-shaped rooms was designated as a place for a cooling system to keep heat out. Another was set aside for his grandparents, and yet another, for his parents. William noted that the volcano had died and no longer "spit out lava," because the cooling system worked so well. I remarked that now people might feel safe living inside it, or coming to observe it because it was no longer dangerous to do so. I asked if I could draw friendly tourists with binoculars and climbing gear on the side of his volcano. We ended up doing this tranquilly together. It is noteworthy that during a session a year previously William had concocted a game in which he had me repeatedly walk puppets over a gate that hid a ditch with a volcano in it. Each time a puppet walked on the gate he had the volcano spit lava at it and William proceeded to throw it wildly across the room.

It would not be implausible to propose that William's depiction symbolically represents the high degree of self-organization he had acquired at this juncture in his life. Indeed, one could even construe William's depiction as a rather elegant illustration of Freud's structural model of the mind, with the lava representing the id, the cooling system the superego, and the chambers for people to retreat to, the ego. Along these lines, his "neutralization" of the lava can even be thought of as his id no longer being the dominant force in his overall personality structure. From an attachment/systemic standpoint, the drawing also seems to suggest that William no longer perceived his home life as the chaotic environment it once was, with overly permeable emotional boundaries, intergenerational strife, and inconsistently accessible caregivers. Evidently, my meetings with his parents had borne fruit.

The mere fact that we could have a low-key, talk-oriented, give-and-take interaction together, in and of itself, speaks volumes. So too does the mere fact that William was able to start and finish a complex drawing entailing higher-order, representational processing of experience—I call your attention to my first meeting with him, where his drawings amounted to jumbled lines and scribbles. His task persistence and frustration tolerance had definitely progressed. In the end, I like to think that the "volcano drawing event," that is, the content of the drawing and the interpersonal processes surrounding its creation, represents a variety of socioemotional milestones attained by William, not the least of which is a capacity to experience emotion (lava) in de-intensified, modulated ways and a willingness to allow others into his personal space, to see him up close, without this being emotionally impinging and evocative of aggressive assertion of boundaries. Above all else, I like to think that William's volcano drawing, complete with the admiring tourists, is a quiet revelation that he no longer believed himself to be an aggressive, impulsive, disorganized, unlikable child, but instead, one who was self-collected, approachable, and lovable.

I selected the cases of Sam and William because I believe them to be fairly typical of the children who are commonly brought in for outpatient therapy due to ADHD. I chose to go with boys over girls, because when it comes to ADHD it is boys that are more likely to be ascribed the diagnosis and whom we treat in disproportionate numbers. Clinicians poring over these cases may see in Sam and William traces of the kind of proclivities embodied by child clients they routinely encounter. In providing detailed descriptions of my active play interventions with Sam and William—at the level of affect—I hope readers can garner something useful in their own clinical work with ADHD children, something implementable, if not some sophisticated rationale for staying with playing.

REFERENCES

Ainsworth, M. D. S., Blehar, M. C., Waters, E., and Wall, S. 1978. *Patterns of attachment*. Hillsdale, NJ: Erlbaum.

Allen, E. R., Singer, H. S., Brow, J. E., and Salem, M. M. 1992. Sleep disorders in Tourette's syndrome: A primary or unrelated problem. *Pediatric Neurology* 8, 275–80.

Allen, S. T. 2001. Attachment status, affect regulation, and behavioral control in young adults. Unpublished doctoral dissertation. University of Connecticut.

American Psychiatric Association. 1994. *Diagnostic and statistical manual of mental disorders*, 4th Ed. Washington, DC: American Psychiatric Association.

Aron, L. 1996. *A meeting of minds: Mutuality in psychoanalysis*. Hillsdale, NJ: The Analytic Press.

Barkley, R. A. 1999. Theories of attention–deficit/hyperactivity disorder. In H. C. Quay and A. E. Hogan (Eds.), *Handbook of disruptive behavior disorders*, 295–313. New York: Plenum.

———. 2006. *Attention-deficit/hyperactivity disorder: A handbook for diagnosis and treatment*. New York: Guildford.

Beebe, B., and Lachmann, F. M. 1994. Representations and internalization in infancy: Three principles of salience. *Psychoanalytic Psychology* 11, 127–65.

Belsky, J. 1999. Interactional and contextual determinants of attachment security. In J. Cassidy and P. R. Shaver (Eds.), *Handbook of attachment: Theory, research and clinical applications*, 249–64. New York: Guildford.

Benjamin, J. 1988. *The bonds of love: Psychoanalysis, feminism and the problem of domination*. New York: Pantheon Books.

———. 1995. *Like subjects, love objects*. New Haven, CT: Yale University Press.

Bonello, P. J. 1998. Emotional competence in children with ADHD: The contribution of symptom severity. Unpublished doctoral dissertation, Wayne State University, Michigan.

Bowlby, J. 1969. *Attachment and loss: Vol. 1. Attachment*. New York: Basic Books.

———. 1973. *Attachment and loss: Vol. 2. Separation: Anxiety and anger*. New York: Basic Books.

189

Bradley, S. J. 2000. *Affect regulation and the development of psychopathology.* New York: Guilford Press.

Brisch, K. H. 2002. *Treating attachment disorders: From theory to therapy.* New York: Guilford.

Buss, A. H., and Plomin, R. 1984. *Temperament: Early developing personality traits.* Hillsdale, NJ: Erlbaum.

Cadesky, E. B., Mota, V. L., and Schachar, R. J. 2000. Beyond words: How do problem children with ADHD and/or conduct problems process nonverbal information about affect? *Journal of American Academy of Child and Adolescent Psychiatry* 39, 1160–67.

Caillois, R. 2001. *Man, play and games.* Chicago: University of Illinois Press.

Carlson, E. A., Jacobvitz., D., and Sroufe, L. A. 1995. A developmental investigation of inattentiveness and hyperactivity. *Child Development* 66, 37–54.

Cassidy, J. 1994. Emotion regulation: Influences of attachment relations. In N.A. Fox (Ed.), *The development of emotion regulation: Biological and behavioral considerations. Monographs of the Society for Research in Child Development,* 59 (2–3 Serial No. 240), 228–49.

Cassidy, J., and Shaver, P. R. Eds. 1999. *Handbook of attachment: Theory, research and clinical applications.* New York: Guilford.

Charach, A., Ickowicz, A., and Schachar, R. 2004. Stimulant treatment over five years: Adherence, effectiveness, and adverse effects. *Journal of the American Academy of Child and Adolescent Psychiatry* 43, 559–67.

Chess, S., and Thomas, A. 1996. *Temperament theory and practice.* New York: Brunner/Mazel.

Chethik, M. 2000. *Techniques of child therapy,* 2nd Ed. New York: Guilford.

Chused, J. F. 1998. The evocative power of enactments. In P. Beren (Ed.), *Narcissistic disorders in children and adolescents: Diagnosis and treatment,* 225–43. Northvale, NJ: Aronson.

Ciulla, J. B. 2000. *The working life: The promise and betrayal of modern work.* New York: Times Books.

Clarke, L., Ungerer, J., Chahoud, K., Johnson, S., and Steifel, I. 2002. Attention-deficit/hyperactivity disorder is associated with attachment insecurity. *Clinical Child Psychology and Psychiatry* 7, 179–98.

Connors, C. K., Epstein, J., and March, J. 2001. Multi-modal treatment of ADHD (MTA): An alternative outcome analysis. *Journal of the American Academy of Child and Adolescent Psychiatry* 40, 159–67.

Connors, C. K., March, J. S., Frances, A., Wells, K. C., and Ross, R. 2001. Treatment of attention-deficit/hyperactivity disorder: Expert consensus guidelines. *Journal of Attention Disorders* 4, 7–128.

Corbett, B., and Glidden, H. 2000. Processing affective stimuli in children with attention-deficit/hyperactivity disorder. *Child Neuropsychology* 6, 144–55.

DeGrandpre, R. 1999. *Ritalin nation: Rapid-fire culture and the transformation of human consciousness.* New York: Norton.

DeKlyen, M. 1996. Disruptive behavior disorders and intergenerational attachment patterns: A comparison of normal and clinic-referred preschoolers and their mothers. *Journal of Consulting and Clinical Psychology* 64, 357–65.

Denham, S. A. 1998. *Emotional development in young children*. New York: Guilford.

Douglas, V. I. 2005. Cognitive deficits in children with attention-deficit/hyperactivity disorder. *Canadian Psychology* 46, 23–31.

Edward, J., Ruskin, N., and Turrini, P. 1991. *Separation-individuation*. New York: Gardner Press.

Eisenberg, N., Fabes, R., Miller, P. A., Fultz, J., Shell, R., Mathy, R., and Reno, R. 1989. Relation of sympathy and personal distress to prosocial behavior: A multi-method study. *Journal of Personality and Social Psychology* 58, 55–66.

Eisenberg, N., Fabes, R. A., Shepard, S. A., Guthrie, I. K., Murphy, B. C., and Reiser, M. 1999. Parental reactions to children's negative emotions: Longitudinal relations to quality of children's social functioning. *Child Development* 70, 513–34.

Ekstein, R. 1966. *Children of time and space, of action and impulse*. New York: Appleton-Century-Crofts.

Elkind, D. 1994. *Ties that stress*. Cambridge, MA: Harvard University Press.

Erikson, E. 1999. Play and cure. In C. E. Schaefer (Ed.), *The therapeutic use of child's play*, 79–93. Northvale, NJ: Aronson.

Fancher, R. E. 1973. *Psychoanalytic psychology: The development of Freud's thought*. New York: Norton.

Fitzpatrick, P. A., Klorman, R., Brumaghim, J. T., and Borgstedt, A. D. 1992. Effect of sustained-release and standard preparations of methylphenidate on attention deficit disorder. *Journal of the American Academy of Child and Adolescent Psychiatry* 31, 226–34.

Fonagy, P. 2001. *Attachment theory and psychoanalysis*. New York: Other Press.

Fox, N. A., and Card, J. A. 1999. Psychophysiological measures in the study of attachment. In J. Cassidy and P. R. Shaver (Eds.), *Handbook of attachment: Theory, research and clinical applications*, 226–45. New York: Guilford.

Frank, K. A. 1999. *Psychoanalytic participation: Action, interaction and integration*. Hillsdale, NJ: The Analytic Press.

Freud, A. 1946. *The psychoanalytic treatment of children*. New York: International Universities Press.

Gallardo, K. A. 2005. A psychiatric resident's reflections on the nonmedical use of prescription stimulants. *Psychiatric Annals* 35, 264–69.

Ginott, H. D. 1993. Interpretations and child therapy. In E. Hammer (Ed.), *Use of interpretation in treatment: Technique and art*, 291–99. Northvale, NJ: Aronson.

Glassner, B. 1999. *The culture of fear*. New York: Basic Books.

Gnaulati, E. 1999. Enhancing the self-esteem and social competence of hyperactive children: A semi-structured activity group therapy model. *Group* 23, 87–101.

Gnaulati, E., and North, S. 2006. Peacemaking with preschoolers. Unpublished manuscript.

Goldschmidt, W. 2006. *The bridge to humanity: How affect hunger trumps the selfish gene*. New York: Oxford University Press.

Gorman, E. B., Klorman, R., Thatcher, J. E., and Borgstedt, A. D. 2006. Effects of methylphenidate on subtypes of attention-deficit/hyperactivity disorder. *Journal of the American Academy of Child and Adolescent Psychiatry* 45, 808–16.

Gorsuch, S. E. 1990. Shame and acting out in psychotherapy. *Psychotherapy:Theory, Research and Practice* 27, 585–90.

Greene, R. W., Biederman, J., Faraone, S. V., and Ouellette, C. A. 1996. Toward a new psychometric definition of social disability in children with attention-deficit/hyperactivity disorder. *Journal of the American Academy of Child and Adolescent Psychiatry* 35, 571–78.

Greenspan, S. I. 1982. The "second other": The role of the father in early personality formation and the dyadic-phallic phase of development. In S. H. Cath, A. R. Gurwitt, and J. M. Ross (Eds.), *Father and child: Developmental and clinical perspectives*. Boston: Little Brown and Company.

Guignon, C., and Hiley, D. R. Eds. 2003. *Richard Rorty*. New York: Cambridge University Press.

Haber, S. N., and Fudge, J. L. 1997. The interface between dopamine neurons and the amygdala: Implications for schizophrenia. *Schizophrenia Bulletin* 23, 471–82.

Henker, B., and Whalen, C. K. 1999. The child with attention-deficit/hyperactivity disorder in school and peer settings. In H. C. Quay and A. E. Hogan (Eds.), *Handbook of disruptive behavior disorders,* 157–78. New York: Plenum.

Himelstein, J., Schultz, K. P., Newcorn, J. H., and Halperin, J. M. 2000. The neurobiology of attention-deficit/hyperactivity disorder. *Frontiers in Biosciences* 5, 461–78.

Hinshaw, S. P., Carte, E. T., Fan, C., Jassy, J. S., Owens, E. B. 2007. Neurological functioning in girls with attention-deficit/hyperactivity disorder followed prospectively into adolescence: Evidence for continuing deficits. *Neuropsychology* 21, 263–73.

Hoza, B., Pelham, W. E., Milich, R., Pillow, D., and McBride, K. 1993. The self-perceptions and attributions of attention deficit hyperactivity disordered and nonreferred boys. *Journal of Abnormal Child Psychology* 21, 271–86.

Johnson, M. H., and Magaro, P. A. 1987. Effects of mood and severity on memory processes in depression and mania. *Psychological Bulletin* 101, 28–40.

Johnson, S. J. 1987. *Humanizing the narcissistic style*. New York: Norton.

Johnston, C. 1996. Parent characteristics and parent-child interactions in families of non-problem children and ADHD children with higher levels of oppositional-defiant behavior. *Journal of Abnormal Child Psychology* 24, 85–104.

Kagan, J. 1989. The concept of behavioral inhibition to the unfamiliar. In J. S. Reznick (Ed.), *Perspectives on behavioral inhibition,* 1–23. Chicago: University of Chicago Press.

Kagan, J., Reznick, J. S., and Gibbons, J. 1989. Inhibited and uninhibited types of children. *Child Development* 60, 838–45.

Kataria, S., Swanson, M. S., and Trevathan, G. E. 1987. Persistence of sleep distur-
bances in preschool children. *The Journal of Pediatrics* 110, 642–46.

Klein, M. 1932. *The psychoanalysis of children*. London: Hogarth Press.

Klimkeit, E. I., Mattingley, J. B., Sheppard, D. M., Lee, P., and Bradshaw, P. L.
2005. Motor preparation, motor execution, attention and executive functions in
attention deficit/hyperactivity disorder [ADHD]. *Child Neuropsychology* 11,
153–73.

Kohut, H. 1977. *The restoration of the self*. New York: International Universities
Press.

———. 1985. *Self psychology and the humanities*. New York: Norton.

Kris, E. 1952. *Psychoanalytic explorations in art*. New York: International Universities
Press.

Landau, S., and Moore, L. A. 1991. Social skills deficits in children with attention-
deficit hyperactivity disorder. *School Psychology Review* 20, 235–51.

Lansky, M. R. 1992. *Fathers who fail: Shame and psychopathology in the family system*.
Hilsdale, NJ: The Analytic Press.

Lewis, C., and Lamb, M. E. 2003. Fathers' influence on children's development:
The evidence from two-parent families. *European Journal of Psychology of Education*
18, 211–28.

Lewit, E. M., and Baker, L. S. 1995. School readiness. *The Future of Children* 5,
128–39.

Lomas, P. 1987. *The limits of interpretation*. Northvale, NJ: Aronson.

Losoya, S. H. 1995. Patterns of emotional responding in children with and without attention-deficit/hyperactivity disorder. *Dissertation Abstracts International*
55(11-B), ISSN No. 0419-4217.

Louv, R. 2006. *Last child in the woods*. Chapel Hill, NC: Algonquin Books.

Lyons-Ruth, K. 1998. Implicit relational knowing: Its role in development and psychoanalytic treatment. *Infant Mental Health Journal*, 19, 282–89.

Lyons-Ruth, K., Zoll, D., Connell, D. B., and Grunebaum, H. 1989. The depressed mother and her one-year-old infant: Environmental context, mother-
infant interaction and attachment, and infant development. In E. Tronick and
T. Field (Eds.), *Maternal depression and infant disturbance*, 61–82. San Francisco:
Jossey Bass.

Mahler, M. S., Bergman, A., and Pine, F. 1975. *The psychological birth of the human
infant*. New York: Basic Books.

Main, M., and Hesse, E. 1990. Parents' unresolved traumatic experiences are related
to infant disorganized attachment status: Is frightened and/or frightening parental
behavior the linking mechanism? In M. T. Greenberg, D. Cicchett, and E. M.
Cummings (Eds.), *Attachment in the preschool years: Theory, research and intervention*,
161–82. Chicago: University of Chicago Press.

Mangione, C. L. 2003. Boys with ADHD in frustrating peer competition: Towards
a theory of behavioral disinhibition and emotional reactivity. *Dissertation Abstracts
International* 63(9-B), ISSN No. 0419-4217.

McKenna, J. J. 1993. Infant-parent co-sleeping in an evolutionary perspective. *Sleep* 16, 263–82.

Meichenbaum, D. 1975. A self-instructional approach to stress management: A proposal for stress-innoculation training. In C. Speilberger and I. Saranson (Eds.), *Stress and anxiety,* 237–63. New York: Wiley.

Melnick S. M., and Hinshaw, S. P. 2000. Emotion regulation and parenting in AD/HD and comparison boys: Linkages with social behaviors and peer preference. *Journal of Abnormal Child Psychology* 28, 73–86.

Michalson, L., and Lewis, M. 1985. What do children know about emotions and when do they know it? In M. Lewis and C. Saarni (Eds.), *The socialization of emotions,* 117–39. New York: Plenum.

Miller, J. P. 1996. *Using self psychology in child psychotherapy: The restoration of the child.* Northvale, NJ: Aronson.

Mitchell, S. A. 1993. *Hope and dread in psychoanalysis.* New York: Basic Books.

———. 1997. *Influence and autonomy in psychoanalysis.* Hillsdale, NJ: The Analytic Press.

———. 2000. *Relationality: From attachment to intersubjectivity.* Hillsdale, NJ: The Analytic Press.

Morrison, A. P. Ed. 1986. *The essential papers on narcissism.* New York: New York University Press.

Murphy, D. A., Pelham, W. E., and Lang, A. R. 1992. Aggression in boys with attention-deficit/hyperactivity disorder: Methylphenidate effects on naturalistically observed aggression, response to provocation, and social information processing. *Journal of Abnormal Child Psychology* 20, 451–66.

Murphy, K. 2005. Psychosocial treatments for ADHD in teens and adults. *Journal of Clinical Psychology* 61, 607–19.

Nathanson, D. L. 1992. *Shame and pride: Affect, sex, and the birth of the self.* New York: Norton.

———. 1997. Attentional disorders and the compass of shame. In M. R. Lansky and A. P. Morrison (Eds.), *The widening scope of shame,* 366–78. Hillsdale, NJ: Analytic Press.

National Institutes of Health Consensus Statement. 1998 (November). *Diagnosis and treatment of attention-deficit/hyperactivity disorder.*

Norvilitis, J. M., Casey, R. J., Brooklier, K. M., and Bonello, P. J. 2000. Emotion appraisal in children with attention deficit/hyperactivity disorder and their parents. *Journal of Attention Disorders* 4, 15–26.

Panksepp, J. 1998. Attention-deficit/hyperactivity disorders, psychostimulants, and intolerance of child playfulness: A tragedy in the making? *Current Directions in Psychological Science* 10, 91–98.

Pelham, W. E., Burrows-Maclean, L., Gnagy, E. M., Fabiano, G. A., Coles, E. K., Tresco, K. E., Chacko, A., Wymbs, B. T., Wienke, A. L., Walker, K. S., and Hoffman, M. T. 2005. Transdermal methylphenidate, behavioral, and combined treatment for children with ADHD. *Experimental and Clinical Psychopharmacology* 13, 111–26.

Pellegrini, A. D., Huberty, P. D., and Jones, I. 1995. The effects of recess timing on children's playground and classroom behavior. *British Journal of Educational Psychology* 63, 88–95.

Piaget, J. 1962. *Play, dreams, and imitation in childhood.* New York: Norton.

Raine, A. 1997. Autonomic nervous system factors underlying disinhibited, antisocial and violent behavior. *Annals of the New York Academy of Sciences* 794, 46–59.

Reich, A. (1954). Early identification as archaic elements in the superego. *Journal of the American Psychoanalytic Association* 2, 218–38.

Ross, A. 2003. *No-collar: The humane workplace and its hidden costs.* New York: Basic Books.

Saarni, C. 1999. *The development of emotional competence.* New York: Guilford.

Sadeh, A., Raviv, A., and Gruber, R. 2000. Sleep patterns and sleep disruptions in school-age children. *Developmental Psychology* 36, 291–301.

Sartre, J. P. 1956. *Being and nothingness: An essay on phenomenological nothingness* (H. Barnes, Trans.). New York: Philosophical Library.

Schachter, H. M., Ba' Pham, P., King, J., Langford, S., and Moher, D. 2001. How efficacious and safe is short-acting methylphenidate for the treatment of attention-deficit disorder in children and adolescents: A meta-analysis. *Canadian Medical Association Journal* 165, 1475–88.

Scheff, T. J., and Retzinger, S. M. 1991. *Emotions and violence.* Lexington, MA: Lexington Books.

Schore, A. N. 2003. *Affect regulation and the repair of the self.* New York: Norton.

Siegel, H. I. 1997. Emotion socialization and affect regulation in children with attention deficit hyperactivity disorder. *Dissertation Abstracts International* 57(9-B), ISSN No. 0419-4217.

Slade, A. 1994. Making meaning and making believe: Their role in the clinical process. In A. Slade and D.W. Wolf (Eds.), *Children at play: Clinical and developmental approaches to meaning and representations,* 81–107. New York: Oxford University Press.

Smirnoff, V. 1971. *The scope of child analysis.* New York: International Universities Press.

Spiegel, S. 1989. *An interpersonal approach to child therapy.* New York: Columbia University Press.

Sroufe, L. A. 1997. *Emotional development: The organization of emotional life in the early years.* New York: Cambridge University Press.

Stark, M. 1999. *Modes of therapeutic action.* Northvale, NJ: Aronson.

Stern, D. B. 1997. *Unformulated experience: From dissociation to imagination in psychoanalysis.* Hillsdale, NJ: The Analytic Press.

Stern, D. N. 1971. A micro-analysis of mother-infant interaction: Behaviors regulating social contact between a mother and her three-and-a-half-month-old twins. *Journal of American Academy of Child Psychiatry* 10, 501–517.

———. 1977. *The first relationship: Infant and mother.* Cambridge, MA: Harvard University Press.

———. 1985. *The interpersonal world of the infant*. New York: Basic Books.

Stolorow, R. D., and Atwood, G. E. 1992. *Contexts of being: The intersubjective foundations of psychological life*. Hillsdale, NJ: The Analytic Press.

Stolorow, R. D., Atwood, G. E., and Orange, D. M. 2002. *Worlds of experience: Interweaving philosophical and clinical dimensions in psychoanalysis*. New York: Basic Books.

Suess, G., Grossman, K. E., and Sroufe, L. A. 1992. Effects of infant attachment to mother and father on quality of adaptation in preschool: From dyadic to individual organization of the self. *International Journal of Behavioral Development* 15, 43–66.

Sullivan, H. S. 1953. *The interpersonal theory of psychiatry*. New York: Norton.

Swanson, J. M., McBurnett, K., Christian, D. L., and Wigal, T. 1995. Stimulant medication and treatment of children with ADHD. In T. H. Ollendick and R. J. Prinz (Eds.), *Advances in clinical child psychology*, Vol. 17, 265–322. New York: Plenum Press.

Taylor, A. F., Kuo, F. E., and Sullivan, W. C. 2001. Coping with ADD: The surprising connection to green play settings. *Environment and Behavior* 33, 54–77.

Taylor, E., Chadwick, O., Heptinstall, E., and Danckaerts, M. 1996. Hyperactivity and conduct problems as risk factors for adolescent development. *Journal of the American Academy of Child and Adolescent Psychiatry* 39, 1213–26.

Thompson, R. A. 1990. Emotion and self regulation. In R. A. Thompson (Ed.), *Nebraska Symposium on Motivation: Vol. 36. Socioemotional development*, 367–467. Lincoln: University of Nebraska Press.

———. 1991. Emotion regulation and emotional development. *Educational Psychology Review* 3: 269–307.

———. 1994. Emotion regulation: A theme in search of definition. In N. Fox (Ed.), *The development of emotion regulation: Behavioral and biological considerations. Monographs of the Society for Research in Child Development, 59* (Serial No. 240), 25–52.

Tikotzky, L., and Sadeh, A. 2001. Sleep patterns and sleep disruptions in kindergarten children. *Journal of Clinical Child Psychology* 30, 581–91.

Trevarthen, C., and Aitken, K. J. 2001. Infant intersubjectivity: Research, theory and clinical applications. *Journal of Child Psychology and Psychiatry* 42, 3–48.

Trevathan, W., Smith, N., and McKenna, J. 1999. *Evolutionary medicine*. Oxford: Oxford University Press.

Trites, R. L., and Laprade, K. 1983. Evidence for an independent syndrome of hyperactivity. *Journal of Child Psychology and Psychiatry* 24, 573–86.

Tronick, E. Z. 1989. Emotions and emotional communication in infants. *American Psychologist* 44, 112–19.

Vygotsky, L. 1978. *Mind in society: The development of higher psychological processes*. Cambridge, MA: Harvard University Press.

Wachtel, P. L. 1987. *Action and insight*. New York: Guilford.

Waelder, R. 1999. Psychoanalytic theory of play. In C. E. Schaefer (Ed.), *The therapeutic use of child's play*, 79–93. Northvale, NJ: Aronson.

Walraich, M. L. 2006. Stimulant medications and their adverse events and the Food and Drug Administration: What can we conclude? *Journal of Developmental and Behavioral Pediatrics* 27, 177–78.

Whalen, C. K., and Henker, B. 1991. Therapies for hyperactive children: Comparisons, combinations and compromises. *Journal of Consulting and Clinical Psychology* 59, 126–37.

———. 1998. Attention-deficit/hyperactivity disorders. In T. H. Ollendick and M. Hersen (Eds.), *Handbook of child psychopathology*, 3rd ed., 181–211. New York: Plenum.

Wheeler, J., and Carlson, C. L. 1994. The social functioning of children with ADD with hyperactivity and ADD without hyperactivity: A comparison of their peer relationships and social deficits. *Journal of Emotional and Behavioral Disorders* 2, 2–12.

Wineman, R. F. 1957. *The aggressive child.* New York: Free Press.

Winnicott, D. W. 1944. *The child, the family, and the outside world.* Middlesex, England: Penguin Books.

———. 1971. *Playing and reality.* London: Tavistock Publications.

———. 1992. Hate in the countertransference. In *Through pediatrics to psychoanalysis,* 194–203. New York: Brunner/Mazel.

Wurmser, L. 1981. *The mask of shame.* Baltimore, MD: John Hopkins University Press.

INDEX

Affect: contagious nature of, 51; differentiated relatedness, at level of, 56, 58; flooding, 31, 46, 80; as form of social communication, 83; mutual regulation of, 76–79, 131; Ancillary play activity, in therapy, 99

Asynchronous interactions, mother-infant, 7–8

Attachment: avoidant type, 24, 45; disorganized type, 26, 46; insecure type, 24–26, 46; problems and ADHD symptoms, 43–47, 148–151; secure type, 24; sensitivity, 47

Attention-deficit/hyperactivity disorder (ADHD): diagnostic criteria for, 29; neurocognitive position on, xi–xiii, 29–30, 40, 136–137, 141; role of emotion dysregulation, 29–31, 35–36, 101; Attention-deficit/hyperactivity disordered (ADHD) children, problems with: affect-modulation, 35–35; attachment style, 30–31, 43–47, 148–151, 184; autonomous functioning, 38; emotional reactivity, 33–35, 152, 154; empathy skills, 34; exhibitionistic tendencies, 106–108;

externalization of blame, 40–42, 93, 108–111; frustration tolerance, 38–39, 130–131; narcissistic vulnerability, 30, 42–43, 85–86, 108–110, 126; play style, 50–53, 54–57, 59–60, 67–69, 83–84, 88, 103, 115; self-other differentiation , 33–35; social-know how, 70, 84–87, 118; symbolic processing, 36–37, 82–83

Barkley, R. A., 29
Benjamin, J., 85

Countertransference, 59, 83, 155

Differentiated emotional responsiveness: parental, 13–14, 152–155; therapist, 89, 98–99

Emotion regulation: defined, 1–5; infancy, 7–9; neurobiological factors, 26–28; influence of pre-school pedagogy, 18–20; role of parental responsiveness, 13–15; role of sleep, 17–18; school-age years, 20–23; social referencing, 17; toddlerhood, 9–15

Ego-ideal, 87–88

ABOUT THE AUTHOR

Enrico Gnaulati Ph.D., is a graduate of the doctoral program in clinical psychology at Teachers College, Columbia University and a former faculty member in the child and family studies department at California State University, Los Angeles. His previous published works are on adolescent development, sibling therapy, group work with ADHD children, and peacemaking skills with preschoolers. Dr. Gnaulati maintains a private practice in Pasadena, California, and is a frequent public speaker on child development and parenting issues. For more information please visit Dr. Gnaulati's webpage at www.gnaulati.net.